Relative Importance:
1 2 3 4 5

Strength of Evidence:
1 2 3 4 ○

Research–Based
Web Design &
Usability Guidelines

Forewords by:
Michael O. Leavitt
Secretary of Health and Human Services

Ben Shneiderman
Professor of Computer Science, University of Maryland

GSA

U.S. GOVERNMENT OFFICIAL EDITION NOTICE

Use of ISBN

This is the Official U.S. Government edition of this publication and is herein identified to certify its authenticity. Use of the 0-16 ISBN prefix (if agency uses own block of ISBN, list full ISBN in this space) is for U.S. Government Printing Office Official Editions only. The Superintendent of Documents of the U.S. Government Printing Office requests that any reprinted edition clearly be labeled as a copy of the authentic work with a new ISBN.

Legal Status and Use of Seals and Logos

The seal and logo of the U.S. Department of Health and Human Services (HHS) and the U.S. General Services Administration (GSA) authenticates the Research-Based Web Design & Usability Guidelines as the official codification of Federal regulations established under the Federal Register Act. The HHS seal and logo displayed in this book are protected under the provisions of 42 U.S.C. 1320b-10. The GSA seal and logo displayed in this book are protected under the provisions of 18 U.S.C 506. The unauthorized use of these seals and logos in a publication is prohibited and subject to a civil penalty of up to $5,000 for each unauthorized copy of it that is reprinted or distributed.

It is prohibited to use the HHS or GSA seal or logo displayed in this book without the express, written permission. To request permission to use the HHS seal or logo, please submit a request to:
The U.S. Department of Health and Human Services
200 Independence Avenue, S.W.
Washington, DC 20201

To request permission to use the GSA seal or logo, please submit a request to:
U.S. General Services Administration
1800 F Street, N.W.
Washington, DC 20405

For sale by the Superintendent of Documents,
U.S. Government Printing Office, Internet: bookstore.gpo.gov
Phone: toll free (866) 512-1800; DC area (202) 512-1800;
Fax: (202) 512-2250 Mail: Stop IDCC, Washington, DC 20402-0001

ISBN 0-16-076270-7

ISBN 0-16-076270-7

9 780160 762703   90000

Foreword—Secretary Michael O. Leavitt

I am pleased to announce this new edition of the

U.S. Department of Health and Human Services' (HHS) Research-Based Web Design and Usability Guidelines. These Guidelines reflect HHS' commitment to identifying innovative, research-based approaches that result in highly responsive and easy-to-use Web sites for the public.

The Federal government is the largest single producer, collector, consumer, and disseminator of information in the United States. The Internet provides the most efficient and effective way of making this information available to the widest possible audience. Record numbers of citizens are accessing government sites 24 hours a day to find information and services that will improve their daily lives. This makes it all the more essential that the Federal government deliver Web technologies that enable and empower citizens.

These Guidelines help move us in that direction by providing practical, yet authoritative, guidance on a broad range of Web design and communication issues. Having access to the best available research helps to ensure we make the right decisions the first time around and reduces the possibility of errors and costly mistakes.

Since their introduction in 2003, the Guidelines have been widely used by government agencies and the private sector, implemented in academic curriculum, and translated into several foreign languages. I encourage all government agencies to use these Guidelines to harness the Web in support of the President's vision of a Federal government that is citizen-centered and results-oriented.

– **Michael O. Leavitt**
Secretary of Health and Human Services

Foreword—Dr. Ben Shneiderman

Background

These new HHS Web usability Guidelines carry

forward one of the most enduring success stories in user interface design. They continue the noble tradition of thoughtful practitioners who have hacked their way through the unruly design landscape and then distilled their experience into compact and generalizable aphorisms or patterns.

Compilations of such guidelines offer newcomers a clearer roadmap to follow, helping them to avoid some of the swamps and potholes. Guidelines serve experienced experts and busy managers by giving them an overview and reminding them of the wide range of issues. Most importantly, guidelines provoke discussions among designers and researchers about which guidelines are relevant and whether a refined or new guideline should be added.

Guidelines should be more than one person's lightly-considered opinion, but they are not rigid standards that can form the basis of a contract or a lawsuit. Guidelines are not a comprehensive academic theory that has strong predictive value, rather they should be prescriptive, in the sense that they prescribe practice with useful sets of DOs and DON'Ts. Guidelines should be presented with justifications and examples.

Like early mapmakers, the pioneering developers of user interface guidelines labored diligently. Working for IBM in the mid-1970s, Stephen Engel and Richard Granda recorded their insights in an influential document. Similarly, Sid Smith and Jane Mosier in the early 1980s, collected 944 guidelines in a 500-page volume (available online at http://hcibib.org/sam/contents.html). The design context in those days included aircraft cockpits, industrial control rooms, and airline reservation systems and the user community emphasized regular professional users. These admirable efforts influenced many designers and contributed to the 1980s corporate design guidelines from Apple, Microsoft, and others covering personal computers, desktop environments, and public access kiosks.

Then, the emergence of the World Wide Web changed everything. The underlying principles were similar, but the specific decisions that designers had to make required new guidelines. The enormously growing community of designers eagerly consulted useful guidelines from sources as diverse as Yale University, Sun Microsystems, the Library of Congress, and Ameritech. Many of these designers had little experience and were desperate for any guidance about screen features and usability processes. Sometimes they misinterpreted or misapplied the guidelines, but at least they could get an overview of the issues that were important.

As Web usability guidelines became more widely used and consulted, discrepancies and contradictions became subjects of lively discussion at usability conferences and human-computer interaction research seminars. For example, many early Web guidelines documents were vague about appropriate numbers of links per page, sometimes falling back to mention George Miller's famous notion of seven plus or minus two. His work dealt with short-term memory capacity, but in studying a Web page, this factor has little bearing. As controversy grew, researchers collected dramatic empirical evidence that broader shallow trees were superior in information presentation websites.

Fortunately, the remarkable growth of the professional community of Web designers was matched by a healthy expansion of the academic community in psychology, computer science, information systems, and related disciplines. The research community went to work on the problems of menu design, navigation, screen layout, response time, and many more. Not every experiment is perfect, but the weight of validated results from multiple studies provides crucial evidence that can be gainfully applied in design.

This newest set of guidelines from the prestigious team assembled by the Department of Health and Human Services makes important contributions that will benefit practitioners and researchers. They have done the meticulous job of scouring the research literature to find support for design guidelines, thereby clarifying the message, resolving inconsistencies, and providing sources for further reading. Researchers will also benefit by this impressive compilation that will help them understand the current state of the art and see what problems are unresolved. Another impact will be on epistemologists and philosophers of science who argue about the relevance of research to practice. It is hard to recall a project that has generated as clear a demonstration of the payoff of research for practice.

The educational benefits for those who read the guidelines will be enormous. Students and newcomers to the field will profit from the good survey of issues that reminds them of the many facets of Web design. Experienced designers will find subtle distinctions and important insights. Managers will appreciate the complexity of the design issues and gain respect for those who produce effective websites.

Enthusiasms and Cautions

My enthusiasms for this HHS guidelines project and its product are great, but they are tempered by several cautions. To put it more positively, the greatest benefits from these research-based guidelines will accrue to those who create effective processes for their implementation. My advice is to recognize the Guidelines as a 'living document' and then apply the four Es: education, enforcement, exemption, and enhancement.

Foreword

Education: Delivering a document is only the first stage in making an organization's guidelines process effective. Recipients will have to be motivated to read it, think about it, discuss it, and even complain about it. Often a live presentation followed by a discussion can be effective in motivating use of guidelines.

Enforcement: While many designers may be willing to consider and apply the guidelines, they will be more diligent if there is a clear process of interface review that verifies that the guidelines have been applied. This has to be done by a knowledgeable person and time has to be built into the schedule to handle deviations or questions.

Exemption: Creative designers may produce innovative compelling Web page designs that were not anticipated by the Guidelines writers. To support creative work, managers should balance the enforcement process with an exemption process that is simple and rapid.

Enhancement: No document is perfect or complete, especially a guidelines document in a fast changing field like information technology. This principle has two implications. First, it means that HHS or another organization should produce an annual revision that improves the Guidelines and extends them to cover novel topics. Second, it means that adopting organizations should consider adding local guidelines keyed to the needs of their community. This typically includes guidelines for how the organization logo, colors, titles, employee names, contact information, etc. are presented. Other common additions are style guides for terminology, templates for information, universal usability requirements, privacy policies, and legal guidance.

Finally, it is important to remember that as helpful as these research-based guidelines are, that they do not guarantee that every website will be effective. Individual designers make thousands of decisions in crafting websites. They have to be knowledgeable about the content, informed about the user community, in touch with the organizational goals, and aware of the technology implications of design decisions. Design is difficult, but these new research-based guidelines are an important step forward in providing assistance to those who are dedicated to quality.

– **Ben Shneiderman, Ph.D.**
University of Maryland

Contributors

The following experts assigned 'Strength of Evidence' ratings for these guidelines and provided many sources listed in this book.

Robert W. Bailey, Ph.D.
President, Computer Psychology, Inc.

Carol Barnum, Ph.D.
Professor of Technical Communication, Southern Polytechnic State University

John Bosley, Ph.D.
Cognitive Psychologist, Bureau of Labor Statistics (U.S. Bureau of Census)

Barbara Chaparro, Ph.D.
Director of the Software Usability Research Laboratory, Wichita State University

Joseph Dumas, Ph.D.
Senior Human Factors Specialist, The Design and Usability Center, Bentley College

Melody Y. Ivory, Ph.D.
Assistant Professor, University of Washington

Bonnie John, Ph.D.
Associate Professor and Director of the Masters Program for Human Computer Interaction, Carnegie Mellow University

Hal Miller-Jacobs, Ph.D.
Managing Director, Human Factors International

Sanjay J. Koyani
Senior Usability Specialist, U.S. Department of Health and Human Services

James R. Lewis, Ph.D.
Senior Human Factors Engineer, IBM

Stanley Page
Usability Manager, The Church of Jesus Christ of Latter-day Saints

Judith Ramey, Ph.D.
Professor & Department Chair, University of Washington

Janice (Ginny) Redish, Ph.D.
President, Redish & Associates, Inc.

Jean Scholtz, Ph.D.
Computer Science Researcher, National Institute of Standards and Technology

Steve Wigginton
Architecture Manager, Amdocs

Cari A. Wolfson
President, Focus on U!

Larry E. Wood, Ph.D.
User Experience Consultant and Managing Partner, Parallax, LC

Don Zimmerman, Ph.D.
Professor of Journalism and Technical Communications, Colorado State University

Introduction

The Research-Based Web Design & Usability Guidelines (*Guidelines*) were developed by the U.S. Department of Health and Human Services (HHS), in partnership with the U.S. General Services Administration. This new edition of the *Guidelines* updates the original set of 187 guidelines, and adds 22 new ones. Many of the guidelines were edited, and numerous new references have been added. There are now 209 guidelines.

The *Guidelines* were developed to assist those involved in the creation of Web sites to base their decisions on the most current and best available evidence. The *Guidelines* are particularly relevant to the design of information-oriented sites, but can be applied across the wide spectrum of Web sites.

Who Are the *Guidelines* for?

The primary audiences for the *Guidelines* are Web site managers, designers, and others involved in the creation or maintenance of Web sites. A secondary audience is researchers who investigate Web design issues. This resource will help researchers determine what research has been conducted, and where little or no research exists.

Why Were the *Guidelines* Created?

HHS created this set of guidelines for several reasons:

1) To create better and more usable health and human service Web sites. HHS is mandated to provide clear information in an efficient and effective manner to patients, health professionals, researchers, and the public. Translating the latest Web design research into a practical, easy-to-use format is essential to the effective design of HHS' numerous Web sites. The approach taken to produce the *Guidelines* is consistent with HHS' overall health information dissemination model that involves rapidly collecting, organizing, and distributing information in a usable format to those who need it.

2) To provide quantified, peer-reviewed Web site design guidelines. This resource does not exist anywhere else. Most Web design guidelines are lacking key information needed to be effective.
   For example, many guideline sets:

   • Are based on the personal opinions of a few experts;
   • Do not provide references to support them;
   • Do not provide any indication as to whether a particular guideline represents a consensus of researchers, or if it has been derived from a one-time, non-replicated study; and
   • Do not give any information about the relative importance of individual guidelines.

By addressing these issues, the *Guidelines* will help enable organizations to make more effective design decisions. Each guideline in this book shows a rating of its 'Relative Importance' to the success of a Web site, and a rating of the 'Strength of Evidence' supporting the guideline. Professional Web designers, usability specialists, and academic researchers contributed to these ratings. The ratings allow the user to quickly ascertain which guidelines have the greatest impact on the success of a Web site, and to determine the nature and quality of the supporting evidence. The 'Relative Importance' and 'Strength of Evidence' ratings are unique to this set of guidelines.

3) To stimulate research into areas that will have the greatest influence on the creation of usable Web sites. There are numerous Web design questions for which a research-based answer cannot be given. While there are typically more than 1,000 papers published each year related to Web design and usability, much of this research is not based on the most important (or most common) questions being asked by Web designers. By providing an extensive list of sources and 'Strength of Evidence' ratings in the *Guidelines*, HHS hopes to highlight issues for which the research is conclusive and attract researchers' attention to the issues most in need of answers.

How to Contribute Additional References?

The authors of the *Guidelines* attempted to locate as many references and source documents as possible. However, some important *Guidelines* may not have been created, and some applicable references may have been missed. Readers who are aware of an original reference pertaining to an existing guideline, or who have a suggestion for a new research-based guideline, should submit an email to: info@usability.gov.

Please include the following information in your email:

- Reference information—author, title, publication date, source, etc. (Remember, books are usually not original references.);
- The guideline to which the reference applies;
- If suggesting a new guideline, a draft of the guideline; and
- A copy of the source (or a link to it), if available.

This information will help the authors maintain the *Guidelines* as a current and accurate resource.

Is There an Online Version of these *Guidelines*?

HHS has created an online version that can be found at www.usability.gov. The online version provides users with the opportunity to search for specific topics.

How to Use the Guidelines

Successful use of the *Guidelines* depends on how they are disseminated and used within an organization. Simply providing the *Guidelines* to designers and managers may not be enough to spur the adoption and use of these guidelines.

The *Guidelines* offer benefits to four key audiences:

- **Designers**
  The *Guidelines* provide a clear sense of the range of issues that designers—especially those new to the field—need to consider when planning and designing a Web site. Applying the *Guidelines* will help to reduce the negative impacts of 'opinion-driven' design, and referring to evidence-based guidance can reduce the clashes resulting from differences of opinion between design team members.

- **Usability Specialists**
  The *Guidelines* will help usability specialists evaluate the designs of Web sites. For example, usability specialists can use the *Guidelines* as a checklist to aid them during their review of Web sites. They also can create customized checklists that focus on the 'Relative Importance' and 'Strength of Evidence' scales associated with each guideline. For example, a usability specialist can create a checklist that only focuses on the top 25 most important issues related to the success of a Web site.

- **Managers**
  The *Guidelines* will provide managers with a good overview and deep understanding of the wide range of usability and Web design issues that designers may encounter when creating Web sites. The *Guidelines* also provide managers with a 'standard of usability' for their designers. Managers can request that designers follow relevant portions of the *Guidelines* and can use the *Guidelines* to set priorities. For example, during timeframes that require rapid design, managers can identify guidelines deemed most important to the success of a Web site—as defined by the 'Relative Importance' score associated with each guideline—and require designers to focus on implementing those selected guidelines.

- **Researchers**
  Researchers involved in evaluating Web design and Web process issues can use this set of *Guidelines* to determine where new research is needed. Researchers can use the sources of evidence provided for each guideline to assess the research that has been

conducted, and to determine the need for additional research to increase the validity of the previous findings, or to challenge these findings. Perhaps more importantly, researchers also can use the *Guidelines* and their sources to formulate new and important research questions.

Options for Implementing the *Guidelines*

There are a variety of ways to use the *Guidelines* in Web site development efforts. Users can read the book from beginning to end to become familiar with all of the guidelines. The book also can be used as a reference to answer specific Web site design questions. The *Guidelines* can be customized to fit most organizations' needs. The customization process can be approached in several ways:

- Encourage key stakeholders and/or decision makers to review the full set of guidelines and identify key guidelines that meet their Web design needs. For example, an organization may be developing portal Web sites that focus exclusively on linking to other Web sites (as opposed to linking to content within its own Web site). Therefore, it may focus more on selecting guidelines from the 'designing links' and 'navigation' chapters and less from the content-related chapters.

- Selected guidelines can be merged with existing standards and guidelines currently used within an organization. This may reduce the number of documents or online tools that designers must reference, and improve the adoption and use of existing standards and the *Guidelines*.

- The 'Relative Importance' and 'Strength of Evidence' scales can be used to prioritize which guidelines to implement. For example, on page 205 of this book, the guidelines are listed in order of relative importance. Using this list, designers can focus on implementing the 25 or 50 most important guidelines. In turn, the 'Strength of Evidence' ratings on page 210 can be used to determine the guidelines in which a designer can place the greatest confidence. Conversely, the guidelines with the lowest 'Strength of Evidence' ratings could indicate where more time should be devoted during usability testing. To help readers customize these guidelines to meet their organization's needs, an electronic copy of the *Guidelines* is posted at http://usability.gov/.

- Finally, Ben Shneiderman, Ph.D., suggests four ways to enhance the application of the *Guidelines*: education, enforcement, exemption, and enhancement. Please read his foreword to consider other ways to successfully implement the *Guidelines*.

Considerations Before Using the *Guidelines*

The guidelines are intended to improve the design and usability of information-based Web sites, but also can be applied across the wide spectrum of Web sites. When using the guidelines, it is helpful to remember that:

- Within each chapter of this book, the guidelines are ordered according to their 'Relative Importance' ratings. That is, the most important guidelines are toward the beginning of a chapter and the less important ones are toward the end.

- Readers may have a tendency to think that guidelines with one or two bullets on the 'Relative Importance' scale are not important. However, it is crucial to note that all guidelines in this book were rated as at least 'somewhat important' by the review team, otherwise they would not have been selected for inclusion in the book. Therefore, a guideline with one or two bullets is still important, just relatively less so than a guideline with four or five bullets.

- The guidelines may not be applicable to all audiences and contexts. For example, they may not apply to Web sites used by audiences with low literacy skills that have special terminology and layout needs. In general, these guidelines apply to English language Web sites designed for adults who are between 18 and 75 years of age.

- The guidelines may not adequately consider the experience of the designer. For example, a designer may have specialized knowledge about designing for a particular audience or context. These guidelines are adaptable and are not fixed rules.

- The guidelines may not reflect all evidence from all disciplines related to Web design and usability. Considerable effort has been made to include research from a variety of fields including human factors, cognitive psychology, computer science, usability, and technical communication. However, other disciplines may have valuable research that is not reflected in the guidelines.

- Some 'Strength of Evidence' ratings are low because there is a lack of research for that particular issue. The 'Strength of Evidence' scale used to rate each guideline was designed to put a high value on research-based evidence, but also to acknowledge experience-based evidence including expert opinions. Low 'Strength of Evidence' ratings should encourage the research of issues that are not currently investigated.

Background and Methodology

The U.S. Department of Health and Human Services (HHS) Research-Based Web Design & Usability Guidelines (*Guidelines*) project began in March of 2000. Since that time, each guideline presented in this book has undergone an extensive internal and external review. The process used to create the *Guidelines* is presented here.

Step 1: Creating the Initial Set of Guidelines
HHS wanted to develop a set of guidelines that could help designers build Web sites that are based on the best available research. The initial set of guidelines were drawn from existing Web design guideline and style guides, published research articles, research summaries, publicly available usability test reports, and lessons learned from in-house usability tests. This effort resulted in more than 500 guidelines.

Step 2: Reviewing the Initial Set of Guidelines
The initial seat of 500 guidelines was far too many for Web site designers to use effectively. An internal review process was conducted to:

* identify and combine duplicate guidelines.

* identify and resolve guidelines that conflicted with each other; and

* reword unclear guidelines.

Each of the reviewers had experience in Web site design, usability engineering, technical communication, software design, computer programming and/or human-computer interaction. This internal review reduced the initial set of guidelines to 398.

Step 3: Determining the 'Relative Importance' of Each Guideline
To determine the 'Relative importance' of each guideline, 16 external reviewers were recruited. Half of these reviewers were Web site designers and half were usability specialists. Each reviewer evaluated each guideline and assigned a rating based on the question, 'How important is this guideline to the success of a Web site?' Those guidelines that were rated as having little importance to the success of a Web site were eliminated. The set of guidelines now was reduced to 287.

Step 4: Determining the 'Strength of Evidence' for Each Guideline
The next step was to generate a 'Strength of Evidence' rating for each guideline. To do this, a group of eight usability researchers, practitioners and authors were recruited. These reviewers were all published researchers with doctoral degrees, experienced peer reviewers, and knowledgeable of experimental design. These reviewers constructed a set of criteria for judging the strength of the evidence for each guideline, which was used as the 'Strength of Evidence' scale.

Step 5: Finding Graphic Examples for the *Guidelines*

Most of the guidelines required a graphic example to ensure that users clearly understand the meaning of the guideline. The project team identified and reviewed several possible examples for each guideline, and selected the best examples. During this activity, the number of guidelines was further reduced.

Step 6: Grouping, Organizing, and Usability Testing the *Guidelines*

To ensure that the information about specific Web design issues is easy to find, a group of 20 Web site designers were asked to participate in a formal 'grouping' of the guidelines by participating in a card-sorting exercise. Each of the twenty individuals put the guidelines into groups that reflected how they think about Web design issues, and then provided a name for each group. Data from this exercise was analyzed with specially developed software and formed the chapters of this book.

Several draft page layouts in print format were developed for this book. These drafts were usability tested to determine how best to facilitate readers' ability to locate and understand information on a page. These findings, as well as readers' preferences, served as the basis for the final page layout. The final set that was published in 2004 contained 187 guidelines.

Step 7: Updating the Set of *Guidelines*

Since publishing the 2004 edition of the *Research-Based Web Design and Usability Guidelines*, the research literature has been continually searched for new and useful research-based information. We identified new relevant research that enabled us to substantially revise (update) 21 existing guidelines, and to add 22 new guidelines. Minor editing changes were made to a few other guidelines. The new and revised guidelines were edited by three different, independent groups of computer professionals. After editing, the final number of guidelines was 209.

The 'Relative Importance' ratings were revised based on a new survey in which 36 Web site professionals responded to an online survey. Each of these people reviewed each of the existing 209 guidelines and rated each one on a Likert-like importance scale with the anchors set at 'Important' to 'Very Important.'

The 'Strength of Evidence' ratings were revised for those guidelines where new research was reported. In this case, 13 usability professionals rated each of the new and revised guidelines, and assigned 'Strength of Evidence' ratings. The raters all were very familiar the research literature, all had conducted their own studies, and there was a high level of agreement in their ratings (Cronbach's alpha = .92). The criteria used for making the 'Strength of Evidence' estimates is shown on the next page.

The 'Strength of Evidence' ratings were revised for those guidelines where new research was reported. In this case, 13 usability professionals rated each of the new and revised guidelines, and assigned 'Strength of Evidence' ratings. The raters all were very familiar the research literature, all had conducted their own studies, and there was a high level of agreement in their ratings (Cronbach's alpha = .92). The criteria used for making the 'Strength of Evidence' estimates is shown below:

5 – Strong Research Support ①②③④⑤
- Cumulative and compelling, supporting research-based evidence
- At least one formal, rigorous study with contextual validity
- No known conflicting research-based findings
- Expert opinion agrees with the research

4 – Moderate Research Support ①②③④○
- Cumulative research-based evidence
- There may or may not be conflicting research-based findings
- Expert opinion
  - Tends to agree with the research, and
  - A consensus seems to be building

3 – Weak Research Support ①②③○○
- Limited research-based evidence
- Conflicting research-based findings may exist
  - and/or -
- There is mixed agreement of expert opinions

2 – Strong Expert Opinion Support ①②○○○
- No research-based evidence
- Experts tend to agree, although there may not be a consensus
- Multiple supporting expert opinions in textbooks, style guides, etc.
- Generally accepted as a 'best practice' or reflects 'state of practice'

1 – Weak Expert Opinion Support ①○○○○
- No research-based evidence
- Limited or conflicting expert opinion

Design Process and Evaluation

There are several usability-related issues,

methods, and procedures that require careful consideration when designing and developing Web sites. The most important of these are presented in this chapter, including 'up-front' issues such as setting clear and concise goals for a Web site, determining a correct and exhaustive set of user requirements, ensuring that the Web site meets user's expectations, setting usability goals, and providing useful content.

To ensure the best possible outcome, designers should consider a full range of user-interface issues, and work to create a Web site that enables the best possible human performance. The current research suggests that the best way to begin the construction of a Web site is to have many different people propose design solutions (i.e., parallel design), and then to follow up using an iterative design approach. This requires conducting the appropriate usability tests and using the findings to make changes to the Web site.

1:1 Provide Useful Content

Relative Importance:
①②③④⑤

Strength of Evidence:
①②③④⑤

Guideline: Provide content that is engaging, relevant, and appropriate to the audience.

Comments: Content is the information provided on a Web site. Do not waste resources providing easy access and good usability to the wrong content. One study found that content is the most critical element of a Web site. Other studies have reported that content is more important than navigation, visual design, functionality, and interactivity.

Sources: Asher, 1980; Badre, 2002; Baldwin, Peleg-Bruckner and McClintock, 1985; Celsi and Olson, 1988; Evans, 1998; Levine, 1996; Nielsen and Tahir, 2002; Nielsen, 1997b; Nielsen, 2000; Rajani and Rosenberg, 1999; Sano, 1996; Sinha, et al., 2001; Spyridakis, 2000; Stevens, 1980.

1:2 Establish User Requirements

Relative Importance:
①②③④⑤

Strength of Evidence:
①②③④○

Guideline: Use all available resources to better understand users' requirements.

Comments: The greater the number of exchanges of information with potential users, the better the developers' understanding of the users' requirements. The more information that can be exchanged between developers and users, the higher the probability of having a successful Web site. These could include customer support lines, customer surveys and interviews, bulletin boards, sales people, user groups, trade show experiences, focus groups, etc. Successful projects require at least four (and average five) different sources of information. Do not rely too heavily on user intermediaries.

The information gathered from exchanges with users can be used to build 'use cases.' Use cases describe the things that users want and need the Web site to be able to do. In one study, when compared with traditional function-oriented analyses, use cases provided a specification that produced better user performance and higher user preferences.

Sources: Adkisson, 2002; Brinck, Gergle and Wood, 2002; Buller, et al., 2001; Coble, Karat and Kahn, 1997; Keil and Carmel, 1995; Li and Henning, 2003; Norman, 1993; Osborn and Elliott, 2002; Ramey, 2000; Vora, 1998; Zimmerman, et al., 2002.

See page xxii
for detailed descriptions
of the rating scales
①②③④○

Guideline: Ensure that the Web site format meets user expectations, especially related to navigation, content, and organization.

Relative Importance:
① ② ③ ④ ⑤

Strength of Evidence:
① ② ③ ○ ○

Comments: One study found that users define 'usability' as their perception of how consistent, efficient, productive, organized, easy to use, intuitive, and straightforward it is to accomplish tasks within a system. It is important for designers to develop an understanding of their users' expectations through task analyses and other research. Users can have expectations based on their prior knowledge and past experience. One study found that users acted on their own expectations even when there were indications on the screen to counter those expectations.

The use of familiar formatting and navigation schemes makes it easier for users to learn and remember the layout of a site. It's best to assume that a certain percentage of users will not use a Web site frequently enough to learn to use it efficiently. Therefore, using familiar conventions works best.

Sources: Carroll, 1990; Detweiler and Omanson, 1996; Lynch and Horton, 2002; McGee, Rich and Dumas, 2004; Spool, et al., 1997; Wilson, 2000.

Example:

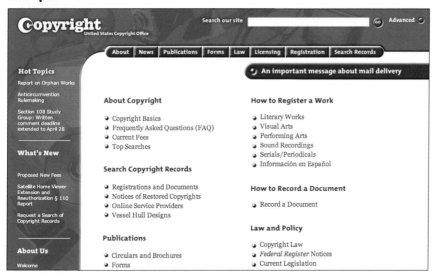

The Copyright Office Web site meets user expectations—links to the most likely user activities or queries (searching records, licensing and registering works, etc.) are prominently displayed and logically ordered, and there are very few distractions on the page.

1:4 Involve Users in Establishing User Requirements

Guideline: Involve users to improve the completeness and accuracy of user requirements.

Relative Importance:
①②③④⑤

Strength of Evidence:
①②③○○

Comments: One of the basic principles of user-centered design is the early and continual focus on users. For this reason, user involvement has become a widely accepted principle in the development of usable systems. Involving users has the most value when trying to improve the completeness and accuracy of user requirements. It is also useful in helping to avoid unused or little-used system features. User involvement may improve the level of user acceptance, although the research is not yet clear that it does in all cases. There is little or no research suggesting that user involvement leads to more effective and efficient use of the system. Finally, the research suggests that users are not good at helping make design decisions. To summarize, users are most valuable in helping designers know what a system should do, but not in helping designers determine how best to have the system do it.

Sources: Barki and Hartwick, 1991; Baroudi, Olson and Ives, 1986; Foster and Franz, 1999; Heinbokel, et al., 1996; Ives and Olson, 1984; Kujala, 2003; McKeen and Guimaraes, 1997.

1:5 Set and State Goals

Relative Importance:
①②③④⑤

Strength of Evidence:
①②○○○

Guideline: Identify and clearly articulate the primary goals of the Web site before beginning the design process.

Comments: Before starting design work, identify the primary goals of the Web site (educate, inform, entertain, sell, etc.). Goals determine the audience, content, function, and the site's unique look and feel. It is also a good idea to communicate the goals to, and develop consensus for the site goals from, management and those working on the Web site.

Sources: Badre, 2002; Coney and Steehouder, 2000; Detweiler and Omanson, 1996.

1:6 Focus on Performance Before Preference

Guideline: If user performance is important, make decisions about content, format, interaction, and navigation before deciding on colors and decorative graphics.

Relative Importance:
①②③④○

Strength of Evidence:
①②③○○

Comments: Focus on achieving a high rate of user performance before dealing with aesthetics. Graphics issues tend to have little impact, if any, on users' success rates or speed of performance.

Sources: Baca and Cassidy, 1999; Grose, et al., 1999; Tractinsky, 1997.

1:7 Consider Many User Interface Issues

Relative Importance:
①②③④○

Guideline: Consider as many user interface issues as possible during the design process.

Strength of Evidence:
①②③○○

Comments: Consider numerous usability-related issues during the creation of a Web site. These can include: the context within which users will be visiting a Web site; the experience levels of the users; the types of tasks users will perform on the site; the types of computer and connection speeds used when visiting the site; evaluation of prototypes; and the results of usability tests.

Sources: Bailey, 1996; Buller, et al., 2001; Graham, Kennedy and Benyon, 2000; Mayhew, 1992; Miller and Stimart, 1994; Zimmerman, et al., 2002.

See page xxii for detailed descriptions of the rating scales
①②③④○

1:8 Be Easily Found in the Top 30

Relative Importance:
①②③④○

Strength of Evidence:
①②③④○

Guideline: In order to have a high probability of being accessed, ensure that a Web site is in the 'top 30' references presented from a major search engine.

Comments: One study showed that users usually do not look at Web sites that are not in the 'top 30.' Some of the features required to be in the 'top 30' include appropriate meta-content and page titles, the number of links to the Web site, as well as updated registration with the major search engines.

Sources: Amento, et al., 1999; Dumais, Cutrell and Chen, 2001; Lynch and Horton, 2002; Spink, Bateman and Jansen, 1999.

Example:

The below snippet of html code illustrates one important way of ensuring that a Web site will be found by search engines—embedding keyword metatags. These keywords are read by search engines and used to categorize Web sites; understanding typical users will provide clues as to what keywords should be used.

> <meta name="description" content="The Official Website of the Federal Bureau of Investigation">
>
> <meta name="title" content="Federal Bureau of Investigation">
>
> <meta name="subject" content="Federal Bureau of Investigation, FBI, F.B.I., The Bureau, G-man, G-men, Mueller, Intelligence, Terrorism, Counterterrorism, Counterintelligence, Espionage, Crime, Most Wanted, J. Edgar Hoover, Department of Justice, Fraud, Money Laundering, Public Corruption, Cyber, Fingerprints, Be Crime Smart, Submit A Crime Tip, E-Scams, forensics, Kids Page, jobs, careers">

1:9 Set Usability Goals

Relative Importance:

Strength of Evidence:

Guideline: Set performance goals that include success rates and the time it takes users to find specific information, or preference goals that address satisfaction and acceptance by users.

Comments: Setting user performance and/or preference goals helps developers build better Web sites. It can also help make usability testing more effective. For example, some intranet Web sites have set the goal that information will be found eighty percent of the time and in less than one minute.

Sources: Baca and Cassidy, 1999; Bradley and Johnk, 1995; Grose, et al., 1999; Sears, 1995.

1:10 Use Parallel Design

Relative Importance:

Strength of Evidence:

Guideline: Have several developers independently propose designs and use the best elements from each design.

Comments: Do not have individuals make design decisions by themselves or rely on the ideas of a single designer. Most designers tend to adopt a strategy that focuses on initial, satisfactory, but less than optimal, solutions. Group discussions of design issues (brainstorming) do not lead to the best solutions.

The best approach is parallel design, where designers independently evaluate the design issues and propose solutions. Attempt to 'saturate the design space' before selecting the ideal solution. The more varied and independent the ideas that are considered, the better the final product will be.

Sources: Ball, Evans and Dennis., 1994; Buller, et al., 2001; Macbeth, Moroney and Biers, 2000; McGrew, 2001; Ovaska and Raiha, 1995; Zimmerman, et al., 2002.

Design Process and Evaluation

See page xxii for detailed descriptions of the rating scales

Design Process and Evaluation

1:11 Use Personas

Relative Importance:
❶○○○○

Strength of Evidence:
❶❷○○○

Guideline: Use personas to keep the design team focused on the same types of users.

Comments: Personas are hypothetical 'stand-ins' for actual users that drive the decision making for interfaces. They are not real people, but they represent real people. They are not 'made up,' but are discovered as a by-product of an investigative process with rigor and precision. Interfaces should be constructed to satisfy the needs and goals of personas.

Some usability specialists feel that designers will have far more success designing an interface that meets the goals of one specific person, instead of trying to design for the various needs of many. The design team should develop a believable persona so that everybody will accept the person. It is usually best to detail two or three technical skills to give an idea of computer competency, and to include one or two fictional details about the persona's life. Even though a few observational studies have been reported, there are no research studies that clearly demonstrate improved Web site success when personas are used.

Keep the number of personas for each Web site relatively small – use three to five. For each persona include at least a first name, age, photo, relevant personal information, and work and computer proficiency.

Sources: Cooper, 1999; Goodwin, 2001; Head, 2003.

See page xxii
for detailed descriptions
of the rating scales
❶❷❸❹○

2

Optimizing the User Experience

Web sites should be designed to facilitate and

encourage efficient and effective human-computer interactions.
Designers should make every attempt to reduce the user's workload
by taking advantage of the computer's capabilities. Users will make the
best use of Web sites when information is displayed in a directly usable
format and content organization is highly intuitive. Users also benefit
from task sequences that are consistent with how they typically do their
work, that do not require them to remember information for more than
a few seconds, that have terminology that is readily understandable,
and that do not overload them with information.

Users should not be required to wait for more than a few seconds
for a page to load, and while waiting, users should be supplied with
appropriate feedback. Users should be easily able to print information.
Designers should never 'push' unsolicited windows or graphics to users.

2:1 Do Not Display Unsolicited Windows or Graphics

Guideline: Do not have unsolicited windows or graphics 'pop-up' to users.

Relative Importance:
①②③④⑤

Comments: Users have commented that unsolicited windows or graphics that 'pop up' are annoying and distracting when they are focusing on completing their original activity.

Strength of Evidence:
①②③○○

Sources: Ahmadi, 2000.

2:2 Increase Web Site Credibility

Relative Importance:
①②③④○

Guideline: Optimize the credibility of information-oriented Web sites.

Strength of Evidence:
①②③○○

Comments: Based on the results of two large surveys, the most important Web site-related actions that organizations can do to help ensure high Web site credibility are to:

- Provide a useful set of frequently asked questions (FAQ) and answers;
- Ensure the Web site is arranged in a logical way;
- Provide articles containing citations and references;
- Show author's credentials;
- Ensure the site looks professionally designed;
- Provide an archive of past content (where appropriate);
- Ensure the site is as up-to-date as possible;
- Provide links to outside sources and materials; and
- Ensure the site is frequently linked to by other credible sites.

Sources: Fogg, 2002; Fogg, et al., 2001; Lightner, 2003; Nielsen, 2003.

See page xxii for detailed descriptions of the rating scales
①②③④○

2:3 Standardize Task Sequences

Relative Importance:
①②③④○

Strength of Evidence:
①②③④⑤

Guideline: Allow users to perform tasks in the same sequence and manner across similar conditions.

Comments: Users learn certain sequences of behaviors and perform best when they can be reliably repeated. For example, users become accustomed to looking in either the left or right panels for additional information. Also, users become familiar with the steps in a search or checkout process.

Sources: Bovair, Kieras and Polson, 1990; Czaja and Sharit, 1997; Detweiler and Omanson, 1996; Foltz, et al., 1988; Kieras, 1997; Polson and Kieras, 1985; Polson, Bovair and Kieras, 1987; Polson, Muncher and Engelback, 1986; Smith, Bubb-Lewis and Suh, 2000; Sonderegger, et al., 1999; Ziegler, Hoppe and Fahnrich, 1986.

Example:

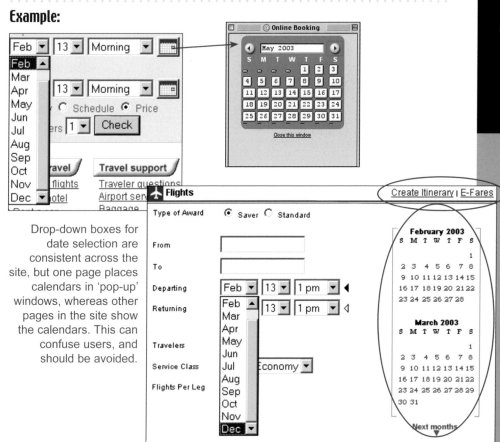

Drop-down boxes for date selection are consistent across the site, but one page places calendars in 'pop-up' windows, whereas other pages in the site show the calendars. This can confuse users, and should be avoided.

Optimizing the User Experience

2:4 Reduce the User's Workload

Relative Importance:

Strength of Evidence:

Guideline: Allocate functions to take advantage of the inherent respective strengths of computers and users.

Comments: Let the computer perform as many tasks as possible, so that users can concentrate on performing tasks that actually require human processing and input. Ensure that the activities performed by the human and the computer take full advantage of the strengths of each. For example, calculating body mass indexes, remembering user IDs, and mortgage payments are best performed by computers.

Sources: Gerhardt-Powals, 1996; Moray and Butler, 2000; Sheridan, 1997.

Example:

Calculators

How Much is Your Monthly Payment?

The following information is needed to calculate your monthly payment. After providing the information, click on "Calculate Single Payment" for your payment calculation. For a payment schedule, click on "Calculate Payment Schedule." You can reset the values you entered by clicking on the "Reset Values" option.

* = Required field

In Calculators

Fannie Mae True Cost Calculator

How Much House Can You Afford?

What Monthly Payment Is Needed for a House with a Specific Sales Price?

How Much House Can You Afford with a Specific Monthly Payment?

How Much Is Your Monthly Payment?

Is Now a Good Time to Refinance?

Loan balance: *

Mortgage term: *   30 Years ⬍

Interest rate: *   %

Calculate Single Payment

Calculate Payment Schedule

Reset Values

Enter your ID and password to sign in

ID:

Password:

☐ Remember my ID on this computer

Sign In

Mode: Standard | Secure

When looking to buy a house, users will know the value of variables necessary to calculate a monthly payment (interest rate, loan amount, etc.), but are incapable of quickly calculating it themselves.

See page xxii for detailed descriptions of the rating scales

Guideline: Do not require users to remember information from place to place on a Web site.

Relative Importance:
①②③④○

Comments: Users can remember relatively few items of information for a relatively short period of time. This 'working memory' capacity tends to lessen even more as people become older. One study compared the working memory performance of age groups 23-44 years and 61-68 years. The younger group performed reliably better than the older group.

Strength of Evidence:
①②③④⑤

When users must remember information on one Web page for use on another page or another location on the same page, they can only remember about three or four items for a few seconds. If users must make comparisons, it is best to have the items being compared side-by-side so that users do not have to remember information—even for a short period of time.

Sources: Ahlstrom and Longo, 2001; Baddeley, 1992; Bailey, 2000a; Broadbent, 1975; Brown, 1958; Cockburn and Jones, 1996; Curry, McDougall and de Bruijn, 1998; Evans, 1998; Kennedy and Wilkes, 1975; LeCompte, 1999; LeCompte, 2000; MacGregor, 1987; McEneaney, 2001; Nordby, Raanaas and Magnussen, 2002; Raanaas, Nordby and Magnussen, 2002; Spyridakis, 2000.

2:6 Minimize Page Download Time

Relative Importance:
①②③④○

Guideline: Minimize the time required to download a Web site's pages.

Strength of Evidence:
①②③④○

Comments: The best way to facilitate fast page loading is to minimize the number of bytes per page.

Sources: Barber and Lucas, 1983; Bouch, Kuchinsky and Bhatti, 2000; Byrne, et al., 1999; Evans, 1998; Lynch and Horton, 2002; Nielsen, 1997d; Spool, et al., 1997; Tiller and Green, 1999.

Optimizing the User Experience

2:7 Warn of 'Time Outs'

Relative Importance:
①②③④○

Strength of Evidence:
①②③○○

Guideline: Let users know if a page is programmed to 'time out,' and warn users before time expires so they can request additional time.

Comments: Some pages are designed to 'time out' automatically (usually because of security reasons). Pages that require users to use them within a fixed amount of time can present particular challenges to users who read or make entries slowly.

Sources: Koyani, 2001a; United States Government, 1998.

Example:

Email Member

 For your protection, this page will time out in 45 minutes. Please send your email before time is up.

First contact? It's easy. Just let this person know what caught your eye, and what makes

---

Microsoft Internet Explorer timeout problems.

Microsoft Internet Explorer ("IE") users, please note that if you are running reports on large chapter 11 cases, such as PG&E, the IE browser may "time out" before the report is completed. Unfortunately, the "time out" problem is beyond the court's control.

Although the current version of WebPACER was developed specifically for Netscape 4.x, other browsers such as IE may also work. If you are using IE and you receive the "This page can not be displayed" message, please increase the "time out" settings on your browser. We apologize for any inconvenience.

To obtain a copy of the latest version of Netcape.
Instructions for Microsoft IE browsers.

Timeout Warning

Your session is about to expire.

You can extend your session by clicking on the "Continue Session" button.

(Continue Session)

See page xxii for detailed descriptions of the rating scales
①②③④○

Guideline: Display data and information in a format that does not require conversion by the user.

Relative Importance:
①②③④○

Strength of Evidence:
①②③○○

Comments: Present information to users in the most useful and usable format possible. Do not require users to convert or summarize information in order for it to be immediately useful. It is best to display data in a manner that is consistent with the standards and conventions most familiar to users.

To accommodate a multinational Web audience, information should be provided in multiple formats (e.g., centigrade and Fahrenheit for temperatures) or the user should be allowed to select their preferred formats (e.g., the 12-hour clock for American audiences and the 24-hour clock for European audiences).

Do not require users to convert, transpose, compute, interpolate, or translate displayed data into other units, or refer to documentation to determine the meaning of displayed data.

Sources: Ahlstrom and Longo, 2001; Casner and Larkin, 1989; Galitz, 2002; Gerhardt-Powals, 1996; Navai, et al., 2001; Smith and Mosier, 1986.

Example:

FASTATS Home | NCHS Home | CDC/NCHS Privacy Policy Notice
Accessibility | Search NCHS | Data Definitions | Contact us

Birthweight and Gestation
(All figures are for U.S.)

- Median Weight at Birth: **3,000--3,499 grams (2000)**
- Annual Number of Babies Born Low Birthweight: **307,030 (2000)**
- Annual Percent Born Low Birthweight: **7.6 (2000)**
- Annual Percent Born Very Low Birthweight: **1.4 (2000)**
- Annual Number of Preterm Births: **467,201 (2000)**
- Annual Percent Born Preterm: **11.6 (2000)**
- *Source: National Vital Statistics Reports, Vol. 50, No. 5*

Comprehensive Data
- Live Births by Birthweight, Period of Gestation, and Race of Mother, 2000
  View/download PDF

Displaying time in a 24-hour clock format is not suitable for U.S. civilian audiences.

Recognize that there is a difference between the data units used in science and medicine and those used generally. Data should be presented in the generally-accepted manner of the intended audience—in this case, pounds and ounces.

US NAVAL OBSERVATORY MASTER CLOCK	Ticks Left
Fri May 12 14:14:47 2006 UTC	22

Optimizing the User Experience

Optimizing the User Experience

2:9 Format Information for Reading and Printing

Guideline: Prepare information with the expectation that it will either be read online or printed.

Relative Importance:
① ② ③ ④ ○

Comments: Documents should be prepared that are consistent with whether users can be expected to read the document online or printed. One study found that the major reason participants gave for

Strength of Evidence:
① ② ③ ○ ○

deciding to read a document from print or to read it online was the size of the document. Long documents (over five pages) were printed, and short documents were read online. In addition, users preferred to print information that was related to research, presentations, or supporting a point. They favore reading it online if for entertainment.

Users generally favored reading documents online because they could do it from anywhere at anytime with 24/7 access. Users were inclined to print (a) i the online document required too much scrolling, (b) if they needed to refer t the document at a later time, or (c) the complexity of the document required them to highlight and write comments.

Sources: Shaikh and Chaparro, 2004.

2:10 Provide Feedback when Users Must Wait

Guideline: Provide users with appropriate feedback while they are waiting.

Relative Importance:
① ② ③ ④ ○

Comments: If processing will take less than 10 seconds, use an hourglass to indicate status. If processing will take up to sixty seconds or longer, use a process indicator that shows progress toward

Strength of Evidence:
① ② ③ ④ ○

completion. If computer processing will take over one minute, indicate this t the user and provide an auditory signal when the processing is complete.

Users frequently become involved in other activities when they know they m wait for long periods of time for the computer to process information. Under these circumstances, completion of processing should be indicated by a non-disruptive sound (beep).

Sources: Bouch, Kuchinsky and Bhatti, 2000; Meyer, Shinar and Leiser, 1990; Smith and Mosier, 1986.

Example:

Step 1: Initialization
Step 2: Retrieve parameter values
Step 3: Set new values for parameters
80%
Cancel   Show details...

Guideline: Indicate to users the time required to download an image or document at a given connection speed.

Relative Importance:
①②③④○

Strength of Evidence:
①②③○○

Comments: Providing the size and download time of large images or documents gives users sufficient information to choose whether or not they are willing to wait for the file to download. One study concluded that supplying users with download times relative to various connection speeds improves their Web site navigation performance.

Sources: Campbell and Maglio, 1999; Detweiler and Omanson, 1996; Evans, 1998; Nielsen, 2000.

Example:

- Virtual U 1.3 Original Tutorial Download

  22mb Zipped Archive (8/25/00)

  Approximate download time (in minutes)

28.8	33.6	56.6	DSL/CABLE/T1
110 - 160	90 - 135	60 - 90	5 - 30

If you CNR this product, it will take approximately:

> 56 Kbps: 7 minutes 26 seconds
> DSL/Cable Modem: 1 minute 14 seconds
> T1 or LAN: 18 seconds

These are averages. Your actual download time will vary and depends on your particular Internet connection speed, Internet traffic, time of day, your computer's speed, etc.

To use CNR to install this program, return to the Warehouse listing and click on the green button with the running man.

See page xxii for detailed descriptions of the rating scales
①②③④○

Optimizing the User Experience

2:12 Develop Pages that Will Print Properly

Guideline: If users are likely to print one or more pages, develop pages with widths that print properly.

Relative Importance:
①②③④○

Strength of Evidence:
①②○○○

Comments: It is possible to display pages that are too wide to print completely on standard 8.5 x 11 inch paper in portrait orientation. Ensure that margin to margin printing is possible.

Sources: Ahlstrom and Longo, 2001; Evans, 1998; Gerhardt-Powals, 1996; Lynch and Horton, 2002; Spyridakis, 2000; Tullis, 2001; Zhang and Seo, 2001.

Example:

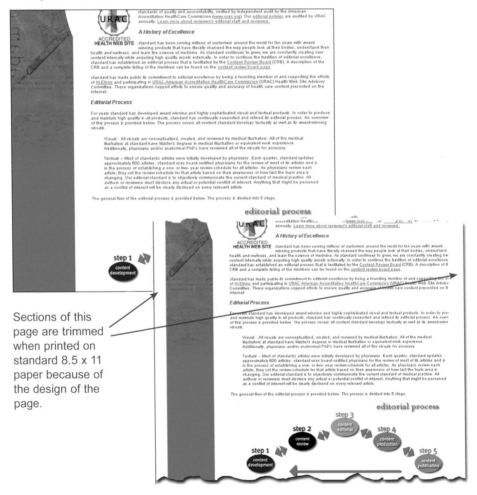

Sections of this page are trimmed when printed on standard 8.5 x 11 paper because of the design of the page.

2:13 Do Not Require Users to Multitask While Reading

Guideline: If reading speed is important, do not require users to perform other tasks while reading from the monitor.

Relative Importance:

Strength of Evidence:

Comments: Generally, users can read from a monitor as fast as they can from paper, unless they are required to perform other tasks that require human 'working memory' resources while reading. For example, do not require users to look at the information on one page and remember it while reading the information on a second page. This can reliably slow their reading performance.

Sources: Baddeley, 1986; Evans, 1998; Mayes, Sims and Koonce, 2000; Spyridakis, 2000.

2:14 Use Users' Terminology in Help Documentation

Guideline: When giving guidance about using a Web site, use the users' terminology to describe elements and features.

Relative Importance:
①②③○○

Strength of Evidence:
①②③○○

Comments: There is varied understanding among users as to what many Web site features are called, and in some cases, how they are used. These features include 'breadcrumbs,' changing link colors after they've been clicked, the left and right panels on the homepage, the tabs at the top of many homepages, and the search capability. For example, if the term 'breadcrumb' is used in the help section, give enough context so that a user unfamiliar with that term can understand your guidance. If you refer to the 'navigation bar,' explain to what you are referring. Even if users know how to use an element, the terms they use to describe it may not be the same terms that a designer would use.

Sources: Bailey, Koyani and Nall, 2000; Foley and Wallace, 1974; Furnas, et al., 1987; Scanlon and Schroeder, 2000.

See page xxii for detailed descriptions of the rating scales ①②③④○

Optimizing the User Experience

2:15 Provide Printing Options

Relative Importance:
①②③○○

Strength of Evidence:
①②○○○

Guideline: Provide a link to a complete printable or downloadable document if there are Web pages, documents, resources, or files that users will want to print or save in one operation.

Comments: Many users prefer to read text from a paper copy of a document. They find this to be more convenient, and it allows them to make notes on the paper. Users sometimes print pages because they do not trust the Web site to have pages for them at a later date, or they think they will not be able to find them again.

Sources: Detweiler and Omanson, 1996; Levine, 1996; Lynch and Horton, 2002; Nielsen, 1997e.

Example: Clicking on the 'Print Friendly' link will open a new browser window that allows the user to choose the sections of the document they wish to print. This is particularly useful for long documents, where users may only be interested in a particular section.

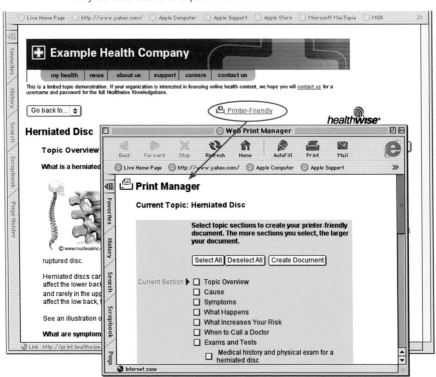

2:16 Provide Assistance to Users

Relative Importance:
①②◯◯◯

Strength of Evidence:
①②③◯◯

Guideline: Provide assistance for users who need additional help with the Web site.

Comments: Users sometimes require special assistance. This is particularly important if the site was designed for inexperienced users or has many first time users. For example, in one Web site that was designed for repeat users, more than one-third of users (thirty-six percent) were first time visitors. A special link was prepared that allowed new users to access more information about the content of the site and described the best way to navigate the site.

Sources: Covi and Ackerman, 1995; Morrell, et al., 2002; Nall, Koyani and Lafond, 2001; Plaisant, et al., 1997.

Example:

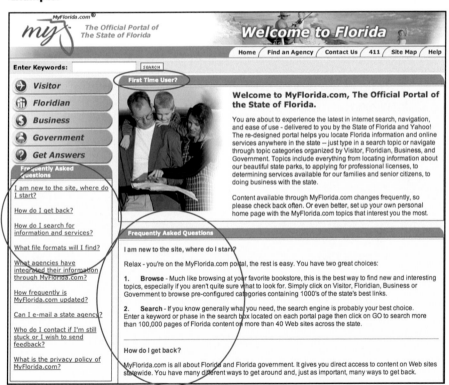

See page xxii
for detailed descriptions
of the rating scales
①②③④◯

3

Accessibility

Web sites should be designed to ensure that

everyone, including users who have difficulty seeing, hearing, and making precise movements, can use them. Generally, this means ensuring that Web sites facilitate the use of common assistive technologies. All United States Federal Government Web sites must comply with the Section 508 Federal Accessibility Standards.

With the exception of Guideline 2:7 and Guideline 9:6, all accessibility-related guidelines are found in this chapter. The sample of users who organized these guidelines assigned these two guidelines to other chapters. (See page xxv, Step 7 for more on how the guidelines were organized.)

Some of the major accessibility issues to be dealt with include:
- Provide text equivalents for non-text elements;
- Ensure that scripts allow accessibility;
- Provide frame titles;
- Enable users to skip repetitive navigation links;
- Ensure that plug-ins and applets meet the requirements for accessibility; and
- Synchronize all multimedia elements.

Where it is not possible to ensure that all pages of a site are accessible, designers should provide equivalent information to ensure that all users have equal access to all information.

For more information on Section 508 and accessibility, see www.section508.gov

3:1 Comply with Section 508

Relative Importance: *
①②③④⑤

Strength of Evidence:
①②○○○

Guideline: If a Web site is being designed for the United States government, ensure that it meets the requirements of Section 508 of the Rehabilitation Act. Ideally, all Web sites should strive to be accessible and compliant with Section 508.

Comments: Section 508 requires Federal agencies to ensure that their procurement of information technology takes into account the needs of all users—including people with disabilities. About eight percent of the user population has a disability that may make the traditional use of a Web site very difficult or impossible. About four percent have vision-related disabilities, two percent have movement-related issues, one percent have hearing-related disabilities, and less than one percent have learning-related disabilities.

Compliance with Section 508 enables Federal employees with disabilities to have access to and use of information and data that is comparable to that provided to others. This also enhances the ability of members of the public with disabilities to access information or services from a Federal agency.

For additional information on Section 508 and accessibility:
- http://www.section508.gov
- http://www.w3.org/WAI/

Sources: GVU, Georgia Institute of Technology, 1998; United States Government, 1998.

3:2 Design Forms for Users Using Assistive Technologies

Guideline: Ensure that users using assistive technology can complete and submit online forms.

Relative Importance: *
①②③④⑤

Strength of Evidence:
①②○○○

Comments: Much of the information collected through the Internet is collected using online forms. All users should be able to access forms and interact with field elements such as radio buttons and text boxes.

Sources: Covi and Ackerman, 1995; Morrell, et al., 2002; United States Government, 1998.

---

* Regardless of the 'Relative Importance' rating assigned by the reviewers, U.S. Federal Web sites must adhere to all Section 508 guidelines (see Guideline 3:1).

3:3 Do Not Use Color Alone to Convey Information

Guideline: Ensure that all information conveyed with color is also available without color.

Relative Importance: *
①②③④⑤

Strength of Evidence:
①②③④○

Comments: Never use color as the only indicator for critical activities. About eight percent of males and about one-half of one percent of females have difficulty discriminating colors. Most users with color deficiencies have difficulty seeing colors in the green portion of the spectrum.

To accommodate color-deficient users, designers should:
- Select color combinations that can be discriminated by users with color deficiencies;
- Use tools to see what Web pages will look like when seen by color deficient users;
- Ensure that the lightness contrast between foreground and background colors is high;
- Increase the lightness contrast between colors on either end of the spectrum (e.g., blues and reds); and
- Avoid combining light colors from either end of the spectrum with dark colors from the middle of the spectrum.

Sources: Bailey, 1996; Chisholm, Vanderheiden and Jacobs, 1999c; Evans, 1998; Hess, 2000; Levine, 1996; Murch, 1985; Rigden, 1999; Smith and Mosier, 1986; Sullivan and Matson, 2000; Thorell and Smith, 1990; Tullis, 2001; United States Government, 1998; Vischeck, 2003; Wolfmaier, 1999.

3:4 Enable Users to Skip Repetitive Navigation Links

Guideline: To aid those using assistive technologies, provide a means for users to skip repetitive navigation links.

Relative Importance: *
①②③④○

Strength of Evidence:
①②○○○

Comments: Developers frequently place a series of routine navigational links at a standard location—usually across the top, bottom, or side of a page. For people using assistive devices, it can be a tedious and time-consuming task to wait for all of the repeated links to be read. Users should be able to avoid these links when they desire to do so.

Sources: United States Government, 1998.

See page xxii for detailed descriptions of the rating scales
①②③④○

Guideline: Provide a text equivalent for every non-text element that conveys information.

Relative Importance: *
① ② ③ ④ ○

Strength of Evidence:
① ② ○ ○ ○

Comments: Text equivalents should be used for all non-text elements, including images, graphical representations of text (including symbols), image map regions, animations (e.g., animated GIFs), applets and programmatic objects, ASCII art, frames, scripts, images used as list bullets, spacers, graphical buttons, sounds, stand-alone audio files, audio tracks of video, and video.

Sources: Chisholm, Vanderheiden and Jacobs, 1999a; Nielsen, 2000; United States Government, 1998.

Example:

Alt text allows the with visual impairments user to understand the meaning of the picture.

President Discusses Immigration Reform with Members of the Senate

President George W. Bush places his hands on the arm of U.S. Senate Majority leader Senator Bill Frist, R-Tenn., and U.S. Senate Democratic leader Senator Harry Reid, D-Nev., right, at the conclusion of a meeting with legislators Tuesday, April 25, 2006 at the White House to discuss immigration reform. President Bush thanked both Republican and Democratic members of the Senate for their hard work to get a comprehensive immigration bill out of the U.S. Senate and hopefully to his desk before the end of the year.

White House photo by Eric Draper **full story**

* Regardless of the 'Relative Importance' rating assigned by the reviewers, U.S. Federal Web sites must adhere to all Section 508 guidelines (see Guideline 3:1).

Accessibility

3:6 Test Plug-Ins and Applets for Accessibility

Guideline: To ensure accessibility, test any applets, plug-ins or other applications required to interpret page content to ensure that they can be used by assistive technologies.

Relative Importance: *
①②③❹○

Strength of Evidence:
❶❷○○○

Comments: Applets, plug-ins and other software can create problems for people using assistive technologies, and should be thoroughly tested for accessibility.

Sources: United States Government, 1998.

3:7 Ensure that Scripts Allow Accessibility

Guideline: When designing for accessibility, ensure that the information provided on pages that utilize scripting languages to display content or to create interface elements can be read by assistive technology.

Relative Importance: *
①②❸○○

Strength of Evidence:
❶❷○○○

Comments: Whenever a script changes the content of a page, the change must be indicated in a way that can be detected and read by a screen reader. Also, if 'mouseovers' are used, ensure that they can be activated using a keyboard.

Sources: United States Government, 1998.

3:8 Provide Equivalent Pages

Relative Importance: *
①②❸○○

Strength of Evidence:
❶❷○○○

Guideline: Provide text-only pages with equivalent information and functionality if compliance with accessibility provisions cannot be accomplished in any other way.

Comments: When no other solution is available, one option is to design, develop, and maintain a parallel Web site that does not contain any graphics. The pages, in such a Web site should be readily accessible, and facilitate the use of screen readers and other assistive devices.

As a rule, ensure that text-only pages are updated as frequently and contain all of the same information as their non-text counterparts. Also inform users that text-only pages are exactly equivalent and as current as non-text counterparts.

Sources: Chisholm, Vanderheiden and Jacobs, 1999e; United States Government, 1998.

See page xxii for detailed descriptions of the rating scales
①②③④○

3:9 Provide Client-Side Image Maps

Relative Importance: *
①②③◯◯

Strength of Evidence:
①②③◯◯

Guideline: To improve accessibility, provide client-side image maps instead of server-side image maps.

Comments: Client-side image maps can be made fully accessible, whereas server-side image maps cannot be made accessible without employing a text alternative for each section of the map. To make client-side image maps accessible, each region within the map should be assigned alt text that can be read by a screen reader or other assistive device. Designers must ensure that redundant text links are provided for each active region of a server-side image map.

Sources: United States Government, 1998.

3:10 Synchronize Multimedia Elements

Relative Importance: *
①②③◯◯

Strength of Evidence:
①②◯◯◯

Guideline: To ensure accessibility, provide equivalent alternatives for multimedia elements that are synchronized.

Comments: For multimedia presentations (e.g., a movie or animation), synchronize captions or auditory descriptions of the visual track with the presentation.

Sources: Ahlstrom and Longo, 2001; Chisholm, Vanderheiden and Jacobs, 1999b; Galitz, 2002; Mayhew, 1992; United States Government, 1998.

3:11 Do Not Require Style Sheets

Relative Importance: *
①②③◯◯

Strength of Evidence:
①◯◯◯◯

Guideline: Organize documents so they are readable without requiring an associated style sheet.

Comments: Style sheets are commonly used to control Web page layout and appearance. Style sheets should not hamper the ability of assistive devices to read and logically portray information.

Sources: United States Government, 1998.

> * Regardless of the 'Relative Importance' rating assigned by the reviewers, U.S. Federal Web sites must adhere to all Section 508 guidelines (see Guideline 3:1).

3:12 Provide Frame Titles

Relative Importance: *
①②○○○

Strength of Evidence:
①②○○○

Guideline: To ensure accessibility, provide frame titles that facilitate frame identification and navigation.

Comments: Frames are used to divide the browser screen into separate areas, with each area presenting different, but usually related, information. For example, a designer may use a frame to place navigational links in the left page, and put the main information in a larger frame on the right side. This allows users to scroll through the information section without disturbing the navigation section. Clear and concise frame titles enable people with disabilities to properly orient themselves when frames are used.

Sources: Chisholm, Vanderheiden and Jacobs, 1999f; United States Government, 1998.

Example: Providing frame titles like that circled will allow users with visual impairments to understand the purpose of the frame's content or its function. Note that the right frame does not contain a title, and thus poses accessibility concerns.

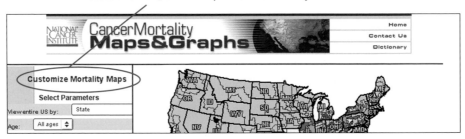

3:13 Avoid Screen Flicker

Relative Importance: *
①②○○○

Strength of Evidence:
①○○○○

Guideline: Design Web pages that do not cause the screen to flicker with a frequency greater than 2 Hz and lower than 55 Hz.

Comments: Five percent of people with epilepsy are photosensitive, and may have seizures triggered by certain screen flicker frequencies. Most current monitors are unlikely to provoke seizures.

Sources: United States Government, 1998.

> * Regardless of the 'Relative Importance' rating assigned by the reviewers, U.S. Federal Web sites must adhere to all Section 508 guidelines (see Guideline 3:1).

4

Hardware and Software

Designers are rarely free to do whatever comes

to mind. Just as designers consider their users' needs for specific information, they must also consider any constraints imposed on them by their users' hardware, software, and speed of connection to the Internet. Today, a single operating system (Microsoft's XP) dominates personal computer market. Similarly, only two Web site browsers are favored by the vast majority of users. More than ninety percent of users have their monitors set to 1024x768, 800x600 or 1280x1024 pixel resolution. And while most users at work have high-speed Internet access, many home users still connect using dial-up.

Within the constraints of available time, money, and resources, it is usually impossible to design for all users. Therefore, identify the hardware and software used by your primary and secondary audiences and design to maximize the effectiveness of your Web site.

Hardware and Software

4:1 Design for Common Browsers

Relative Importance:
❶❷❸❹○

Strength of Evidence:
❶❷○○○

Guideline: Design, develop and test for the most common browsers.

Comments: Designers should attempt to accommodate ninety-five percent of all users. Ensure that all testing of a Web site is done using the most popular browsers.

Sources of information about the most commonly used browsers:
- http://www.google.com/press/zeitgeist.html
- http://www.thecounter.com/stats/

Sources: Evans, 1998; Jupitermedia Corporation, 2003; Morrell, et al., 2002; Nielsen, 1996b.

Example:

This site, when rendered on a Macintosh, falls apart (right). The website should display properly on all platforms, as it does below when rendered on a PC.

See page xxii for detailed descriptions of the rating scales
❶❷❸❹○

4:2 Account for Browser Differences

Relative Importance:
①②③④○

Strength of Evidence:
①②○○○

Guideline: Do not assume that all users will have the same browser features, and will have set the same defaults.

Comments: Users with visual impairments tend to select larger fonts, and some users may turn off backgrounds, use fewer colors, or overrides font. The designer should find out what settings most users are using, and specify on the Web site exactly what assumptions were made about the browser settings.

Sources: Evans, 1998; Levine, 1996.

Example:

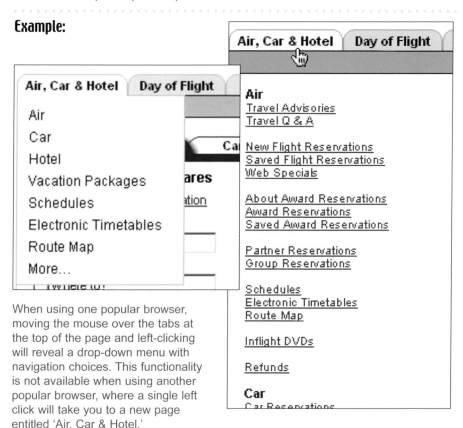

When using one popular browser, moving the mouse over the tabs at the top of the page and left-clicking will reveal a drop-down menu with navigation choices. This functionality is not available when using another popular browser, where a single left click will take you to a new page entitled 'Air, Car & Hotel.'

4:3 Design for Popular Operating Systems

Guideline: Design the Web site so it will work well with the most popular operating systems.

Comments: Designers should attempt to accommodate ninety-five percent of all users. Ensure that all testing of a Web site is done using the most common operating systems.

Relative Importance:

Strength of Evidence:
①②○○○

Currently, the most popular operating system is Microsoft's Windows XP which has over 80 of the market share. The second is Windows 2000 (eight percent), then Windows 98 (five percent), and the Macintosh (three percent). Designers should consult one of the several sources that maintain current figures to help ensure that they are designing to accommodate as many users as possible.

Sources: www.thecounter.com., 2006; Jupitermedia Corporation, 2003.

Example:

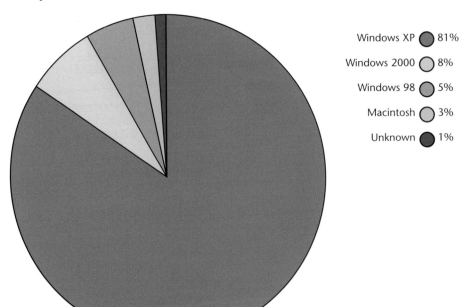

Windows XP 81%
Windows 2000 8%
Windows 98 5%
Macintosh 3%
Unknown 1%

Most popular operating systems, as reported by the counter.com, for June 2006.

See page xxii for detailed descriptions of the rating scales
①②③④○

Hardware and Software

Guideline: Design for the connection speed of most users.

Relative Importance:
①②③④○

Strength of Evidence:
①②○○○

Comments: At work in the United States, at least eighty-nine percent of users have high speed access, while less than eleven percent are using fifty-six K (or slower) modems. At home, more than two-thirds of users have high speed access. These figures are continually changing. Designers should consult one of the several sources that maintain current figures.

Sources: Nielsen/NetRatings, 2006; Forrester Research, 2001; Nielsen, 1999a; Web Site Optimization, 2003.

4:5 Design for Commonly Used Screen Resolutions

Guideline: Design for monitors with the screen resolution set at 1024x768 pixels.

Relative Importance:
①②③○○

Strength of Evidence:
①②○○○

Comments: Designers should attempt to accommodate ninety-five percent of all users. As of June 2006, 56% of users have their screen resolution set at 1024x768. By designing for 1024x768, designers will accommodate this most common resolution, as well as those at any higher resolution. Ensure that all testing of Web sites is done using the most common screen resolutions.

Sources: www.thecounter.com., 2006; Evans, 1998; Jupitermedia Corporation, 2003.

Example:

Resolution Stats

Thu Jun 1 00:01:02 2006 - Wed Jun 7 14:58:01 2006   6.6 Days

Resolution	Count	Percent
1024x768	13014406	(56%)
800x600	4053231	(17%)
1280x1024	3978242	(17%)
Unknown	839963	(3%)
1152x864	813277	(3%)
1600x1200	168204	(0%)
640x480	63251	(0%)

Hardware and Software

5

The Homepage

The homepage is different from all other Web

site pages. A well-constructed homepage will project a good first impression to all who visit the site.

It is important to ensure that the homepage has all of the features expected of a homepage and looks like a homepage to users. A homepage should clearly communicate the site's purpose, and show all major options available on the Web site. Generally, the majority of the homepage should be visible 'above the fold,' and should contain a limited amount of prose text. Designers should provide easy access to the homepage from every page in the site.

5:1 Enable Access to the Homepage

Relative Importance:
①②③④⑤

Strength of Evidence:
①②③○○

Guideline: Enable users to access the homepage from any other page on the Web site.

Comments: Many users return to the homepage to begin a new task or to start a task over again. Create an easy and obvious way for users to quickly return to the homepage of the Web site from any point in the site.

Many sites place the organization's logo on the top of every page and link it to the homepage. While many users expect that a logo will be clickable, many other users will not realize that it is a link to the homepage. Therefore, include a link labeled 'Home' near the top of the page to help those users.

Sources: Bailey, 2000b; Detweiler and Omanson, 1996; IBM, 1999; Levine, 1996; Lynch and Horton, 2002; Nielsen and Tahir, 2002; Spool, et al., 1997; Tullis, 2001.

Example:

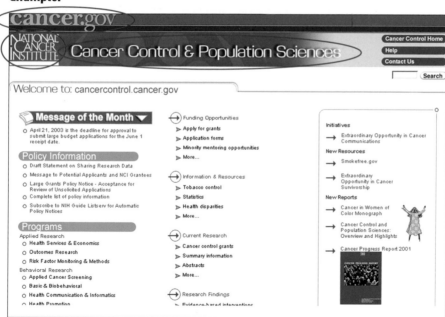

This Web page provides links to both the main organization homepage (clickable 'National Cancer Institute' logo in the upper left corner) as well as the sub-organization homepage ('Cancer Control Home' link placed in the upper right corner). These logos and their placement remain constant throughout the Web site.

5:2 Show All Major Options on the Homepage

Guideline: Present all major options on the homepage.

Comments: Users should not be required to click down to the second or third level to discover the full breadth of options on a Web site. Be selective about what is placed on the homepage, and make sure the options and links presented there are the most important ones on the site.

Relative Importance:
①②③④⑤

Strength of Evidence:
①②○○○

Sources: Farkas and Farkas, 2000; Koyani, 2001a; Nielsen and Tahir, 2002; Nielsen, 2001b.

Example:

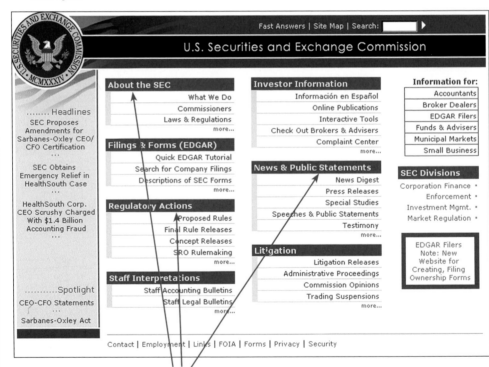

All major topic areas and categories are presented at the homepage level.

See page xxii for detailed descriptions of the rating scales
①②③④○

The Homepage

Guideline: Treat your homepage as the key to conveying the quality of your site.

Relative Importance:
①②③④⑤

Comments: In terms of conveying quality, the homepage is probably the most important page on a Web site. One study found that when asked to find high quality Web sites, about half of the time participants looked only at the homepage. You will not get a second chance to make a good first impression on a user.

Strength of Evidence:
①②③④○

Sources: Amento, et al., 1999; Coney and Steehouder, 2000; Mahlke, 2002; Nielsen and Tahir, 2002.

Example: This homepage creates a positive first impression:
- Tag line increases users' understanding of site;
- Key topic areas are presented in order of importance and are easy to scan; and
- Up-to-date news stories are available.

United States Department of Health & Human Services
Leading America to Better Health, Safety and Well-Being

- HHS Home
- Questions?
- Contact HHS
- Site Map

Search

Diseases & Conditions
- Heart Disease, Cancer, HIV/AIDS, Diabetes...
- Mental Health
- Treatment, Prevention, Genetics
- Clinical Trials
- Addictions, Substance Abuse

Safety & Wellness
- Eating Right
- Exercise, Fitness
- Safety Tips & Programs
- Smoking, Drinking
- Traveler's Health

Drug & Food Information
- Drugs, Dietary Supplements
- Food Safety
- Recalls & Safety Alerts
- Medical Devices

Disasters & Emergencies
- Bioterrorism
- Homeland Security
- Natural Disasters
- Hurricane Katrina Recovery

Grants & Funding

Families & Children
- Medicaid, Other Health Insurance
- Child Support, Child Care, Adoption
- Domestic Violence, Child Abuse
- Vaccines

Aging
- Medicare
- Health Issues
- Coping & Caring

Specific Populations
- Women, Men, Children, Seniors
- Disabilities
- Racial & Ethnic Minorities
- Homeless

Resource Locators
- Hospitals & Nursing Homes
- Other Health Care Facilities
- Physicians, Other Healthcare Providers

Policies & Regulations
- Policies, Guidelines
- Laws, Regulations
- Testimony

About HHS

In the Spotlight
- Mumps Outbreak in Midwest
- Medicare Prescription Drug Coverage
- Pandemic Flu / Avian Flu

News
- April 27, 2006 — HHS Assistant Secretary Simonson Travels to Bangladesh and India to Enhance Planning for a Potential Influenza Pandemic More >>
- April 20, 2006 — Statement by Mike Leavitt, Secretary of Health and Human Services On Resignation of David J. Brailer, National Coordinator for Health IT More >>
- April 20, 2006 — 30 Million Medicare Beneficiaries Now Receiving Prescription Drug Coverage More >>
- Daily HealthBeat Tip
- **All HHS News**

Other Highlights
- Secretary Mike Leavitt's Priorities
- HHS Pandemic Influenza Plan
- Improving Medicaid
- Privacy of Health Information/HIPAA
- Health Information Technology

Guideline: Clearly and prominently communicate the purpose and value of the Web site on the homepage.

Relative Importance:
①②③④○

Strength of Evidence:
①②③○○

Comments: Most people browsing or searching the Web will spend very little time on each site. Emphasize what the site offers that is of value to users, and how the site differs from key competitors. Many users waste time because they misunderstand the purpose of a Web site. In one study, most users expected that a site would show the results of research projects, not merely descriptions of project methodology.

In some cases the purpose of a Web site is easily inferred. In other cases, it may need to be explicitly stated through the use of brief text or a tagline. Do not expect users to read a lot of text or to click into the Site to determine a Site's purpose. Indicating what the Site offers that is of value to users, and how the Site differs from key competitors is important because most people will spend little time on each Site.

Sources: Coney and Steehouder, 2000; Nall, Koyani and Lafond, 2001; Nielsen, 2003.

Example: Concise taglines help users understand your site's purpose.

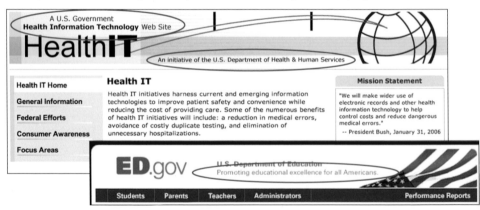

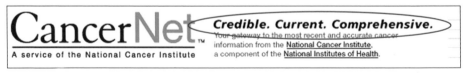

Guideline: Limit the amount of prose text on the homepage.

Comments: The first action of most users is to scan the homepage for link titles and major headings. Requiring users to read large amounts of prose text can slow them considerably, or they may avoid reading it altogether.

Relative Importance:
①②③④○

Strength of Evidence:
①②③○○

Sources: Bailey, Koyani and Nall, 2000; Farkas and Farkas, 2000; Morkes and Nielsen, 1998.

Example:

Clean, prose-free design allows users to quickly discern the primary headings and sub-headings without the distraction of paragraphs of text.

See page xxii
for detailed descriptions
of the rating scales
①②③④○

5:6 Ensure the Homepage Looks like a Homepage

Guideline: Ensure that the homepage has the necessary characteristics to be easily perceived as a homepage.

Relative Importance:
①②③④〇

Strength of Evidence:
①②③④〇

Comments: It is important that pages 'lower' in a site are not confused with the homepage. Users have come to expect that certain actions are possible from the homepage. These actions include, among others, finding important links, accessing a site map or index, and conducting a search.

Sources: Farkas and Farkas, 2000; Ivory and Hearst, 2002; Ivory, Sinha and Hearst, 2000; Lynch and Horton, 2002; Nall, Koyani and Lafond, 2001; Nielsen and Tahir, 2002; Tullis, 2001.

Example:

This homepage has characteristics that help ensure that it is distinct from second and third tier pages:
• Masthead with tagline;
• Distinct and weighted category links listed in order of priority; and
• All major content categories are available.

The second and third tier pages use a less visually imposing masthead and specific content.

5:7 Limit Homepage Length

Relative Importance:
①②③○○

Strength of Evidence:
①②○○○

Guideline: Limit the homepage to one screenful of information, if at all possible.

Comments: Any element on the homepage that must immediately attract the attention of users should be placed 'above the fold.' Information that cannot be seen in the first screenful may be missed altogether—this can negatively impact the effectiveness of the Web site. If users conclude that what they see on the visible portion of the page is not of interest, they may not bother scrolling to see the rest of the page.

Some users take a long time to scroll down 'below the fold,' indicating a reluctance to move from the first screenful to subsequent information. Older users and novices are more likely to miss information that is placed below the fold.

Sources: Badre, 2002; IBM, 1999; Lynch and Horton, 2002; Nielsen and Tahir, 2002; Spyridakis, 2000.

Example: Users can view all of the information on this homepage without scrolling.

See page xxii for detailed descriptions of the rating scales
①②③④○

5:8 Announce Changes to a Web Site

Relative Importance:

Strength of Evidence:

Guideline: Announce major changes to a Web site on the homepage—do not surprise users.

Comments: Introducing users to a redesigned Web site can require some preparation of expectations. Users may not know what to do when they are suddenly confronted with a new look or navigation structure. Therefore, you should communicate any planned changes to users ahead of time. Following completion of changes, tell users exactly what has changed and when the changes were made. Assure users that all previously available information will continue to be on the site.

It may also be helpful to users if you inform them of site changes at other relevant places on the Web site. For example, if shipping policies have changed, a notification of such on the order page should be provided.

Sources: Levine, 1996; Nall, Koyani and Lafond, 2001.

Example: Creating Web pages that introduce a new look or changes in the navigation structure is one way of re-orienting users after a site redesign.

Your resource for designing usable, useful and accessible Web sites and user interfa

New Usability.gov Design to be Launched in late May 2006

Usability Basics

- What is usability?
- Why is usability important
- How much does it cost?

Accessibility Resources

- Federal guidelines (Section 508)

Usability.gov

Usability.gov Announcement

New Usability.gov Design to be Launched in late May 2006

Usability.gov serves as a front door to usability information from across government. To better serve Web managers, designers, usability specialists and other audiences, we are updating Usability.gov's design, navigation, and content. Changes include:

- Easier access to usability methods, templates and examples
- A new step-by-step process to guide users through the user-centered design process
- Updated content on defining user requirements, writing usability statements of work, conducting usability testing, and writing usable content for the Web.
- A fresh new look and navigation based on usability testing with Web designers, managers, and usability specialists

Usability.gov■

Your guide for developing usable & useful Web sites

OUR NEW SITE

Our new look website has all the information you need, whether you are planning your journey, checking train times, or looking out for the latest special offers.

Our new site is updated in real-time so we have the most up to date rail and travel information for your needs.

Our site is also more accessible and PDA-friendly and easier to use. **Tell us what you think**. **Find out more about our new site**

5:9 Attend to Homepage Panel Width

Relative Importance:
①②〇〇〇

Strength of Evidence:
①②③〇〇

Guideline: Ensure that homepage panels are of a width that will cause them to be recognized as panels.

Comments: The width of panels seems to be critical for helping users understand the overall layout of a Web site. In one study, users rarely selected the information in the left panel because they did not understand that it was intended to be a left panel. In a subsequent study, the panel was made narrower, which was more consistent with other left panels experienced by users. The newly designed left panel was used more.

Sources: Evans, 1998; Farkas and Farkas, 2000; Nall, Koyani and Lafond, 2001.

Example:

The width of these panels (wide enough to clearly present links and navigation information, but narrow enough so that they do not dominate the page) allow the user to recognize them as navigation and content panels.

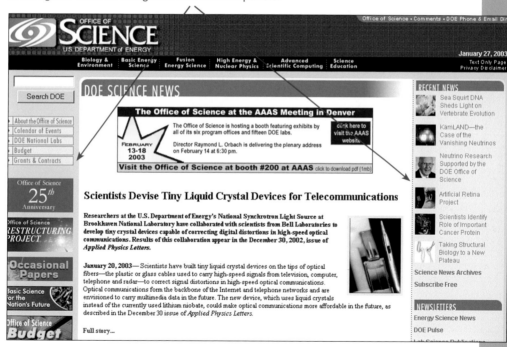

See page xxii for detailed descriptions of the rating scales
①②③④〇

6

Page Layout

All Web pages should be structured for ease of

comprehension. This includes putting items on the page in an order that reflects their relative importance. Designers should place important items consistently, usually toward the top and center of the page. All items should be appropriately aligned on the pages. It is usually a good idea to ensure that the pages show a moderate amount of white space—too much can require considerable scrolling, while too little may provide a display that looks too 'busy.' It is also important to ensure that page layout does not falsely convey the top or bottom of the page, such that users stop scrolling prematurely.

When a Web page contains prose text, choose appropriate line lengths. Longer line lengths usually will elicit faster reading speed, but users tend to prefer shorter line lengths. There are also important decisions that need to be made regarding page length. Pages should be long enough to adequately convey the information, but not so long that excessive scrolling becomes a problem. If page content or length dictates scrolling, but the page's table of contents needs to be accessible, then it is usually a good idea to use frames to keep the table of contents readily accessible and visible in the left panel.

6:1 Avoid Cluttered Displays

Relative Importance:
①②③④⑤

Strength of Evidence:
①②③○○

Guideline: Create pages that are not considered cluttered by users.

Comments: Clutter is when excess items on a page lead to a degradation of performance when trying to find certain information. On an uncluttered display, all important search targets are highly salient, i.e., clearly available. One study found that test participants tended to agree on which displays were least cluttered and those that were most cluttered.

Sources: Rosenholtz, et al., 2005.

Example:

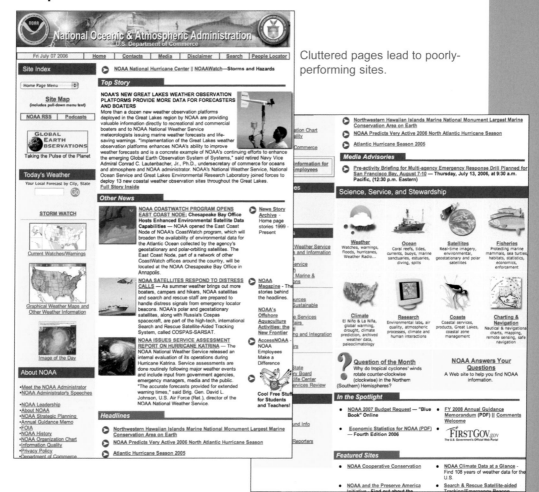

Cluttered pages lead to poorly-performing sites.

6:2 Place Important Items Consistently

Relative Importance:
①②③④⑤

Strength of Evidence:
①②③④○

Guideline: Put important, clickable items in the same locations, and closer to the top of the page, where their location can be better estimated.

Comments: Users will try to anticipate where items will appear on their screen. They will start 'searching' a page before the layout appears on their screen. When screen items remain constant, users learn their location on a page, and use this knowledge to improve task performance. Experienced users will begin moving their mouse to the area of the target before the eye detects the item. Users can anticipate the location of items near the top much better than those farther down the page.

Sources: Badre, 2002; Bernard, 2001; Bernard, 2002; Byrne, et al., 1999; Ehret, 2002; Hornof and Halverson, 2003.

Example: Important items—in this case, primary navigation tabs— are consistently placed at the top of each page.

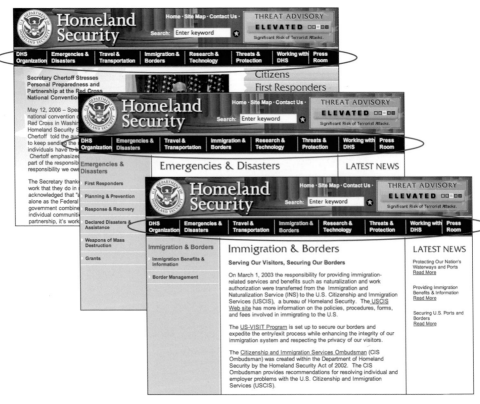

See page xxii for detailed descriptions of the rating scales
①②③④○

Guideline: Put the most important items at the top center of the Web page to facilitate users' finding the information.

Relative Importance:

① ② ③ ④ ⑤

Strength of Evidence:

① ② ③ ④ ○

Comments: Users generally look at the top center of a page first, then look left, then right, and finally begin systematically moving down the total Web page. All critical content and navigation options should be toward the top of the page. Particularly on navigation pages, most major choices should be visible with no, or a minimum of, scrolling.

Sources: Byrne, et al., 1999; Detweiler and Omanson, 1996; Faraday, 2000; Faraday, 2001; Lewenstein, et al., 2000; Mahajan and Shneiderman, 1997; Nielsen, 1996a; Nielsen, 1999b; Nielsen, 1999c; Spyridakis, 2000.

Example: Eye-tracking studies indicate this is the area of the screen where most new users first look when a Web site page loads.

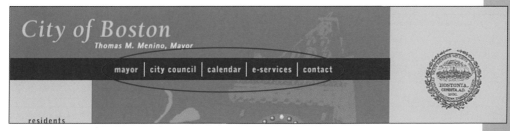

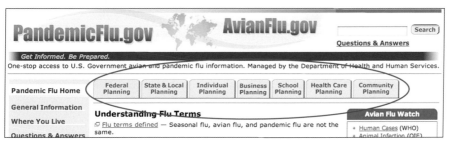

Page Layout

6:4 Structure for Easy Comparison

Guideline: Structure pages so that items can be easily compared when users must analyze those items to discern similarities, differences, trends, and relationships.

Comments: Users should be able to compare two or more items without having to remember one while going to another page or another place on the same page to view a different item.

Sources: Spool, et al., 1997; Tullis, 1981; Williams, 2000.

Example: This page layout is structured to allow users to quickly scan and compare data.

You are now viewing Prescription Drug Plan(s).Click here to view Medicare Advantage Prescription Drug Plan(s).
These results are sorted by the **Estimated Annual Cost**. To sort by another column, click the column name below.

Prescription Drug Plan Comparison

Select To Compare	Plan Summary			Plan Information			What You'll Pay			Enroll
	Plan Name	Estimated Annual Cost	More About This Plan (select option to view)	Mail Order	# of Pharmacies	Annual Deductible	Monthly Drug Premium	Monthly Cost Share	Click to Enroll in Plan
☐	MedicareBlue Rx Option 2 (Contract ID: S5743, Plan ID: 003) *Approved by Medicare*	$1,367.65	Select Below ▼	Yes	4	$0.00	$53.90	$60.07	Available 11/15
☐	MedicareBlue Rx Option 1 (Contract ID: S5743, Plan ID: 001) *Approved by Medicare*	$1,494.82	Select Below ▼	Yes	4	$250.00	$13.58	$96.41	Available 11/15
☐	AdvantraRx Premier (Contract ID: S5674, Plan ID: 033) *Approved by Medicare*	$1,722.36	Select Below ▼	Yes	6	$0.00	$33.43	$110.10	Available 11/15
☐	Prescription Pathway Bronze Plan Reg 25 (Contract ID: S5597, Plan ID: 090) *Approved by Medicare*	$1,768.35	Select Below ▼	Yes	4	$250.00	$25.29	$106.94	Available 11/15
☐	AdvantraRx Premier Plus (Contract ID: S5674, Plan ID: 035) *Approved by Medicare*	$1,784.88	Select Below ▼	Yes	6	$0.00	$43.64	$105.10	Available 11/15

<Previous 1 2 Next>   Plans per page: 5 ▼

The Monthly Cost Share is the amount you will pay for drugs after you've met any applicable deductible, but before you reach any coverage limits. Please select "View Cost Details" for more information.

Compare up to 3 Plans

See page xxii for detailed descriptions of the rating scales
①②③④◯

6:5 Establish Level of Importance

Relative Importance:
①②③④◯

Strength of Evidence:
①②③◯◯

Guideline: Establish a high-to-low level of importance for information and infuse this approach throughout each page on the Web site.

Comments: The page layout should help users find and use the most important information. Important information should appear higher on the page so users can locate it quickly. The least used information should appear toward the bottom of the page. Information should be presented in the order that is most useful to users.

People prefer hierarchies, and tend to focus their attention on one level of the hierarchy at a time. This enables them to adopt a more systematic strategy when scanning a page, which results in fewer revisits.

Sources: Detweiler and Omanson, 1996; Evans, 1998; Hornof and Halverson, 2003; Kim and Yoo, 2000; Marshall, Drapeau and DiSciullo, 2001; Nall, Koyani and Lafond 2001; Nielsen and Tahir, 2002; Nygren and Allard, 1996; Spyridakis, 2000.

Example: Priority information and links appear in order based on users' needs. The order was determined by surveys, log analyses, and interviews.

6:6 Optimize Display Density

Relative Importance:
①②③④○

Strength of Evidence:
①②③○○

Guideline: To facilitate finding target information on a page, create pages that are not too crowded with items of information.

Comments: Density can be defined as the number of items per degree of visual angle within a visually distinct group. This density either can be crowded with many items, or sparse with few items. One study found that locating a target in a crowded area took longer than when the target was in a sparse area. Also, participants searched and found items in the sparse areas faster than those in the crowded areas. Participants used fewer fixations per word in the crowded areas, but their fixations were much longer when viewing items in the crowded areas. Finally, participants tended to visit sparse areas before dense groups. To summarize, targets in sparse areas of the display (versus crowded areas) tended to be searched earlier and found faster.

Sources: Halverson and Hornof, 2004.

Example:

This homepage, though quite dense with information, gives the user's eyes a rest with areas of white space.

This page doesn't allow for quick scanning because of it's density.

See page xxii for detailed descriptions of the rating scales
①②③④○

Guideline: Visually align page elements, either vertically or horizontally.

Comments: Users prefer consistent alignments for items such as text blocks, rows, columns, checkboxes, radio buttons, data entry fields, etc. Use consistent alignments across all Web pages.

Sources: Ausubel, 1968; Bailey, 1996; Esperet, 1996; Fowler, 1998; Lawless and Kulikowich, 1996; Marcus, Smilonich and Thompson 1995; Mayer, Dyck and Cook, 1984; Parush, Nadir and Shtub, 1998; Spyridakis, 2000; Trollip and Sales, 1986; Voss, et al., 1986; Williams, 1994; Williams, 2000.

Example: The design of these list columns makes them extremely difficult to scan, and thus will slow users' attempts to find information.

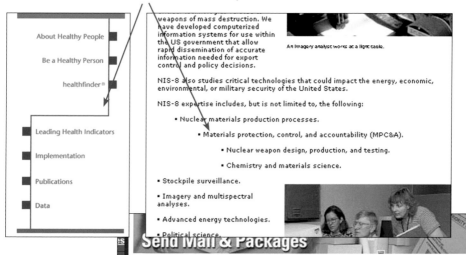

These columns are horizontally aligned, allowing the information to fall easily to the eye.

6:8 Use Fluid Layouts

Relative Importance:
①②③○○

Strength of Evidence:
①②③○○

Guideline: Use a fluid layout that automatically adjusts the page size to monitor resolution settings that are 1024x768 pixels or higher.

Comments: When web page layouts are fixed either to the left or centered, much of the available screen space is not used. It is best to take advantage of as much of the screen space as possible because this will help move more information above the fold. There has been no degradation in user performance when using the non-fluid layouts. However, most users prefer the fluid layout. One 2003 study reported a compliance rate for this guideline of twenty-eight percent, and a 2001 study found that only twenty-three percent of top Web sites used a fluid layout. Keep in mind that large monitors and higher pixel resolutions allow viewing of more than one window at a time.

Sources: Bernard and Larsen, 2001; Nielsen, 2003.

Example: Flexible, or liquid, layouts allow users to adjust Web pages to fit their screen space.

See page xxii
for detailed descriptions
of the rating scales
①②③④○

6:9 Avoid Scroll Stoppers

Relative Importance:
①②③○○

Strength of Evidence:
①②③④○

Guideline: Ensure that the location of headings and other page elements does not create the illusion that users have reached the top or bottom of a page when they have not.

Comments: In one study, three headings were positioned in the center of a page below a section of introductory text—the headings were located about one inch below the navigation tabs. When users scrolled up the page from the bottom and encountered these headings, they tended to stop, thinking the headings indicated the top of the page.

Similarly, users have been found to not scroll to the true bottom of a page to find a link because they encountered a block of text in a very small font size. This small type led users to believe that they were at the true bottom of the page. Other elements that may stop users' scrolling include horizontal lines, inappropriate placement of 'widgets,' and cessation of background color.

Sources: Bailey, Koyani and Nall, 2000; Ivory, Sinha and Hearst, 2000; Marshall, Drapeau and DiSciullo, 2001; Nygren and Allard, 1996; Spool, Klee and Schroeder, 2000; Spool, et al., 1997.

Example: When scrolling up the page, the design of this header (bold, shadowed, and bordered by bars) might suggest that the user has reached the top of the page, when a quick look at the scroll bar will indicate that much of the page exists above this section.

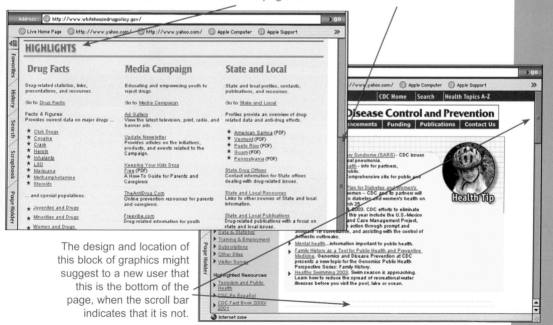

The design and location of this block of graphics might suggest to a new user that this is the bottom of the page, when the scroll bar indicates that it is not.

6:10 Set Appropriate Page Lengths

Relative Importance:
❶❷❸○○

Strength of Evidence:
❶❷❸○○

Guideline: Make page-length decisions that support the primary use of the Web page.

Comments: In general, use shorter pages for homepages and navigation pages, and pages that need to be quickly browsed and/or read online. Use longer pages to (1) facilitate uninterrupted reading, especially on content pages; (2) match the structure of a paper counterpart; (3) simplify page maintenance (fewer Web page files to maintain); and, (4) make pages more convenient to download and print.

Sources: Bernard, Baker and Fernandez, 2002; Evans, 1998; Lynch and Horton, 2002.

Example:

A shorter page is used for this homepage so that most content is visible without scrolling.

The scroll bar on each page is an indication of the amount of information hidden 'below the fold.'

See page xxii for detailed descriptions of the rating scales
❶❷❸❹○

6:11 Use Moderate White Space

Relative Importance:
❶❷❸○○

Strength of Evidence:
❶❷❸❹○

Guideline: Limit the amount of white space (areas without text, graphics, etc.) on pages that are used for scanning and searching.

Comments: 'Density' is the percentage of the screen filled with text and graphics. One study found that higher density is related to faster scanning, and has no impact on user accuracy or preference. Another study found that users prefer moderate amounts of white space, but the amount of white space has no impact on their searching performance. On content (i.e., text) pages, use some white space to separate paragraphs. Too much separation of items on Web pages may require users to scroll unnecessarily.

Sources: Chaparro and Bernard, 2001; Parush, Nadir and Shtub, 1998; Spool, et al., 1997; Staggers, 1993; Tullis, 1984.

Example: This page facilitates users' ability to scan for information by limiting the amount of white space.

Page Layout

6:12 Choose Appropriate Line Lengths

Relative Importance:
❶❷○○○

Strength of Evidence:
❶❷❸❹○

Guideline: If reading speed is most important, use longer line lengths (75-100 characters per line). If acceptance of the Web site is most important, use shorter line lengths (fifty characters per line).

Comments: When designing, first determine if performance or preference is most important. Users read faster when line lengths are long. However, they tend to prefer shorter line lengths, even though reading shorter lines generally slows overall reading speed. One study found that line lengths of about twenty characters reliably slowed reading speed.

When space for text display is limited, display a few longer lines of text rather than many shorter lines of text. Always display continuous text in columns containing at least fifty characters per line.

Research done using a paper-based document found that medium line length was read fastest.

Sources: Bailey, 2002; Duchnicky and Kolers, 1983; Dyson and Haselgrove, 2000; Dyson and Haselgrove, 2001; Dyson and Kipping, 1998; Evans, 1998; Paterson and Tinker, 1940b; Rehe, 1979; Smith and Mosier, 1986; Tinker and Paterson, 1929; Tullis, 1988; Youngman and Scharff, 1999.

Example: Formatting text into narrow columns with very short line lengths will slow users' reading speeds.

About Us	Community	Content	Ethics
Learn more about our history, mission and members. You can also "meet" our **NEW Board of Directors**, and our advisors in this section. If you are interested in learning more about us, please see how to contact us here.	Our community is international in scope and we encourage the open discussion of viewpoints. Enter here if you wish to become a member or a sponsor or learn about our conferences and workshops.	Over the years, we have developed a body of knowledge and opinions from thought leaders in the areas of online privacy, ethics and the use of technology to improve health care. In this area you can find Tips for Consumers, links to articles and presentations by	Since 1999 the Coalition has been actively involved in developing guidelines for the ethical use of the Internet in health care. Here you can find information about our eHealth Ethics Initiative and access the eHealth Code of Ethics in several languages.

Formatting text like this—roughly 100 characters per line—elicits faster reading speeds.

Subscribe to IHC-NEWS
Coali
mail n
notifie
throu
inform

Interagency Working Group on Assistive Technology Mobility Devices
Memorandum for the Secretary of Education, Health and Human Services, Labor, and the Commissioner of Social Security

When President George H. W. Bush signed the Americans with Disabilities Act of 1990, America opened its door to a new age for people with disabilities. Although much progress has been made since then, significant challenges remain for individuals with disabilities who seek full participation in American society.

My Administration is committed to increasing education and employment opportunities for individuals with disabilities. My New Freedom Initiative strives to provide people with disabilities increased opportunities to lead more independent lives by expanding education and job opportunities, and by ensuring that the latest technologies, which often make education and employment possible, are readily available.

Often, individuals with disabilities require assistive technology mobility devices such as powered wheelchairs and scooters in order to access education, training, and competitive employment. While there are several Federal programs, as well as State and local efforts, that help individuals with disabilities obtain these and other assistive technologies, they are not adequately coordinated. Other Federal programs provide funding of assistive technology mobility devices for medical purposes, but the intent of these programs has always been, and should remain, medical rather than educational or

Guideline: Use frames when certain functions must remain visible on the screen as the user accesses other information on the site.

Comments: It works well to have the functional items in one frame and the items that are being acted upon in another frame. This is sometimes referred to as a 'simultaneous menu' because making changes in one frame causes the information to change in another frame. Side-by-side frames seem to work best, with the functions on the left and the information viewing area on the right.

Keep in mind that frames can be confusing to some users. More than three frames on a page can be especially confusing to infrequent and occasional users. Frames also pose problems when users attempt to print, and when they search pages.

Sources: Ashworth and Hamilton, 1997; Bernard and Hull, 2002; Bernard, Hull and Drake, 2001; Detweiler and Omanson, 1996; Kosslyn, 1994; Koyani, 2001a; Lynch and Horton, 2002; Nielsen, 1996a; Nielsen, 1999b; Powers, et al., 1961; Spool, et al., 1997.

Example:

Multi-variable charting applications are one example of an acceptable use of frames. The map of the United States in the right frame is controlled by the menu selections in the left frame. As such, the left frame remains fixed while the right frame regenerates based upon the user-defined selections in the left frame. Such use of frames allows users to continually view the menu selections, avoiding use of the Back button when changing selections and eliminating the need for users to maintain this information in their working memory.

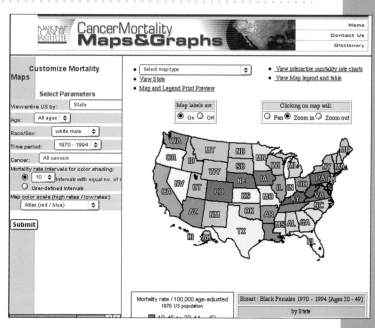

See page xxii for detailed descriptions of the rating scales
① ② ③ ④ ○

Page Layout

7

Navigation

Navigation refers to the method used to find

information within a Web site. A navigation page is used primarily to help users locate and link to destination pages. A Web site's navigation scheme and features should allow users to find and access information effectively and efficiently. When possible, this means designers should keep navigation-only pages short. Designers should include site maps, and provide effective feedback on the user's location within the site.

To facilitate navigation, designers should differentiate and group navigation elements and use appropriate menu types. It is also important to use descriptive tab labels, provide a clickable list of page contents on long pages, and add 'glosses' where they will help users select the correct link. In well-designed sites, users do not get trapped in dead-end pages.

7:1 Provide Navigational Options

Relative Importance:
①②③④○

Strength of Evidence:
①②○○○

Guideline: Do not create or direct users into pages that have no navigational options.

Comments: Many Web pages contain links that open new browser windows. When these browser windows open, the Back button is disabled (in essence, the new browser window knows nothing of the user's past navigation, and thus is disabled). If the new window opens full-screen, users may not realize that they have been redirected to another window, and may become frustrated because they cannot press Back to return to the previous page. If such links are incorporated into a Web site, the newly-opened window should contain a prominent action control that will close the window and return the user to the original browser window.

In addition, designers should not create Web pages that disable the browser's Back button. Disabling the Back button can result in confusion and frustration for users, and drastically inhibits their navigation.

Sources: Detweiler and Omanson, 1996; Lynch and Horton, 2002; Spool, et al., 1997; Tullis, 2001; Zimmerman, Slater and Kendall, 2001.

Example:

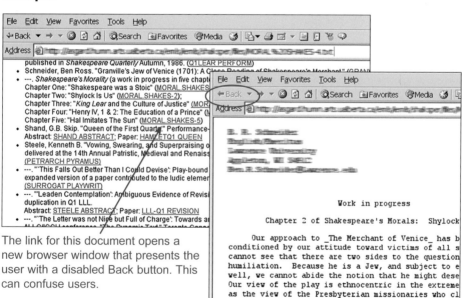

The link for this document opens a new browser window that presents the user with a disabled Back button. This can confuse users.

7:2 Differentiate and Group Navigation Elements

Guideline: Clearly differentiate navigation elements from one another, but group and place them in a consistent and easy to find place on each page.

Relative Importance:
①②③④○

Strength of Evidence:
①②③○○

Comments: Create a common, Web site-wide navigational scheme to help users learn and understand the structure of your Web site. Use the same navigation scheme on all pages by consistently locating tabs, headings, lists, search, site map, etc. Locate critical navigation elements in places that will suggest clickability (e.g., lists of words in the left or right panels are generally assumed to be links).

Make navigational elements different enough from one another so that users will be able to understand the difference in their meaning and destination. Grouping reduces the amount of time that users need to locate and identify navigation elements.

Do not make users infer the label by studying a few items in the group. Finally, make it easy for users to move from label to label (link to link) with a single eye movement. This best can be done by positioning relevant options close together and to using vertical lists.

Sources: Bailey, 2000b; Detweiler and Omanson, 1996; Evans, 1998; Farkas and Farkas, 2000; Hornof and Halverson, 2003; Koyani and Nall, 1999; Lynch and Horton, 2002; Nielsen and Tahir, 2002; Niemela and Saarinen, 2000.

Example:

Navigation elements are grouped (high-level topic areas across the top of the page) and consistently placed across the Web site.

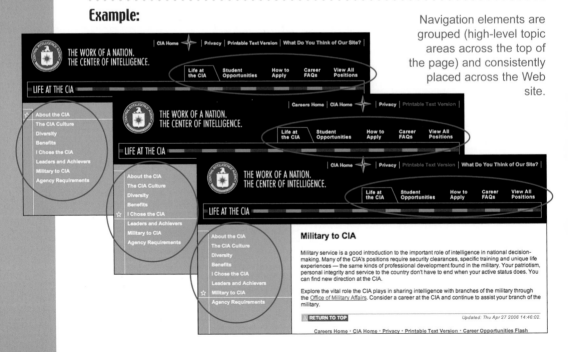

Guideline: On long pages, provide a 'list of contents' with links that take users to the corresponding content farther down the page.

Relative Importance:
①②③④○

Strength of Evidence:
①②③○○

Comments: For long pages with several distinct sections that are not visible from the first screenful, add a short, clickable list of the sections (sometimes called 'anchor' or 'within-page' links) at the top of the page. 'Anchor links' can serve two purposes: they provide an outline of the page so users can quickly determine if it contains the desired information, and they allow users to quickly navigate to specific information.

Since 'anchor links' enable a direct link to content below the first screenful, they are also useful for getting users to specific information quickly when they arrive from a completely different page.

Sources: Bieber, 1997; Farkas and Farkas, 2000; Haas and Grams, 1998; Levine, 1996; Nall, Koyani and Lafond, 2001; Spool, et al., 1997; Spyridakis, 2000; Williams, 2000; Zimmerman, Slater and Kendall, 2001.

Example:

Contents

Abstract

Executive Summary

Introduction

Uses and Benefits of Technology Roadmapping

What is Technology Roadmapping?

What is a Technology Roadmap?

Types of Technology Roadmaps

Planning and Business Development Context for Technology Roadmapping

Knowledge and Skills Required for Technology Roadmapping

Technology Roadmapping Process

What is Technology Roadmapping?
Technology roadmapping is a needs-driven technology planning process to help id select, and develop technology alternatives to satisfy a set of product needs. It bri together a team of experts to develop a framework for organizing and presenting t technology-planning information to make the appropriate technology investment d to leverage those investments. (For an example of this teaming process at the ind see Garcia, Introduction to Technology Roadmapping: The Semiconductor Industr Association's Technology Roadmapping Process.)

Given a set of needs, the technology roadmapping process provides a way to dev organize, and present information about the critical system requirements and perfo targets that must be satisfied by certain time frames. It also identifies technologies to be developed to meet those targets. Finally, it provides the information needed trade-offs among different technology alternatives.

Roadmapping can be done at either of two levels - industry or corporate. These lev different commitments in terms of time, cost, level of effort, and complexity. Howeve levels the resulting roadmaps have the same structure - needs, critical system requ and targets, technology areas, technology drivers and targets, technology alternat recommended alternatives or paths, and a roadmap report - although with different detail. Technology roadmapping within a national laboratory is essentially corporat roadmapping, although a national laboratory may participate in an industry roadma process.
Back to Contents

What is a Technology Roadmap?
A technology roadmap is the document that is generated by the technology roadm process. It identifies (for a set of product needs) the critical system requirements, th and process performance targets, and the technology alternatives and milestones those targets. In effect, a technology roadmap identifies alternate technology "roa meeting certain performance objectives. A single path may be selected and a plan If there is high uncertainty or risk, then multiple paths may be selected and pursue concurrently. The roadmap identifies precise objectives and helps focus resources critical technologies that are needed to meet those objectives. This focusing is imp because it allows increasingly limited R&D investments to be used more effectively.
Back to Contents

Types of Technology Roadmaps
There are different types of technology roadmaps. The product technology roadma by product/process needs. Since the product technology roadmap is the focus of t is usually referred to simply as a technology roadmap.

Another type of technology roadmap, which is used by some corporations, is an er technology roadmap. An emerging technology roadmap differs from a product tech roadmap in two ways:

See page xxii
for detailed descriptions
of the rating scales
①②③④○

Guideline: Provide feedback to let users know where they are in the Web site.

Relative Importance:
①②③④○

Comments: Feedback provides users with the information they need to understand where they are within the Web site, and for proceeding to the next activity. Examples of feedback include providing path and hierarchy information (i.e., 'breadcrumbs'), matching link text to the destination page's heading, and creating URLs that relate to the user's location on the site. Other forms of feedback include changing the color of a link that has been clicked (suggesting that destination has been visited), and using other visual cues to indicate the active portion of the screen.

Strength of Evidence:
①②○○○

Sources: Evans, 1998; Farkas and Farkas, 2000; IBM, 1999; Lynch and Horton, 2002; Marchionini, 1995; Nielsen and Tahir, 2002; Spool, et al., 1997.

Example:

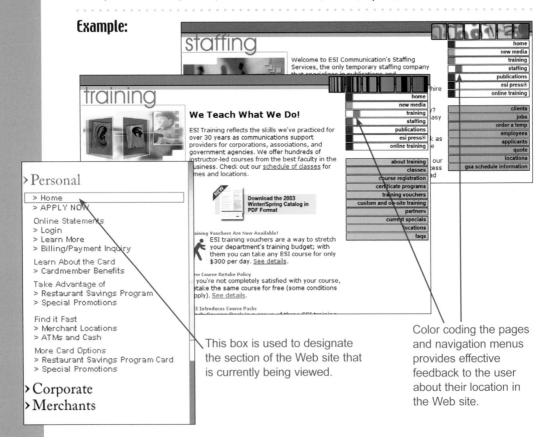

This box is used to designate the section of the Web site that is currently being viewed.

Color coding the pages and navigation menus provides effective feedback to the user about their location in the Web site.

See page xxii for detailed descriptions of the rating scales
①②③④○

Navigation

Guideline: Place the primary navigation menus in the left panel, and the secondary and tertiary menus together.

Relative Importance:
①②③④○

Strength of Evidence:
①②③○○

Comments: One study found that navigation times were faster when the primary menu was located in the left panel. Also, navigation performance was best when the secondary and tertiary menus were placed together. Placing a navigation menu in the right panel was supported as a viable design option by both performance and preference measures. Users preferred having the primary menu in the left panel, and grouping secondary and tertiary menus together, or grouping all three menu levels together. The best performance and preference was achieved when all three menus were placed in the left panel (placing them all in the right panel achieved close to the same performance level).

Sources: Kalbach and Bosenick, 2003; Kingsburg and Andre, 2004.

Example:

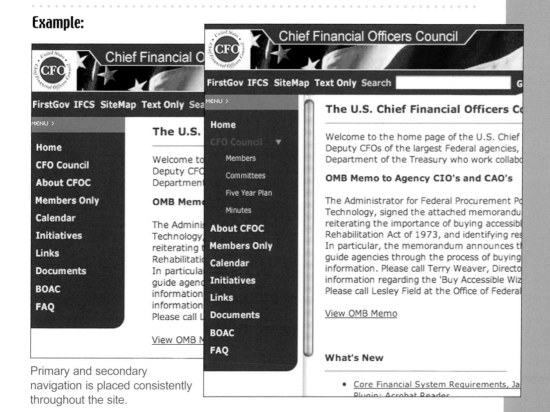

Primary and secondary navigation is placed consistently throughout the site.

7:6 Use Descriptive Tab Labels

Relative Importance:

Strength of Evidence:

Guideline: Ensure that tab labels are clearly descriptive of their function or destination.

Comments: Users like tabs when they have labels that are descriptive enough to allow error-free selections. When tab labels cannot be made clear because of the lack of space, do not use tabs.

Sources: Allinson and Hammond, 1999; Badre, 2002; Koyani, 2001b.

Example:

These tab labels clearly describe the types of information a user can expect to find on the destination pages.

These tab labels are not as descriptive which leaves the user in doubt about the type of information available on the destination pages.

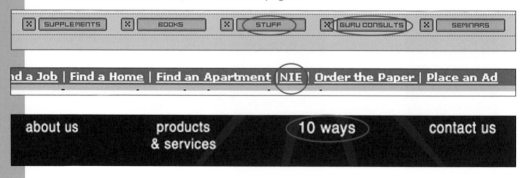

See page xxii for detailed descriptions of the rating scales

Relative Importance:

Strength of Evidence:

Guideline: Ensure that navigation tabs are located at the top of the page, and look like clickable versions of real-world tabs.

Comments: Users can be confused about the use of tabs when they do not look like real-world tabs. Real-world tabs are those that resemble the ones found in a file drawer. One study showed that users are more likely to find and click appropriately on tabs that look like real-world tabs.

Sources: Bailey, Koyani and Nall, 2000; Kim, 1998.

Example: These clickable tabs look just like tabs found in office filing cabinets.

The design of these navigation tabs provides few clues to suggest that they are clickable until a user mouses-over them. Mousing-over is a slow and inefficient way for users to discover navigation elements.

7:8 Keep Navigation-Only Pages Short

Relative Importance:
① ② ○ ○ ○

Strength of Evidence:
① ② ③ ④ ○

Guideline: Do not require users to scroll purely navigational pages.

Comments: Ideally, navigation-only pages should contain no more than one screenful of information. Users should not need to scroll the page, even a small distance. One study showed that users considered the bottom of one screenful as the end of a page, and they did not scroll further to find additional navigational options.

Sources: Piolat, Roussey and Thunin, 1998; Schwarz, Beldie and Pastoor, 1983; Zaphiris, 2000.

Example: Users can view all of the information on these navigation pages without scrolling.

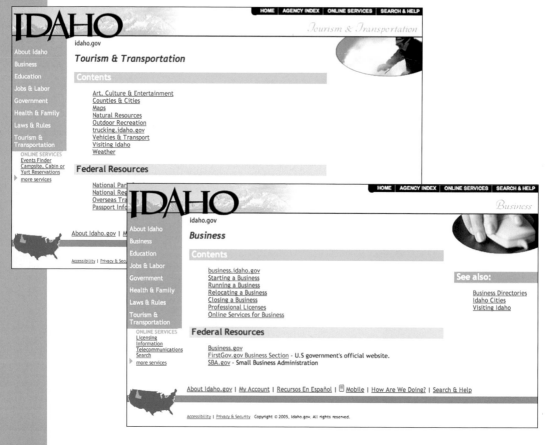

See page xxii for detailed descriptions of the rating scales
① ② ③ ④ ○

7:9 Use Appropriate Menu Types

Relative Importance:
① ② ○ ○ ○

Strength of Evidence:
① ② ③ ④ ○

Guideline: Use 'sequential' menus for simple forward-moving tasks, and use 'simultaneous' menus for tasks that would otherwise require numerous uses of the Back button.

Comments: Most Web sites use familiar 'sequential' menus that require items to be selected from a series of menus in some predetermined order. After each selection is made, another menu opens. The final choice is constrained by the sum total of all previous choices.

Simultaneous menus display choices from multiple levels in the menu hierarchy, providing users with the ability to make choices from the menu in any order. Simultaneous menus are often presented in frames, and are best employed in situations where users would have to make extensive use of the Back button if presented with a sequential menu.

Sources: Card, Moran and Newell, 1980a; Hochheiser and Shneiderman, 2000.

Example:

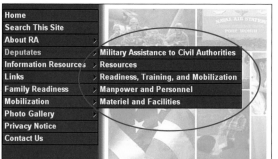

This is an example of a 'sequential' menu. In this case, mousing-over 'Deputates' invokes the circled sub-menu.

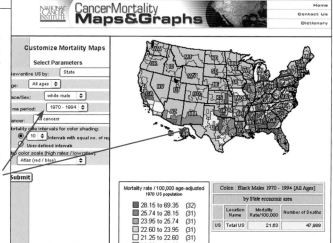

This is a good example of when to use 'simultaneous' menus. The user can repetitively manipulate the many variables shown in the left panel and view the results on the map in the right panel without having to use the Back button.

7:10 Use Site Maps

Relative Importance:
①②◯◯◯

Strength of Evidence:
①②③④◯

Guideline: Use site maps for Web sites that have many pages.

Comments: Site maps provide an overview of the Web site. They may display the hierarchy of the Web site, may be designed to resemble a traditional table of contents, or may be a simple index.

Some studies suggest that site maps do not necessarily improve users' mental representations of a Web site. Also, one study reported that if a site map does not reflect users' (or the domain's) conceptual structure, then the utility of the map is lessened.

Sources: Ashworth and Hamilton, 1997; Billingsley, 1982; Detweiler and Omanson, 1996; Dias and Sousa, 1997; Farkas and Farkas, 2000; Farris, Jones and Elgin, 2001; Kandogan and Shneiderman, 1997; Kim and Hirtle, 1995; McDonald and Stevenson, 1998; McEneaney, 2001; Nielsen, 1996a; Nielsen, 1997a; Nielsen, 1999b; Nielsen, 1999c; Nielsen, 1999d; Stanton, Taylor and Tweedie, 1992; Tullis, 2001; Utting and Yankelovich, 1989.

Example:

This site map effectively presents the site's information hierarchy.

The use of headers, subcategories, and alphabetization make this site map easy to scan.

Guideline: Provide 'glosses' to help users select correct links.

Comments: 'Glosses' are short phrases of information that popup when a user places his or her mouse pointer close to a link. It provides a preview to information behind a link. Users prefer the preview information to be located close to the link, but not placed such that it disturbs the primary text. However, designers should not rely on the 'gloss' to compensate for poorly labeled links.

Relative Importance:

Strength of Evidence:
❶❷○○○

Sources: Evans, 1998; Farkas and Farkas, 2000; Zellweger, Regli and Mackinlay, 2000.

Example:

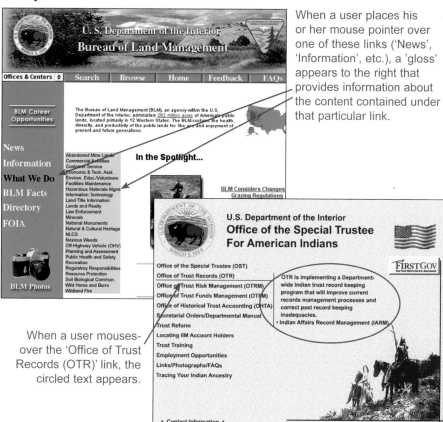

When a user places his or her mouse pointer over one of these links ('News', 'Information', etc.), a 'gloss' appears to the right that provides information about the content contained under that particular link.

When a user mouses-over the 'Office of Trust Records (OTR)' link, the circled text appears.

See page xxii for detailed descriptions of the rating scales
❶❷❸❹○

7:12 Breadcrumb Navigation

Navigation

Relative Importance:
❶○○○○

Strength of Evidence:
❶❷❸○○

Guideline: Do not expect users to use breadcrumbs effectively.

Comments: One study reported no difference in task completion times and total pages visited between groups that had breadcrumbs and those that did not. Participants could have used breadcrumbs thirty-two percent of the time, but only did so six percent of the time. It is probably not worth the effort to include breadcrumbs unless you can show that your Web site's users use them frequently, either to navigate the site, or to understand the site's hierarchy.

One study found that test participants who received instruction on the use of breadcrumbs completed tasks much faster than those who did not. This time savings could result in increased productivity for users that search Web sites on a daily basis.

Sources: Rogers and Chaparro, 2003; Hull, 2004.

Example: Breadcrumbs, when used, allow users to quickly navigate your site.

& Concepts	& Leadership	& Tools	Others	from Others

Home ▶ Discussion ▶ Archives ▶ List View ▶ Message Details

Home ▶ Global Resources ▶ Physical Geography Case Studies ▶ Living at the South Pole

Homepage | Publications | RS8 Transparency and Accountability: Annex A - Research Techniques and Survey findings

You are in: Regions > Southern Region > Drought in the South East > Water Resource Summary

See page xxii for detailed descriptions of the rating scales ❶❷❸❹○

Scrolling and Paging

Designers must decide, early in the design process,

whether to create long pages that require extensive scrolling or shorter pages that will require users to move frequently from page to page (an activity referred to as paging). This decision will be based on considerations of the primary users and the type of tasks being performed. For example, older users tend to scroll more slowly than younger users; therefore, long scrolling pages may slow them down considerably. As another example, some tasks that require users to remember where information is located on a page may benefit from paging, while many reading tasks benefit from scrolling.

Generally, designers should ensure that users can move from page to page as efficiently as possible. If designers are unable to decide between paging and scrolling, it is usually better to provide several shorter pages rather than one or two longer pages. The findings of usability testing should help confirm or negate that decision.

When scrolling is used, a Web site should be designed to allow the fastest possible scrolling. Users only should have to scroll through a few screenfuls, and not lengthy pages. Designers should never require users to scroll horizontally.

8:1 Eliminate Horizontal Scrolling

Relative Importance:
①②③④⑤

Strength of Evidence:
①②③④○

Guideline: Use an appropriate page layout to eliminate the need for users to scroll horizontally.

Comments: Horizontal scrolling is a slow and tedious way to view an entire screen. Common page layouts including fluid and left-justified may require some users to scroll horizontally if their monitor resolution or size is smaller than that used by designers.

Sources: Bernard and Larsen, 2001; Lynch and Horton, 2002; Nielsen and Tahir, 2002; Spyridakis, 2000; Williams, 2000.

Example:

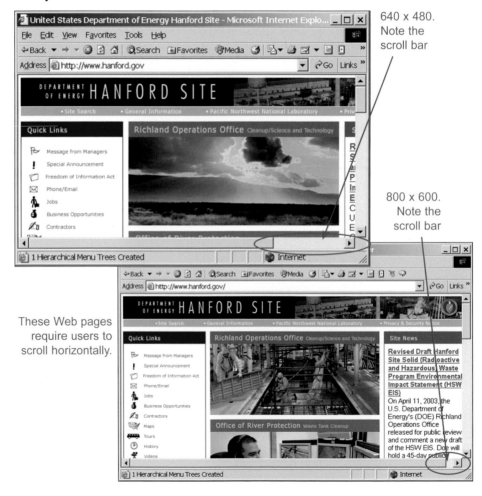

640 x 480. Note the scroll bar

800 x 600. Note the scroll bar

These Web pages require users to scroll horizontally.

Guideline: Facilitate fast scrolling by highlighting major items.

Relative Importance:
①②◯◯◯

Strength of Evidence:
①②③④◯

Comments: Web pages will move quickly or slowly depending on how users elect to scroll. Some users click on the arrows at the ends of the scroll bar, which can be slow but does allow most information to be read during the scrolling process. Other users drag the scroll box, which tends to be much faster. When the scroll box is dragged, the information may move too fast on the screen for users to read prose text, but they can read major headings that are well-designed and clearly placed. Keep in mind that older users (70 and over) will scroll much more slowly than younger users (39 and younger).

Sources: Bailey, Koyani and Nall, 2000; Koyani and Bailey, 2005; Koyani, et al., 2002.

Example:

Bold, large text and an accompanying graphic are effectively used to draw the user's attention during fast scrolling.

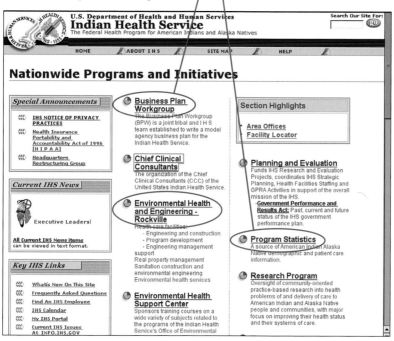

See page xxii for detailed descriptions of the rating scales
①②③④◯

Scrolling and Paging

Scrolling and Paging

8:3 Use Scrolling Pages For Reading Comprehension

Guideline: Use longer, scrolling pages when users are reading for comprehension.

Relative Importance:

Strength of Evidence:

Comments: Make the trade-off between paging and scrolling by taking into consideration that retrieving new linked pages introduces a delay that can interrupt users' thought processes. Scrolling allows readers to advance in the text without losing the context of the message as may occur when they are required to follow links.

However, with pages that have fast loading times, there is no reliable difference between scrolling and paging when people are reading for comprehension. For example, one study showed that paging participants construct better mental representations of the text as a whole, and are better at remembering the main ideas and later locating relevant information on a page. In one study, paging was preferred by inexperienced users.

Sources: Byrne, et al., 1999; Campbell and Maglio, 1999; Piolat, Roussey and Thunin, 1998; Schwarz, Beldie and Pastoor, 1983; Spool, et al., 1997; Spyridakis, 2000.

8:4 Use Paging Rather Than Scrolling

Relative Importance:

Strength of Evidence:

Guideline: If users' system response times are reasonably fast, use paging rather than scrolling.

Comments: Users should be able to move from page to page by selecting links and without having to scroll to find important information.

Sources: Nielsen, 1997e; Piolat, Roosey and Thunin, 1998; Schwarz, Beldie and Pastoor, 1983.

See page xxii
for detailed descriptions
of the rating scales

8:5 Scroll Fewer Screenfuls

Relative Importance:

Strength of Evidence:

Guideline: If users are looking for specific information, break up the information into smaller portions (shorter pages).

Comments: For many Web sites, users deal best with smaller, well-organized pages of information rather than lengthy pages because scrolling can take a lot of time. Older users tend to scroll much more slowly than younger users. One study found that Internet users spend about thirteen percent of their time scrolling within pages. Even though each event takes little time, cumulative scrolling adds significant time.

Sources: Detweiler and Omanson, 1996; Lynch and Horton, 2002; Nielsen, 1996a; Spool, et al., 1997; Spyridakis, 2000.

Example:

Good design of a long, content-rich document. This single document is divided into numerous sections, resulting in each page being no longer than four screenfuls.

IRAS Explanatory Supplement
V. Data Reduction
D. Point Source Confirmation

Chapter Contents | Introduction | Authors | References
Table of Contents | Index | Previous Section | Next Section

Section V.D has been split into multiple files due to its size.

1. Processing Overview
2. Overview of Seconds-Confirmation

   a. Band Seconds-Confirmation
   b. Position Reconstruction
   c. Optical Crosstalk Removal
   d. In-Band Seconds-Confirmation Decision
   e. Double-Detection Mode
   f. Triple-Detection Mode (Edge Detections)
   g. In-Band Seconds-Confirmation Confusion Processing
   h. In-Band Seconds-Confirmation Position Refinement
   i. In-Band Seconds-Confirmation Photometric Refinement
   j. In-Band Seconds-Confirmation Statistical Processing

11. Band-Merging

   a. Overview of Band-Merging
   b. Band Filling

The single-page design of this document requires users to scroll more than twenty-seven screenfuls.

decision is not straight forward.

Fundamentals of Technology Roadmapping

Strategic Business Development Department

Sandia National Laboratories
P.O. Box 5800
Albuquerque, NM 87185-1378

	E-mail:	Phone:	FAX:
Marie L. Garcia	mgarci@sandia.gov	(505) 844-7661	(505) 844-6501
Olin H. Bray	ohbray@sandia.gov	(505) 844-7658	(505) 844-6501

Contacting Us
News and Events
Search
Home

The process identified within "Fundamentals of Technology Roadmapping," was customized to develop the DOE Robotics & Intelligent Machines Technology Roadmap.

Undersecretary Moniz testified to the House Science Committee on September 23, 1998. His testimony highlighted the Robotics and Intelligent Machines roadmap.
A few key phrases:
"good example of a roadmap",
"started with a carefully thought through needs document",
"DOE has the broadest and most demanding needs for robotics",
"we are a leader in defining the future of robotics and intelligent machines for the country",
"DOE must push the leading edge in order to meet its mission requirements."

9

Headings, Titles, and Labels

Most users spend a considerable amount of time

scanning rather than reading information on Web sites. Well-designed headings help to facilitate both scanning and reading written material. Designers should strive to use unique and descriptive headings, and to use as many headings as necessary to enable users to find what they are looking for—it is usually better to use more rather than fewer headings. Headings should be used in their appropriate HTML order, and it is generally a good idea not to skip heading levels.

Designers should ensure that each page has a unique and descriptive page title. When tables are used, designers should make sure that descriptive row and column headings are included that enable users to clearly understand the information in the table. It is occasionally important to highlight certain critical information.

9:1 Use Clear Category Labels

Relative Importance:
①②③④⑤

Strength of Evidence:
①②③④○

Guideline: Ensure that category labels, including links, clearly reflect the information and items contained within the category.

Comments: Category titles must be understood by typical users. Users will likely have difficulty understanding vague, generalized link labels, but will find specific, detailed links, and descriptors easier to use.

Sources: Evans, 1998; Landesman and Schroeder, 2000; Mahajan and Shneiderman, 1997; Marshall, Drapeau and DiSciullo, 2001; Nall, Koyani, and Lafond, 2001; Spyridakis, 2000; Zimmerman, et al., 2002.

Example:

These labels are clear and distinct, allowing users to distinguish paths quickly.

9:2 Provide Descriptive Page Titles

Relative Importance:
①②③④○

Strength of Evidence:
①②○○○

Guideline: Put a descriptive, unique, concise, and meaningfully different title on each Web page.

Comments: Title refers to the text that is in the browser title bar (this is the bar found at the very top of the browser screen). Titles are used by search engines to identify pages. If two or more pages have the same title, they cannot be differentiated by users or the Favorites capability of the browser. If users bookmark a page, they should not have to edit the title to meet the characteristics mentioned above.

Remember that some search engines only list the titles in their search results page. Using concise and meaningful titles on all pages can help orient users as they browse a page or scan hot lists and history lists for particular URLs. They can also help others as they compile links to your pages.

To avoid confusing users, make the title that appears in the heading of the browser consistent with the title in the content area of the pages.

Sources: Evans, 1998; Levine, 1996; Nielsen and Tahir, 2002; Spyridakis, 2000; Williams, 2000.

Example: These titles are unique, concise, and consistent with the titles in the content area.

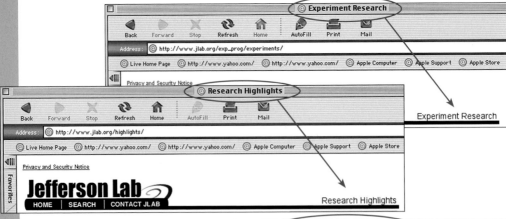

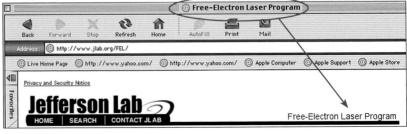

Guideline: Use descriptive headings liberally throughout a Web site.

Relative Importance:
①②③④○

Comments: Well-written headings are an important tool for helping users scan quickly. Headings should conceptually relate to the information or functions that follow them.

Strength of Evidence:
①②③④⑤

Headings should provide strong cues that orient users and inform them about page organization and structure. Headings also help classify information on a page. Each heading should be helpful in finding the desired target.

The ability to scan quickly is particularly important for older adults because they tend to stop scanning and start reading more frequently. If headings are not descriptive or plentiful enough, the user may start reading in places that do not offer the information they are seeking, thereby slowing them down unnecessarily.

Sources: Bailey, Koyani and Nall, 2000; Evans, 1998; Flower, Hayes and Swarts, 1983; Gerhardt-Powals, 1996; Hartley and Trueman, 1983; Ivory and Hearst, 2002; Ivory, Sinha and Hearst, 2000; Lorch and Lorch, 1995; Mayer, Dyck and Cook, 1984; Meyer, 1984; Morkes and Nielsen, 1998; Morrell, et al., 2002; Murphy and Mitchell, 1986; Nielsen, 1999c; Nielsen, 1999d; Schultz and Spyridakis, 2002; Spyridakis, 1989; Spyridakis, 2000; Zimmerman and Prickett, 2000.

Example:

Spending time during the design process to ensure that the site contains many carefully written headings and sub-headings will save users time as they rapidly locate the information for which they are searching.

■ **Common Cancers**
  • Bladder Cancer
  • Breast Cancer
  • Colon Cancer
  • Endometrial Cancer
  • Head and Neck Cancer
  • Leukemia

■ **Childhood/Pediatric Cancers**
  • Childhood Cancers Home Page

■ **Cancers by Body Location/System**
  • AIDS-Related
  • Bone
  • Brain
  • Breast
  • Digestive/Gastrointestinal
  • Endocrine
  • Eye
  • Genitourinary
  • Germ Cell
  • Gynecologic
  • Head and Neck

Headings, Titles, and Labels

See page xxii for detailed descriptions of the rating scales
①②③④○

9:4 Use Unique and Descriptive Headings

Guideline: Use headings that are unique from one another and conceptually related to the content they describe.

Relative Importance:
①②③④○

Strength of Evidence:
①②③○○

Comments: Using poor headings (mismatches between what users were expecting and what they find) is a common problem with Web sites. Ensure that headings are descriptive and relate to the content they introduce. If headings are too similar to one another, users may have to hesitate and re-read to decipher the difference. Identifying the best headings may require extensive usability testing and other methods.

Sources: Bailey, Koyani and Nall, 2000; Gerhardt-Powals, 1996; Morkes and Nielsen, 1998; Williams, 2000.

Example: These headings are well-designed—they are unique from one another and descriptive of the information to which they link.

Alphabetical List of all Topics

Air
Acid Rain, Global Warming, Emissions...

Cleanup
Brownfields, Superfund, Corrective Action...

Compliance & Enforcement
Complaints, Compliance Assistance...

Economics
Cost Benefit Analysis, Grants, Financing...

Ecosystems
Wetland, Watersheds, Endangered Species...

Emergencies
Reporting, Oil Spills, Accidents...

Environmental Management
Smart Growth, Risk Mgmt, Environmental Indicators...

Human Health
Children's Health, Exposure, Risk Assessment, Healthy School Environments ...

Industry
Small Business, Permits, Reporting...

International Cooperation
Border Issues, Technical Assistance...

Pesticides
Insecticides, Registration, Food Safety...

Pollutants/Toxics
Lead, Dioxins, Chemicals, Radiation...

Pollution Prevention
Recycling, Conservation, Energy...

Research
Publications, Laboratories, Models...

Treatment & Control
Treatment Technologies, Pretreatment..

Wastes
Hazardous Wastes, Landfills, Treatment...

Water
Wastewater, Drinking Water, Ground Water...

See page xxii for detailed descriptions of the rating scales
①②③④○

9:5 Highlight Critical Data

Relative Importance:
❶❷❸❹○

Strength of Evidence:
❶❷❸○○

Guideline: Visually distinguish (i.e., highlight) important page items that require user attention, particularly when those items are displayed infrequently.

Comments: Items to highlight might include recently changed data, data exceeding acceptable limits, or data failing to meet some other defined criteria. Highlight is used here in its general sense, meaning to emphasize or make prominent. Highlighting is most effective when used sparingly, i.e., highlighting just a few items on a page that is otherwise relatively uniform in appearance.

Sources: Ahlstrom and Longo, 2001; Engel and Granda, 1975; Levine, 1996; Myers, 1985.

Example: Formatting this text in underline, bold, and red draws attention to the most pressing deadline and instructions.

Event Status

Event Type:	Event Id:	Event Title:	Bidding Opens:	Bids Due:
Internet Auction 269 lots, 1315 items	809	Hawaii & Alaska ➡ **More Info**	**03/25/2003**	03/27/2003
Sealed Bid 1 lots, 1 items	902	Portable Ofc Trailers ➡ **Bid Package & Info**	**02/28/2003**	**03/28/2003**
Internet Auction 1 lots, 1 items	908	Mattresses@St.Juliens ➡ **More Info**	03/31/2003	04/02/2003
Internet Auction 401 lots, 5833 items	810	Norfolk & Richmond, VA ➡ **More Info**	03/31/2003	04/02/2003
Sealed Bid 224 lots, 684 items	812	Marianas US Naval Guam ➡ **Bid Package & Info**	03/28/2003	04/07/2003

Please confirm that the following information is correct.

After you have reviewed your information, click **"Edit"** to edit the information you entered or **"Submit"** to send your request.

YOUR REQUEST WILL NOT BE SENT UNTIL YOU CLICK "SUBMIT".

[Edit] [Submit]

Headings, Titles, and Labels

9:6 Use Descriptive Row and Column Headings

Guideline: Ensure that data tables have clear, concise, and accurate row and column headings.

Relative Importance:
①②③④○

Comments: Use row and column headings to indicate unique cell contents. Users require clear and concise table headings in order to make efficient and effective use of table information. Row and column headings will indicate to screen readers how data points should be labeled or identified, so the user can understand the significance of the cell in the overall scheme of the table.

Strength of Evidence:
①②③○○

Sources: Bransford and Johnson, 1972; Chisholm, Vanderheiden and Jacobs, 1999d; Detweiler and Omanson, 1996; Lynch and Horton, 2002; United States Government, 1998; Wright, 1980.

Example: An example of good table heading design. The non-expert user will have no problem understanding these descriptive row and column headers.

Connecticut Business Starts Index 2006

Click on the 2006 Month/Year Column Header for a
Monthly Detailed Report of Starts

Link --->	Jan-2006 Starts.	Feb-2006 Starts.	Mar-2006 Starts.	Apr-2006 Starts.	May-2006 Starts.	Jun-2006 Starts.	Jul-2006 Starts.	Aug-2006 Starts.	Sep-2006 Starts.	Oct-2006 Starts.	Nov-2006 Starts.	Dec-2006 Starts.
# New Starts	2,836	2,496	3,254									
% Change (M/M)	23.6	-13.6	23.3									
% Change (Y/Y)	3.0	3.2	8.2									

An example of poor table heading design. The non-expert user will have little idea what is meant by 'R', 'J.', and 'Pt.' Unless space constraints dictate otherwise, always use row and column headers that are descriptive enough to be understood by non-expert users.

2005 TERM OPINIONS OF THE COURT

Slip Opinions, *Per Curiams* (PC), and Original Case Decrees (D)

R-	Date	Docket	Name	J.	Pt.
49	04/26/06	04-1495	Hartman v. Moore	DS	547/1
48	04/26/06	04-1477	Jones v. Flowers	R	547/1
47	04/25/06	04-1324	Day v. McDonough	G	547/1
46	04/25/06	04-1618	Northern Ins. Co. of N. Y. v. Chatham County	T	547/1
45	04/24/06	05-	Salinas v. United States	PC	547/1

Guideline: Use headings in the appropriate HTML order.

Relative Importance:
①②③○○

Comments: Using the appropriate HTML heading order helps users get a sense of the hierarchy of information on the page. The appropriate use of H1-H3 heading tags also allows users of assistive technologies to understand the hierarchy of information.

Strength of Evidence:
①②○○○

Sources: Detweiler and Omanson, 1996; Spool, et al., 1997.

Example:

Best Practices in Funding Extramural Research

Receipt and Review H1 nvestigator-Initiated Applications

■ **Communicating about Applications Prior** H2 ubmission

Communication between Program Staff and Applicants
Communication between PDs and CSR (Use of ARA Form)
Communication between Applicants and CSR Staff

■ **Assigning** H2 lications to Review Groups within NIH

Processing Applications in the CSR Division of Receipt and Referral
Notifying Applicants about Assignment to Scientific Review Groups

■ **Processing Applications Assigned to NCI**

Receiving, Recording, and Storing Applications
Assigning Applications to Program Areas
Accepting Applica
Changing the Sta

```
<td valign="top">
  <h1><b>Receipt and Review of Investigator-Initia
      Applications</b></h1>
  <h2><img src="images/red.gif" width="9" height="9
      <a href="#1">Communicating about Applications F
  <ul class="tight">
    <p><a href="#1a">Communication between Program
       <a href="#1b"><br>
       Communication between PDs and CSR (Use of ARF
       Communication between Applicants and CSR Sta
  </ul>
  <h2><img src="images/red.gif" width="9" height="9
      <a href="#2">Assigning Applications to Review (
  <ul class="tight">
    <p><a href="#2a">Processing Applications in the
```

See page xxii for detailed descriptions of the rating scales
①②③④○

9:8 Provide Users with Good Ways to Reduce Options

Headings, Titles, and Labels

Guideline: Provide users with good ways to reduce their available options as efficiently as possible.

Relative Importance:
❶❷◯◯◯

Comments: Users seem willing to reduce their options quickly. Provide all options clearly so that users can focus first on selecting what they consider to be the most important option.

Strength of Evidence:
❶❷◯◯◯

Sources: Bailey, Koyani, and Nall, 2000.

Example: By providing three different options for selecting desired information, users can select the one most important to them.

Types of Cancer

What You Need To Know About™ Cancer Index
Information about detection, symptoms, diagnosis, and treatment of many types of cancer.

▪ **Common Cancers**
- Bladder Cancer
- Breast Cancer
- Colon Cancer
- Endometrial Cancer
- Head and Neck Cancer
- Leukemia

- Lung Cancer
- Melanoma
- Non-Hodgkins Lymphoma
- Ovarian Cancer
- Prostate Cancer
- Rectal Cancer

▪ **Childhood/Pediatric Cancers**
- Childhood Cancers Home Page

▪ **Cancers by Body Location/System**
- AIDS-Related
- Bone
- Brain
- Breast
- Digestive/Gastrointestinal
- Endocrine
- Eye
- Genitourinary
- Germ Cell
- Gynecologic
- Head and Neck

- Hematologic/Blood
- Leukemia
- Lung
- Lymphoma
- Musculoskeletal
- Neurologic
- Pregnancy and Cancer
- Respiratory/Thoracic
- Skin
- Unknown Primary

See page xxii for detailed descriptions of the rating scales
❶❷❸❹◯

Links

Linking means that users will select and click on

a hypertext link on a starting page (usually the homepage), which then causes a new page to load. Users continue toward their goal by finding and clicking on subsequent links.

To ensure that links are effectively used, designers should use meaningful link labels (making sure that link names are consistent with their targets), provide consistent clickability cues (avoiding misleading cues), and designate when links have been clicked.

Whenever possible, designers should use text for links rather than graphics. Text links usually provide much better information about the target than do graphics.

Links

10:1 Use Meaningful Link Labels

Relative Importance:
①②③④⑤

Strength of Evidence:
①②③④○

Guideline: Use link labels and concepts that are meaningful, understandable, and easily differentiated by users rather than designers.

Comments: To avoid user confusion, use link labels that clearly differentiate one link from another. Users should be able to look at each link and learn something about the link's destination. Using terms like 'Click Here' can be counterproductive.

Clear labeling is especially important as users navigate down through the available links. The more decisions that users are required to make concerning links, the more opportunities they have to make a wrong decision.

Sources: Bailey, Koyani and Nall, 2000; Coney and Steehouder, 2000; Evans, 1998; Farkas and Farkas, 2000; IEEE; Larson and Czerwinski, 1998; Miller and Remington, 2000; Mobrand and Spyridakis, 2002; Nielsen and Tahir, 2002; Spool, et al., 1997; Spyridakis, 2000.

Example: 'COOL' refers to an application that allows users to search for all jobs within the Department of Commerce (not just the Census Bureau.) This link does a poor job in explaining itself. The other circled links aren't as descriptive as they could be.

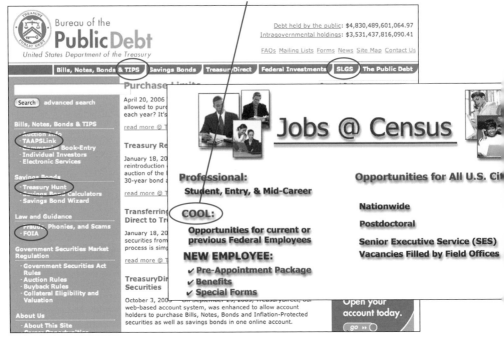

10:2 Link to Related Content

Relative Importance:
①②③④○

Strength of Evidence:
①②○○○

Guideline: Provide links to other pages in the Web site with related content.

Comments: Users expect designers to know their Web sites well enough to provide a full list of options to related content.

Sources: Koyani and Nall, 1999.

Example:

Avian Influenza (Bird Flu)

Influenza (Flu)
›Avian Flu
 ›What You Should
  Know
  ›Key Facts
  ›Current Situation
  ›Infection in Humans
  ›Q & A
 ›Specific Topics
  ›The Virus & Its
   Spread
  ›Prevention
  ›Outbreaks
 ›Info for Specific
  Groups
 ›References
 ›Related Links
›Seasonal Flu
›Pandemic Flu

Related Links on Avian Influenza (Bird Flu)   ✉ E-mail this page
                                                    🖨 Printer-friendly version

U.S. Resources

U.S. Department of Health and Human Services (HHS)
- PandemicFlu.gov
  Official U.S. government website for pandemic influenza
    • HHS Congressional testimony on pandemic and avian influenza
    • Transcripts of HHS press conferences on pandemic and avian influenza
- HHS National Vaccine Program Office: Pandemic Influenza

U.S. Department of Agriculture (USDA)
- USDA Avian Influenza website
  Information on USDA efforts to protect the nation's poultry supply

Related Government Agencies & International Organizations

- European Copyright User Platform
- Federal Communications Commission
- Government Printing Office *Access*
- U.S. Patent & Trademark Office
- WIPO (World Intellectual Property Organization)

Home | Contact Us | Legal Notices | Freedom of Information Act (FOIA) | Library of Congress

U.S. Copyright Office
101 Independence Ave. S.E.
Washington, D.C. 20559-6000
(202) 707-3000

The cloud of Iraq
Rove repeated later in the ques
war was having a widespread d

"The war looms on all political
Americans are not sour on the
circumstances are good; they're feeling good about where they
are…. They're worried about the long haul," he added, and
specifically they're worried about globalization and Social Security.

CLICK FOR RELATED STORIES

- **Curry: What would a Democratic majority do?**
- **Fineman: Rove revamps the Republican strategy**

Evidence of voter happiness, according to Rove: the University of
Michigan's consumer confidence survey has relatively high readings.
He cited a study from some political scientists (whom he didn't

See page xxii
for detailed descriptions
of the rating scales
①②③④○

10:3 Match Link Names with Their Destination Pages

Guideline: Make the link text consistent with the title or headings on the destination (i.e., target) page.

Comments: Closely matched links and destination targets help provide the necessary feedback to users that they have reached the intended page.

Relative Importance:
①②③④○

Strength of Evidence:
①②③④○

If users will have to click more than once to get to a specific target destination, avoid repeating the exact same link wording over and over because users can be confused if the links at each level are identical or even very similar. In one study, after users clicked on a link entitled 'First Aid,' the next page had three options. One of them was again titled 'First Aid.' The two 'First Aid' links went to different places. Users tended to click on another option on the second page because they thought that they had already reached 'First Aid.'

Sources: Bailey, Koyani and Nall, 2000; Levine, 1996; Mobrand and Spyridakis, 2002.

Example: Link text in the left navigation panel is identical to the headings found on the destination page.

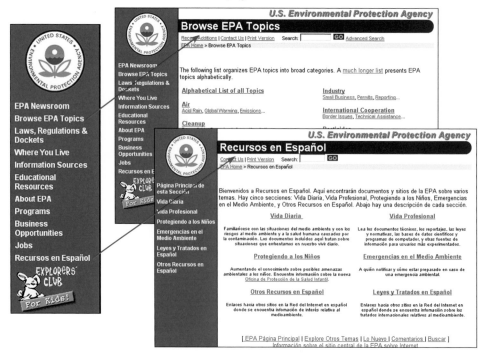

See page xxii for detailed descriptions of the rating scales
①②③④○

Relative Importance:
①②③④○

Strength of Evidence:
①②○○○

Guideline: Ensure that items that are not clickable do not have characteristics that suggest that they are clickable.

Comments: Symbols usually must be combined with at least one other cue that suggests clickability. In one study, users were observed to click on a major heading with some link characteristics, but the heading was not actually a link.

However, to some users bullets and arrows may suggest clickability, even when they contain no other clickability cues (underlining, blue coloration, etc.). This slows users as they debate whether the items are links.

Sources: Bailey, Koyani and Nall, 2000; Evans, 1998; Spool, et al., 1997.

Example:

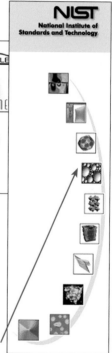

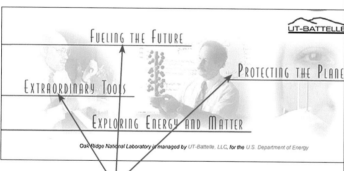

These items appear clickable, but are not. This design may confuse users because the items are underlined and are demonstratively different, and thus attract the users' attention.

This is a good example of misleading the user—blue text and underlined text placed at the top center of the page, and yet none of these are clickable.

Two of these graphics are not clickable—if a user mouses over one of them, they are likely to think that they are all not clickable. If one graphic is clickable, they should all be clickable.

10:5 Repeat Important Links

Relative Importance:
①②③④○

Strength of Evidence:
①②③④○

Guideline: Ensure that important content can be accessed from more than one link.

Comments: Establishing more than one way to access the same information can help some users find what they need. When certain information is critical to the success of the Web site, provide more than one link to the information. Different users may try different ways to find information, depending on their own interpretations of a problem and the layout of a page. Some users find important links easily when they have a certain label, while others may recognize the link best with an alternative name.

Sources: Bernard, Hull and Drake, 2001; Detweiler and Omanson, 1996; Ivory, Sinha and Hearst, 2000; Ivory, Sinha and Hearst, 2001; Levine, 1996; Nall, Koyani and Lafond, 2001; Nielsen and Tahir, 2002; Spain, 1999; Spool, Klee and Schroeder, 2000.

Example:

Multiple links provide users with alternative routes for finding the same information.

If the user misses the 'Hours' link in the left panel, they still have a chance to find the header in the content panel.

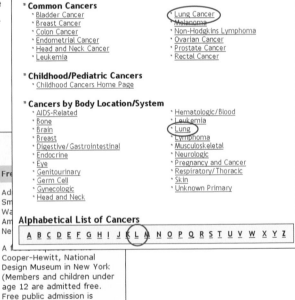

See page xxii for detailed descriptions of the rating scales
①②③④○

10:6 Use Text for Links

Relative Importance:
①②③④○

Strength of Evidence:
①②③④○

Guideline: Use text links rather than image links.

Comments: In general, text links are more easily recognized as clickable. Text links usually download faster, are preferred by users, and should change colors after being selected. It is usually easier to convey a link's destination in text, rather than with the use of an image.

In one study, users showed considerable confusion regarding whether or not certain images were clickable. This was true even for images that contained words. Users could not tell if the images were clickable without placing their cursor over them ('minesweeping'). Requiring users to 'minesweep' to determine what is clickable slows them down.

Another benefit to using text links is that users with text-only and deactivated graphical browsers can see the navigation options.

Sources: Detweiler and Omanson, 1996; Farkas and Farkas, 2000; Koyani and Nall, 1999; Mobrand and Spyridakis, 2002; Nielsen, 2000; Spool, et al., 1997; Zimmerman, et al., 2002.

Example:

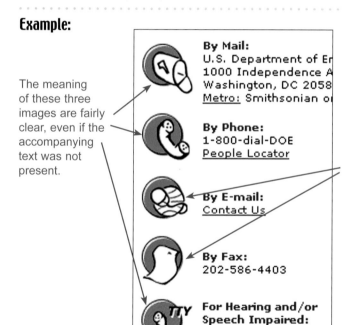

The meaning of these three images are fairly clear, even if the accompanying text was not present.

The meanings of these two image links are not obvious at first glance.

Links

10:7 Designate Used Links

Relative Importance:
①②③④○

Strength of Evidence:
①②○○○

Guideline: Use color changes to indicate to users when a link has been visited.

Comments: Generally, it is best to use the default text link colors (blue as an unvisited location/link and purple as a visited location/link). Link colors help users understand which parts of a Web site they have visited. In one study, providing this type of feedback was the only variable found to improve the user's speed of finding information. If a user selects one link, and there are other links to the same target, make sure all links to that target change color.

One 2003 study indicated a compliance rate of only thirty-three percent for this guideline; a 2002 study showed a compliance rate of thirty-five percent.

Sources: Evans, 1998; Nielsen and Tahir, 2002; Nielsen, 1996a; Nielsen, 1999b; Nielsen, 1999c; Nielsen, 2003; Spool, et al., 2001, Tullis 2001.

Example:

Opportunities

- Access America for Seniors
- Government Benefits
- Nonprofit Gateway
- Procurement
- Small Business Opportunities
- Technology Transfer
- USDA /1890 National Scholars Program
- USDA Debarment and Suspension Contacts
- U.S. State and Local Gateway

Employment:

- USDA
- Intern Programs
- All Federal Government
- USDA Telework Center
- Senior Executive Service Candidate Development Program

A poor design choice. Unvisited links are in green, whereas visited links are in blue—users expect blue to denote an unvisited link.

Schools / IMSOs -- Air Force
Advanced Airlift Tactics Training Center, St Josep
Air Command & Staff College, Maxwell AFB AL
Air Education and Training Command, Randolph
Air Force Institute of Technology, Wright-Patterson
Air University, Maxwell AFB AL
Air War College, Maxwell AFB AL
Altus AFB OK
College for Enlisted Professional Military Educati
Columbus AFB MS
Fairchild AFB WA
Goodfellow AFB TX
Inter-American Air Forces Academy, Lackland AF
Joint Special Operations University, Hurlburt Field
Keesler AFB MS
Lackland AFB TX
Little Rock AFB AR
Luke AFB AZ
Randolph AFB TX
School of Aerospace Medicine, Brooks AFB TX
Sheppard AFB TX,   IMSO
Squadron Officer School, Maxwell AFB AL
Tyndall AFB FL
Vance AFB OK
Wright-Patterson AFB OH

A good design choice—unvisited links are shown in blue, and visited links are shown in purple. Note the conventional use of colors for visited and unvisited links.

Guideline: Provide sufficient cues to clearly indicate to users that an item is clickable.

Relative Importance:
① ② ③ ○ ○

Strength of Evidence:
① ② ○ ○ ○

Comments: Users should not be expected to move the cursor around a Web site ('minesweeping') to determine what is clickable. Using the eyes to quickly survey the options is much faster than 'minesweeping.' Similarly, relying on mouseovers to designate links can confuse newer users, and slow all users as they are uncertain about which items are links.

Be consistent in your use of underlining, bullets, arrows, and other symbols such that they always indicate clickability or never suggest clickability. For example, using images as both links and as decoration slows users as it forces them to study the image to discern its clickability.

Items that are in the top center of the page, or left and right panels have a high probability of being considered links. This is particularly true if the linked element looks like a real-world tab or push button.

Sources: Bailey, 2000b; Bailey, Koyani and Nall, 2000; Farkas and Farkas, 2000; Lynch and Horton, 2002; Nielsen, 1990; Tullis, 2001.

Example:

A bulleted list of blue, underlined text. These are very strong clickability cues for users.

With at least seven non-traditional colors for links, the clickability cues for users might lead to confusion as to which links have been visited or not.

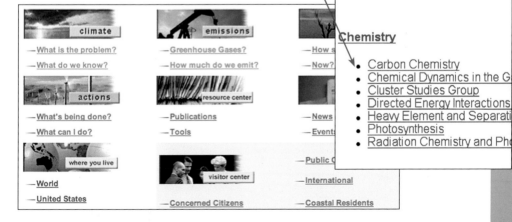

See page xxii for detailed descriptions of the rating scales
① ② ③ ④ ○

Links

10:9 Ensure that Embedded Links are Descriptive

Guideline: When using embedded links, the link text should accurately describe the link's destination.

Comments: Users tend to ignore the text that surrounds each embedded link; therefore, do not create embedded links that use the surrounding text to add clues about the link's destination.

Relative Importance:
① ② ③ ○ ○

Strength of Evidence:
① ② ③ ④ ○

Sources: Bailey, Koyani and Nall, 2000; Bernard and Hull, 2002; Card, et al., 2001; Chi, Pirolli and Pitkow, 2000; Evans, 1998; Farkas and Farkas, 2000; Mobrand and Spyridakis, 2002; Sawyer and Schroeder, 2000; Spool, et al., 1997.

Example: These embedded links are well designed—because the entire organization name is a link, the user does not have to read the surrounding text to understand the destination of the embedded link.

the Intelligence Community and exercises the powers of the Director when the Director's position is vacant or in the Director's absence or disability.

The Associate Director of Central Intelligence for Homeland Security, Office of the Director of Central Intelligence, ensures the flow of intelligence in support of homeland defense. The current director is Winston P. Wiley.

The Executive Director of the Central Intelligence Agency is A.B. Krongard. Assisted by an Executive Board that counts among its membership five mission centers with duties that enable the Agency to carry out its mission--Chief Financial Officer, Chief Information Officer, Security, Human Resources and Global Support, the EXDIR manages the CIA on a day-to-day basis.

The Directorate of Intelligence, the analytical branch of intelligence analysis on key foreign issues. The current director is Jami A. Misck.

The Directorate of Science and Technology creates and mission. The current director is Donald M. Kerr.

The Directorate of Operations is responsible for the clandestine Pavitt.

The Center for the Study of Intelligence maintains the Agency's historical materials and promotes the study of intelligence as a legitimate and serious discipline. The current director is Paul Johnson.

In this example, the user must read the surrounding text to gain clues as to the link's destination. In many cases, users will not read that text.

the economy, efficiency, and effectiveness of the federal government through financial audits, program reviews and evaluations, analyses, legal opinions, investigations, and other services. GAO's activities are designed to ensure the executive branch's accountability to the Congress under the Constitution and the government's accountability to the American people. GAO is dedicated to good government through its commitment to the core values of accountability, integrity, and reliability.

From the Comptroller General
David M. Walker, Comptroller General of the United States. Selected Speeches, Writings, and Press Statements. GAO Press Statement, February 7, 2003 *New!*

GAO's Performance and Accountability Report 2002, Highlights, and related materials including the Strategic Plan 2002-2007

GAO Reports
Updated daily. "Today's Reports," Highlights, Special Collections including Desert Shield and Desert Storm Reports and Testimonies: 1991-1993, Homeland Security.

appropriations, and bid protests, and major federal agency rule GAO's Bid Protest Docket - Information about current and recently closed bid protests. GAO Policy and Procedures Manual for Guidance to Federal Agencies

Federal Agency Issues Highlighting GAO products specifically

Relative Importance:
①②③◯◯

Strength of Evidence:
①②③◯◯

Links

Guideline: 'Pointing-and-clicking,' rather than mousing over, is preferred when selecting menu items from a cascading menu structure.

Comments: One study found that when compared with the mouseover method, the 'point-and-click' method takes eighteen percent less time, elicits fewer errors, and is preferred by users.

Sources: Chaparro, Minnaert and Phipps, 2000.

Example: The below site relies on users to mouse over the main links to reveal the sub-menu links (shown extending to the right in purple and black). The use of these mouseover methods is slower than 'pointing-and-clicking.'

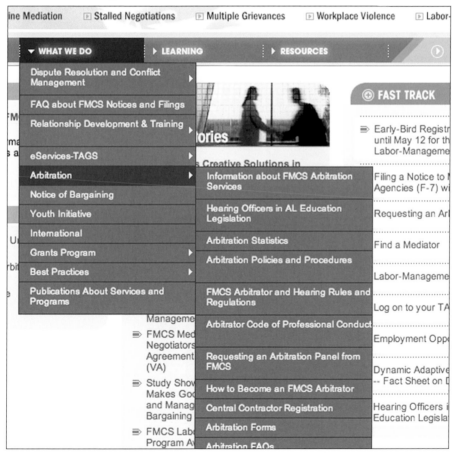

See page xxii
for detailed descriptions
of the rating scales
①②③④◯

10:11 Use Appropriate Text Link Lengths

Guideline: Make text links long enough to be understood, but short enough to minimize wrapping.

Relative Importance:
①②③○○

Strength of Evidence:
①②③○○

Comments: A single word text link may not give enough information about the link's destination. A link that is several words may be difficult to read quickly, particularly if it wraps to another line. Generally, it is best if text links do not extend more than one line. However, one study found that when users scan prose text, links of nine to ten words elicit better performance than shorter or longer links. Keep in mind that it is not always possible to control how links will look to all users because browser settings and screen resolutions can vary.

Sources: Card, et al., 2001; Chi, Pirolli and Pitkow, 2000; Evans, 1998; Levine, 1996; Nielsen and Tahir, 2002; Nielsen, 2000; Sawyer and Schroeder, 2000; Spool, et al., 1997.

Example:

Text links should not wrap to a second line. They should be used to highlight a particular word or short phrase in a sentence, not an entire sentence.

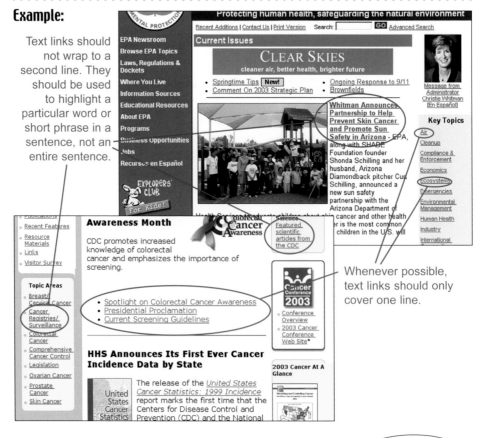

Whenever possible, text links should only cover one line.

See page xxii for detailed descriptions of the rating scales
①②③④○

Guideline: Indicate to users when a link will move them to a different location on the same page or to a new page on a different Web site.

Relative Importance:
❶❷❸◯◯

Strength of Evidence:
❶❷◯◯◯

Comments: One study showed that users tend to assume that links will take them to another page within the same Web site. When this assumption is not true, users can become confused. Designers should try to notify users when they are simply moving down a page, or leaving the site altogether.

Sources: Nall, Koyani and Lafond, 2001; Nielsen and Tahir, 2002; Spool, et al., 1997.

Example:

Add URL addresses below links to help users determine where they are going. By seeing .gov and .com the user is also alerted to the type of site they will visit.

Web Site Guidelines

Research-Based Web Design & Usability Guidelines
http://usability.gov/guidelines

- Provides guidelines for improving Web design, navigation, functionality
- Includes findings from Web design and usability literature identified by the National Cancer Institute and provides references

Web Design Guidelines: Design in Action
http://www-3.ibm.com/ibm/easy/eou_ext.nsf/Publish/572

- Provides guidelines on Web site planning, design, production, and maintenance
- Offers guidelines on e-commerce

Web Publishing Guide
http://www.ieee.org/web/developers/style/

sign, including planning, rmance

Acid Rain Sourcebook
This site is a student's first source book including activities, in about acid rain.

Become an IPM Super Sleuth ⎣EXIT disclaimer ❯⎦
Created with support from EPA and the National Foundation fo can teach you about Integrated Pest Management using word

Best Management Practices for Soil Erosion software
This downloadable program provid worldwide, including what causes

'Exit disclaimer' graphic informs user that the link will take them to a new Web site.

Clicking an outside link leads to this 'interim' page that warns users of their imminent transfer to a non-whitehouse.gov Web site.

You are exiting the White House Web Server

Thank you for visiting our site.

You will now access http://www.achp.gov/

We hope your visit was informative and enjoyable.

To comment on this service, send feedback to the Web Development Team

10:13 Clarify Clickable Regions of Images

Guideline: If any part of an image is clickable, ensure that the entire image is clickable or that the clickable sections are obvious.

Relative Importance:
①②❸○○

Strength of Evidence:
①②❸○○

Comments: Users should not be required to use the mouse pointer to discover clickable areas of images. For example, in a map of the United States, if individual states are clickable, sufficient cues should be given to indicate the clickable states.

Sources: Detweiler and Omanson, 1996; Levine, 1996; Lim and Wogalter, 2000.

Example:

Dramatically different colors delineate clickable regions.

The use of white space between clickable regions in this image map define the boundaries of each individual 'hot' area.

See page xxii for detailed descriptions of the rating scales
①②❸④○

Relative Importance:
❶❷❸○○

Strength of Evidence:
❶❷○○○

Links

Guideline: Provide links to supportive information.

Comments: Use links to provide definitions and descriptions to clarify technical concepts or jargon, so that less knowledgeable users can successfully use the Web site. For example, provide links to a dictionary, glossary definitions, and sections dedicated to providing more information.

Sources: Farkas and Farkas, 2000; Levine, 1996; Morrell, et al., 2002; Zimmerman and Prickett, 2000.

Example:

Tests that examine the breasts are used to detect (find) and diagnose breast cancer.

If an abnormality is found, one or all of the following tests may be used:

- Ultrasound: A test that uses sound waves to create images of areas inside the body. sound waves are bounced off internal tissues and organs. The echoes are changed int called sonograms. The doctor can identify tumors by looking at the sonogram.
- Mammogram: A special x-ray of the breast that may find tumors that are too small to mammogram can be performed with little risk to the fetus. Mammograms in pregnan appear negative even though cancer is present.
- Biopsy: The removal of cells, tissues disease.

Clicking on a highlighted word brings up a 'pop-up' box which provides the user with the definition of the selected word.

The highlighted links below direct the user to a page with a definition of the word.

▆▆▆▆ Definition ▆▆▆▆

sonogram (SON-o-gram):

A computer picture of areas inside the body created by bouncing high-energy sound waves (ultrasound) off internal tissues or organs. Also called an ultrasonogram.

Dictionary

Print this page

Today's featured picture

The **International Space Station** is located in a low Earth orbit, approximately 360 km (220 miles) high. The station has a capacity for a crew of three and there have always been at least two people on board. It has been visited by astronauts from a large number of countries and was also the destination of the first three space tourists.

Photo credit: NASA

Archive - More featured pictures...

Text Appearance

There are several issues related to text

characteristics that can help ensure a Web site communicates effectively with users:

- Use familiar fonts that are at least 12-points;
- Use black text on plain, high-contrast backgrounds; and
- Use background colors to help users understand the grouping of related information.

Even though it is important to ensure visual consistency, steps should be taken to emphasize important text. Commonly used headings should be formatted consistently, and attention-attracting features, such as animation, should only be used when appropriate.

Text Appearance

Guideline: When users are expected to rapidly read and understand prose text, use black text on a plain, high-contrast, non-patterned background.

Comments: Black text on a plain background elicited reliably faster reading performance than on a medium-textured background. When compared to reading light text on a dark background, people read black text on a white background up to thirty-two percent faster. In general, the greater the contrast between the text and background, the easier the text is to read.

Sources: Boyntoin and Bush, 1956; Bruce and Green, 1990; Cole and Jenkins, 1984; Evans, 1998; Goldsmith, 1987; Gould, et al., 1987a; Gould, et al., 1987b; Jenkins and Cole, 1982; Kosslyn, 1994; Muter and Maurutto, 1991; Muter, 1996; Scharff, Ahumada and Hill, 1999; Snyder, et al., 1990; Spencer, Reynolds and Coe, 1977a; Spencer, Reynolds and Coe, 1977b; Treisman, 1990; Williams, 2000.

Example:

11:2 Format Common Items Consistently

Guideline: Ensure that the format of common items is consistent from one page to another.

Relative Importance:
❶❷❸❹○

Strength of Evidence:
❶❷○○○

Comments: The formatting convention chosen should be familiar to users. For example, telephone numbers should be consistently punctuated (800-555-1212), and time records might be consistently punctuated with colons (HH:MM:SS).

Sources: Ahlstrom and Longo, 2001; Engel and Granda, 1975; Mayhew, 1992; Smith and Mosier, 1986; Tufte, 1983.

11:3 Use Mixed-Case for Prose Text

Relative Importance:
❶❷❸❹○

Strength of Evidence:
❶❷❸○○

Guideline: When users must read a lot of information, use lower-case fonts and appropriate capitalization to ensure the fastest possible reading speed.

Comments: Using 'mixed-case' fonts for reading prose text means that most letters will be lowercase, with all letters that should be capitalized being in uppercase. Most users have had considerable experience reading lowercase letters and are therefore very proficient at it.

Sources: Larson, 2004.

Example:

This block of text is an example of displaying continuous (prose) text using mixed upper- and lowercase letters. It's not difficult to read. This is called sentence case.

THIS BLOCK OF TEXT IS AN EXAMPLE OF DISPLAYING CONTINUOUS (PROSE) TEXT USING ALL UPPERCASE LETTERS. IT'S MORE DIFFICULT TO READ. THIS IS NOT CALLED SENTENCE CASE.

See page xxii for detailed descriptions of the rating scales
❶❷❸❹○

11:4 Ensure Visual Consistency

Relative Importance:
①②③④〇

Strength of Evidence:
①②③④〇

Guideline: Ensure visual consistency of Web site elements within and between Web pages.

Comments: Two studies found that the number of errors made using visually inconsistent displays is reliably higher than when using visually consistent displays. Visual consistency includes the size and spacing of characters; the colors used for labels, fonts and backgrounds; and the locations of labels, text and pictures. Earlier studies found that tasks performed on more consistent interfaces resulted in (1) a reduction in task completion times; (2) a reduction in errors; (3) an increase in user satisfaction; and (4) a reduction in learning time.

However, users tend to rapidly overcome some types of inconsistencies. For example, one study found that the use of different-sized widgets (such as pushbuttons, entry fields, or list boxes) does not negatively impact users' performance or preferences.

Sources: Adamson and Wallace, 1997; Adkisson, 2002; Badre, 2002; Card, Moran and Newell, 1983; Cockburn and Jones, 1996; Eberts and Schneider, 1985; Ehret, 2002; Grudin, 1989; Nielsen, 1999d; Osborn and Elliott, 2002; Ozok and Salvendy, 2000; Parush, Nadir and Shtub, 1998; Schneider and Shiffrin, 1977; Schneider, Dumais and Shiffrin, 1984; Tullis, 2001.

Example: An example of good visual consistency: Location and size of pictures, title bar, and font all contribute to visual consistency.

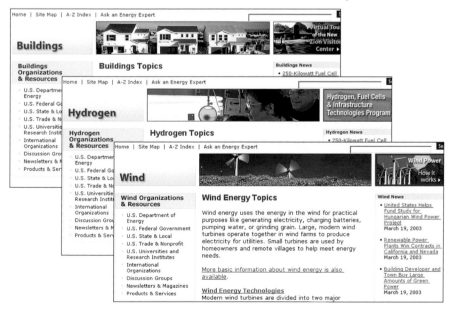

11:5 Use Bold Text Sparingly

Relative Importance:

Guideline: Use bold text only when it is important to draw the user's attention to a specific piece of information.

Strength of Evidence:

Comments: In the following example with the Field Identifiers bolded on the left, users spent about four times as long looking at the bold Field Identifiers than the non-bold Field Values. In the example on the right, participants spent more time looking at the bolded Field Values. In addition, the non-bold Field Values elicited better search accuracy rates than did the bold Field Values. In situations like this example, it is probably best to not use bold for either field identifiers or field values. In general, bold text should be used sparingly.

Sources: Joseph, Knott and Grier, 2002.

Example: The bottom example proves easier to read than either of the top two examples.

Field Identifiers	Field Values	Field Identifiers	Field Values
Previous Bill	$33.84	Previous Bill	**$33.84**
Previous Payment	$32.75	Previous Payment	**$32.75**
Balance	$1.09	Balance	**$1.09**
Current Charges	$18.89	Current Charges	**$18.89**
Total Billed	$19.98	Total Billed	**$19.98**
Penalty	$4.53	Penalty	**$4.53**
Amount Due	$24.51	Amount Due	**$24.51**

Field Identifiers	Field Values
Previous Bill	$33.84
Previous Payment	$32.75
Balance	$1.09
Current Charges	$18.89
Total Billed	$19.98
Penalty	$4.53
Amount Due	$24.51

See page xxii
for detailed descriptions
of the rating scales

Guideline: Use attention-attracting features with caution and only when they are highly relevant.

Relative Importance:
①②③○○

Comments: Draw attention to specific parts of a Web page with the appropriate (but limited) use of moving or animated objects, size differential between items, images, brightly-colored items, and varying font characteristics.

Strength of Evidence:
①②③④⑤

Not all features of a Web site will attract a user's attention equally. The following features are presented in order of the impact they have on users:

- Movement (e.g., animation or 'reveals') is the most effective attention-getting item. Research suggests that people cannot stop themselves from initially looking at moving items on a page. However, if the movement is not relevant or useful, it may annoy the user. If movement continues after attracting attention, it may distract from the information on the Web site.
- Larger objects, particularly images, will draw users' attention before smaller ones. Users fixate on larger items first, and for longer periods of time. However, users will tend to skip certain kinds of images that they believe to be ads or decoration.
- Users look at images for one or two seconds, and then look at the associated text caption. In many situations, reading a text caption to understand the meaning of an image is a last resort. Parts of images or text that have brighter colors seem to gain focus first.

Having some text and graphic items in brighter colors, and others in darker colors, helps users determine the relative importance of elements. Important attention-attracting font characteristics can include all uppercase, bolding, italics, underlining, and increased font size.

Sources: Campbell and Maglio, 1999; Evans, 1998; Faraday and Sutcliffe, 1997; Faraday, 2000; Faraday, 2001; Galitz, 2002; Hillstrom and Yantis, 1994; Lewis and Walker, 1989; McConkie and Zola, 1982; Nygren and Allard, 1996; Treisman, 1988; Williams, 2000.

Example:

Photos, like this one, previously have been shown.

9/11 Pentagon video goes public

Video showing a plane crashing into the Pentagon on September 11, 2001, was officially released to the public today, a judicial watchdog said. "We fought hard to obtain this video because we felt that it was very important to complete the public record with respect to the terrorist attacks of September 11,"

11:7 Use Familiar Fonts

Relative Importance:
①②③○○

Strength of Evidence:
①②③④⑤

Guideline: Use a familiar font to achieve the best possible reading speed.

Comments: Research shows no reliable differences in reading speed or user preferences for twelve point Times New Roman or Georgia (serif fonts), or Arial, Helvetica, or Verdana (sans serif fonts).

Sources: Bernard and Mills, 2000; Bernard, Liao and Mills, 2001a; Bernard, et al., 2002; Bernard, et al., 2001; Boyarski, et al., 1998; Evans, 1998; Tullis, Boynton and Hersh, 1995; Williams, 2000.

Example: Using unfamiliar fonts may slow reading speeds.

See page xxii for detailed descriptions of the rating scales
①②③④○

Relative Importance:
①②❸○○

Strength of Evidence:
①②❸❹○

Text Appearance

Guideline: Use at least a 12-point font (e.g., typeface) on all Web pages.

Comments: Research has shown that fonts smaller than 12 points elicit slower reading performance from users. For users over age 65, it may be better to use at least fourteen-point fonts. Never use less than nine-point font on a Web site.

Traditional paper-based font sizes do not translate well to Web site design. For instance, Windows Web browsers display type two to three points larger than the same font displayed on a Macintosh. User-defined browser settings may enlarge or shrink designer-defined font sizes. Defining text size using pixels will result in differently-sized characters depending upon the physical size of the monitor's pixels and its set resolution, and presents accessibility issues to those individuals who must specify large font settings.

Sources: Bailey, 2001; Bernard and Mills, 2000; Bernard, Liao and Mills, 2001a; Bernard, Liao and Mills, 2001b; Bernard, et al., 2002; Ellis and Kurniawan, 2000; Galitz, 2002; Ivory and Hearst, 2002; Tinker, 1963; Tullis, 2001; Tullis, Boynton and Hersh, 1995.

Example: Examples of cross-platform text-size differences generated on a variety of browsers and platforms by using HTML text in a one-cell table with a width of 100 pixels.

Macintosh 72dpi assumed	PC-Small 96dpi assumed	PC-Large 120dpi assumed
This passage shows the relative sizes of default (size=3) text on different computers using the browser's default (12-point) font setting	This passage shows the relative sizes of default (size=3) text on different computers using the browser's default (12-point) font settings	This passage shows the relative sizes of default (size=3) text on different computers

Text Appearance

11:9 Color-Coding and Instructions

Relative Importance:

Strength of Evidence:

Guideline: When using color-coding on your Web site, be sure that the coding scheme can be quickly and easily understood.

Comments: One study found that participants were able to answer questions significantly faster when the interface was color-coded, but only when information about the color-coding was provided. When both color-coding and information about how to interpret the colors were provided, user performance improved by forty percent. Be sure that the information provided does not require the user to read and comprehend a lot of text to understand it.

Sources: Resnick and Fares, 2004; Wu and Yuan, 2003.

Example:

The key in the bottom left brings clarification to the highlighted sizes in this Men's General Sizing Guidelines.

Men's General Sizing Guidelines

Height

5' 3"	123 lbs	131 lbs	139 lbs	147 lbs	155 lbs	163 lbs	171 lbs	179 lbs	187 lbs				
5' 4"	125 lbs	133 lbs	141 lbs	149 lbs	157 lbs	165 lbs	173 lbs	181 lbs	189 lbs				
5' 5"	127 lbs	135 lbs	143 lbs	151 lbs	159 lbs	167 lbs	175 lbs	183 lbs	191 lbs				
5' 6"	129 lbs	137 lbs	145 lbs	153 lbs	161 lbs	169 lbs	177 lbs	185 lbs	193 lbs				
5' 7"	131 lbs	139 lbs	147 lbs	155 lbs	163 lbs	171 lbs	179 lbs	187 lbs	195 lbs				
5' 8"	133 lbs	141 lbs	149 lbs	157 lbs	165 lbs	173 lbs	181 lbs	189 lbs	197 lbs	213 lbs	229 lbs	245 lbs	
5' 9"	135 lbs	143 lbs	151 lbs	159 lbs	167 lbs	175 lbs	183 lbs	191 lbs	199 lbs	215 lbs	231 lbs	247 lbs	
5' 10"	137 lbs	125 lbs	153 lbs	161 lbs	169 lbs	177 lbs	185 lbs	193 lbs	201 lbs	217 lbs	233 lbs	249 lbs	
5' 11"					171 lbs	179 lbs	187 lbs	195 lbs	203 lbs	219 lbs	235 lbs	251 lbs	267 lbs	283 lbs
6' 0"					173 lbs	181 lbs	189 lbs	197 lbs	205 lbs	221 lbs	237 lbs	253 lbs	269 lbs	285 lbs
6' 1"					175 lbs	183 lbs	191 lbs	199 lbs	207 lbs	223 lbs	239 lbs	255 lbs	271 lbs	287 lbs
6' 2"					177 lbs	185 lbs	193 lbs	201 lbs	209 lbs	225 lbs	241 lbs	257 lbs	273 lbs	289 lbs
6' 3"							195 lbs	203 lbs	211 lbs	227 lbs	243 lbs	259 lbs	275 lbs	291 lbs
6' 4"							197 lbs	205 lbs	213 lbs	229 lbs	245 lbs	261 lbs	277 lbs	293 lbs
6' 5"							199 lbs	207 lbs	215 lbs	231 lbs	247 lbs	263 lbs	279 lbs	295 lbs
6' 6"							201 lbs	209 lbs	217 lbs	233 lbs	249 lbs	265 lbs	281 lbs	297 lbs
6' 7"							203 lbs	211 lbs	219 lbs	235 lbs	251 lbs	267 lbs	283 lbs	300 lbs

Key:
- S
- M
- L
- XL
- XXL

Women's General Sizing Guidelines

Dress Size	2-4	4-6	8-10	12-14	16-18	20-22	24-26
Alpha Size	XS	SM	MED	LG	XL	XXL	XXXL
Numeric Size	32-34	34-36	38-40	42-44	46-48	50-52	54-56

See page xxii for detailed descriptions of the rating scales

11:10 Emphasize Importance

Relative Importance:

Strength of Evidence:

Text Appearance

Guideline: Change the font characteristics to emphasize the importance of a word or short phrase.

Comments: Font characteristics that are different from the surrounding text will dominate those that are routine. Important font characteristics include bolding, italics, font style (serif vs. sans serif), font size (larger is better to gain attention), and case (upper vs. lower). When used well, text style can draw attention to important words.

The use of differing font characteristics has negative consequences as well–reading speed can decrease by almost twenty percent, and thus should be used sparingly in large blocks of prose. Do not use differing font characteristics to show emphasis for more than one or two words or a short phrase. Do not use underlining for emphasis because underlined words on the Web are generally considered to be links.

Sources: Bouma, 1980; Breland and Breland, 1944; DeRouvray and Couper, 2002; Evans, 1998; Faraday, 2000; Foster and Coles, 1977; Lichty, 1989; Marcus, 1992; Paterson and Tinker, 1940a; Poulton and Brown, 1968; Rehe, 1979; Spool, et al., 1997; Tinker and Paterson, 1928; Tinker, 1955; Tinker, 1963; Vartabedian, 1971; Williams, 2000.

Example: Limited use of bolding effectively emphasizes important topic categories.

DoD Sites
DoD on the World Wide Web ✉ Comment

- Air Force
- Army
- Budget
- Business Opportunities
- **Civilian Job Opportunities**
- Coast Guard
- Combined Federal Campaign
- Dear Abby, Operation
- Defend America
- DeploymentLINK
- **Enduring Freedom**
- Environment
- Facts and Statistics
- Family
- Force Transformation(03/27/2003)
  NEW!
- Guard and Reserve
- Homeland Security
- **Iraq**
- Joint Chiefs of Staff
- Korea
- Marine Corps
- Navy
- Organization of DoD
- Pay
- **Pentagon**
- Recruiting
- Secretary of Defense
- **Terrorism and Terrorists**
- Tricare (Military Health System)
- Unified Combatant Commands
- Vaccines

11:11 Highlighting Information

Relative Importance:

Strength of Evidence:

Guideline: Do not use two (or more) different ways to highlight the same information on one page.

Comments: One study found that participants were able to complete tasks faster when the interface contained either color-coding or a form of ranking, but not both. The presence of both seemed to present too much information, and reduced the performance advantage by about half.

Sources: Bandos and Resnick, 2004; Resnick and Fares, 2004.

Example: "Which model has the smallest trunk?" Users were able to complete the focused tasks faster when the diagram contained either color-coding or ranking, but not both. It seems that the presence of both identifiers presented too much information and users had trouble indentifying the information they needed.

Side-By-Side Car Comparison — Mid-Size Luxury Sedans (8 Models)

PRICING	Model 1	Model 2	Model 3	Model 4	Model 5	Model 6	Model 7	Model 8
Base Retail *	$34,150 [6/8]		$30,695 [2/8]	$29,970 [1/8]	$31,350 [4/8]	$32,495 [5/8]	$30,765 [3/8]	
Base Invoice †	$31,091 [6/8]		$28,445 [3/8]	$27,332 [1/8]	$27,653 [2/8]	$29,459 [5/8]	$29,062 [4/8]	
POWERTRAIN	**Model 1**	**Model 2**	**Model 3**	**Model 4**	**Model 5**	**Model 6**	**Model 7**	**Model 8**
Displacement	3.0 [2/8]	3.0 [2/8]	3.2 [1/8]		3.0 [2/8]	3.0 [2/8]		3.2 [1/8]
Compression Ratio	10.1 [3/8]	10.2 [4/8]	10.0 [6/8]	10.3 [2/8]	10.5 [1/8]	10.3 [2/8]		10.0 [6/8]
Valves Per Cylinder	5 [1/8]	4 [2/8]	4 [2/8]	4 [2/8]	4 [2/8]	4 [2/8]	4 [2/8]	
Total Number Valves	30 [1/8]	24 [2/8]	24 [2/8]	24 [2/8]	24 [2/8]	24 [2/8]		18 [7/8]
Horsepower	220 @ 6700 RPM [3/8]	225 @ 5900 RPM [4/8]	220 @ 6000 RPM		215 @ 5800 RPM [6/8]	232 @ 6750 RPM [1/8]		215 @ 5700 RPM [6/8]
Torque	221 @ 3200 RPM [3/8]		220 @ 3400 RPM		218 @ 3000 RPM [6/8]	220 @ 4500 RPM	222 @ 2500 RPM [1/8]	222 @ 3000 RPM [1/8]
EPA City			19 MPG [6/8]	19 MPG [6/8]		20 MPG [1/8]		20 MPG [1/8]
EPA Hwy	26 MPG [2/8]		26 MPG [2/8]	28 MPG [1/8]		26 MPG [2/8]		26 MPG [2/8]
DIMENSIONS	**Model 1**	**Model 2**	**Model 3**	**Model 4**	**Model 5**	**Model 6**	**Model 7**	**Model 8**
Head Room: Front	38.4 in. [6/8]	38.4 in. [6/8]	38.5 in. [5/8]		39.1 in. [3/8]	40.4 in. [1/8]	39.2 in. [2/8]	38.9 in. [4/8]
Head Room: Rear		37.5 in. [2/8]	37.5 in. [2/8]	37.7 in. [1/8]	37.5 in. [2/8]	37.3 in. [6/8]
Leg Room: Front			42.4 in. [2/8]	42.4 in. [2/8]	42.7 in. [1/8]	42.8 in. [1/8]	42.3 in. [5/8]	41.7 in. [6/8]
Leg Room: Rear	34.2 in. [3/8]	34.6 in. [4/8]	37.0 in. [2/8]	34.4 in. [6/8]		37.4 in. [1/8]	35.1 in. [5/8]	
Shoulder Rm: Front	55.1 in. [4/8]	54.4 in. [6/8]	56.1 in. [2/8]	54.5 in. [5/8]		57.7 in. [1/8]	56.3 in. [3/8]	54.3 in. [4/8]
Shoulder Rm: Rear		54.2 in. [5/8]	56.2 in. [2/8]	53.7 in. [6/8]		57.0 in. [1/8]	55.1 in. [3/8]	54.3 in. [4/8]
EPA Trunk or Cargo	13.4 cu.ft. [4/8]		12.8 cu.ft. [5/8]	16.9 cu.ft. [1/8]		13.5 cu.ft. [3/8]	14.8 cu.ft. [2/8]	12.2 cu.ft. [6/8]
WARRANTY	**Model 1**	**Model 2**	**Model 3**	**Model 4**	**Model 5**	**Model 6**	**Model 7**	**Model 8**
Powertrain	4 years or 50000 miles	4 years or [2/8] 50000 miles	4 years or [2/8] 50000 miles	4 years or [2/8] 50000 miles	6 years or [1/8] 70000 miles	4 years or [2/8] 50000 miles	4 years or [2/8] 50000 miles	4 years or 50000 miles
Corrosion/Rust Thru	12 years or [1/8] Unlimited miles	6 years or [2/8] Unlimited miles	6 years or [2/8] 100000 miles	6 years or [2/8] Unlimited miles	6 years or [2/8] Unlimited miles		6 years or [2/8] Unlimited miles	
SPECIFICATIONS	**Model 1**	**Model 2**	**Model 3**	**Model 4**	**Model 5**	**Model 6**	**Model 7**	**Model 8**
Wheel Base		107.3 in. [3/8]	113.4 in. [2/8]	106.7 in. [5/8]		114.5 in. [1/8]	105.3 in. [6/8]	106.9 in. [4/8]
Overall Length	179.0 in. [5/8]		190.1 in. [2/8]	182.9 in. [3/8]	174.4 in.	193.9 in. [1/8]	182.5 in. [4/8]	178.2 in. [6/8]
Width	69.5 in. [4/8]	68.5 in. [6/8]	70.4 in. [2/8]	70.4 in. [2/8]	72.2 in. [1/8]	69.0 in. [5/8]		
Height	56.2 in. [3/8]	55.7 in. [5/8]	54.7 in. [6/8]		55.9 in. [4/8]	56.1 in. [4/8]	56.8 in. [1/8]	
Curb Weight	3462 lbs. [5/8]	3362 lbs. [3/8]		3516 lbs. [6/8]	3285 lbs. [2/8]		3175 lbs. [1/8]	3450 lbs. [4/8]
Turning Radius		14.4 [2/8]		35.7 [4/8]	33.4 [1/8]			35.3 [3/8]
Fuel Capacity	18.5 [1/8]	16.6 [5/8]	17.5 [3/8]		17.5 [3/8]	18.0 [2/8]		16.4 [6/8]

See page xxii for detailed descriptions of the rating scales

Lists

Lists are commonly found on Web sites.

These may be lists of, for example, people, drugs, theaters, or restaurants. Each list should be clearly introduced and have a descriptive title. A list should be formatted so that it can be easily scanned. The order of items in the list should be done to maximize user performance, which usually means that the most important items are placed toward the top of the list. If a numbered list is used, start the numbering at 'one,' not 'zero.' Generally only the first letter of the first word is capitalized, unless a word that is usually capitalized is shown in the list.

Lists

12:1 Order Elements to Maximize User Performance

Guideline: Arrange lists and tasks in an order that best facilitates efficient and successful user performance.

Relative Importance:
① ② ③ ④ ○

Strength of Evidence:
① ② ③ ④ ⑤

Comments: Designers should determine if there is an order for items that will facilitate use of the Web site. If there is, ensure that the site is formatted to support that order, and that all pages follow the same order. For example, ensure that lists of items, sets of links, and a series of tabs are in a meaningful order.

Where no obvious order applies, organize lists alphabetically or numerically. Keep in mind that it is the user's logic that should prevail rather than the designer's logic.

Sources: Bransford and Johnson, 1972; Detweiler and Omanson, 1996; Engel and Granda, 1975; Evans, 1998; Flower, Hayes and Swarts, 1983; Halgren and Cooke, 1993; Morkes and Nielsen, 1998; Nygren and Allard, 1996; Ozok and Salvendy, 2000; Redish, Felker and Rose, 1981; Smith and Mosier, 1986; Spyridakis, 2000.

Example:

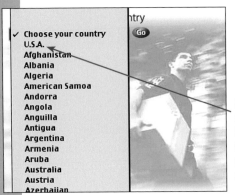

Ordering list by region and then alphabetically by country allows users to rapidly find desired information.

Region/Country
North America
Canada
Mexico
United States
Other
Total
Central & South America
Argentina
Bolivia
Brazil
Chile
Colombia
Costa Rica

If most of your users will be looking for the same item, then place it at the top of your list.

This list should be ordered to read down columns, not across rows.

Alabama	Alaska	Arizona	Arkansas
California	Colorado	Connecticut	Delaware
District of Columbia	Florida	Georgia	Hawaii
Idaho	Illinois	Indiana	Iowa
Kansas	Kentucky	Louisiana	Maine
Maryland	Massachusetts	Michigan	Minnesota
Mississippi	Missouri	Montana	Nebraska
Nevada	New Hampshire	New Jersey	New Mexico
New York	North Carolina	North Dakota	Ohio
Oklahoma	Oregon	Pennsylvania	Rhode Island

Lists

Guideline: Place a list's most important items at the top.

Relative Importance:
①②③④○

Comments: Experienced users usually look first at the top item in a menu or list, and almost always look at one of the top three items before looking at those farther down the list. Research indicates that users tend to stop scanning a list as soon as they see something relevant, thus illustrating the reason to place important items at the beginning of lists.

Strength of Evidence:
①②③④○

Sources: Byrne, et al., 1999; Carroll, 1990; Evans, 1998; Faraday, 2001; Isakson and Spyridakis, 1999; Lewenstein, et al., 2000; Nielsen, 1996a; Nielsen, 1999b; Nielsen, 1999c; Spyridakis, 2000.

Example:

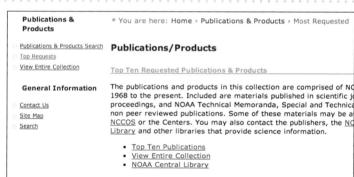

This listing assists users by breaking out the top ten requests in a separate link. The entire collection is then listed next. This tactic can save users time when searching for popular items or topics.

This extensive list of titles contains the most commonly used titles at the top of the list and also in their alphabetically-correct position further down the list. This avoids the need for users to scroll through titles such as 'His Highness.'

See page xxii for detailed descriptions of the rating scales
①②③④○

Lists

12:3 Format Lists to Ease Scanning

Relative Importance:
①②③④〇

Strength of Evidence:
①②③④〇

Guideline: Make lists easy to scan and understand.

Comments: The use of meaningful labels, effective background colors, borders, and white space allow users to identify a set of items as a discrete list.

Sources: Chaparro and Bernard, 2001; Detweiler and Omanson, 1996; Levine, 1996; Nielsen and Tahir, 2002; Nygren and Allard, 1996; Spyridakis, 2000; Treisman, 1982.

Example:

These Web sites use background colors and thin white lines between information groups to make these lists easy to scan.

Video Highlights

- ▶ **Preview 'Brotherhood' episode**
- ▶ Hasselhoff's hilarious ad
- ▶ Perfect grilled salmon
- ▶ Science of the ultimate tsunami
- ▶ All eyes on Danica

Entertainment

Photos: Oprah, Lohan & more
- · 'Miami Vice' sinks 'Pirates' at box office
- · Willie: Dixie Chicks got a 'raw deal'
- · Gossip: Madonna's toilet needs
- · Report: Swank loves to thrill
- · Promising model ID'd as crash victim
- · Fire erupts on James Bond set
- · Photos: Liz Taylor through the years
- · Anderson, Kid Rock marry in St. Tropez
- · Will Ferrell & wife expecting

Find movies, actors and actresses   [Go]

Popular Searches

People Search	Suggested Searches
Robert Charles Browne	Landis doping
Jada Pinkett Smith	Israel-Lebanon border
Tony Blair	NORAD
Reggie Bush	Pakistan Taliban
Colin Farrell	Minimum wage bill

INSIDE EDUCATION

For Teachers
For Students
For University Students & Scholars
Plan a Group Visit
Beyond Our Walls: State Profiles on Holocaust Education

INSIDE RESEARCH

Center for Advanced Holocaust Studies
Collections and Archives
Library
Academic Publications
Web Links
Public Programs Multimedia Archive
Survivors Registry Names Research
Holocaust-Era Assets
Task Force for International Cooperation

INSIDE REMEMBRANCE

Days of Remembrance 2006
Holocaust Remembrance Day 2006–15
Organizing a Remembrance Day
Planning a Military Observance
Survivors Registry
Office of Survivor Affairs

12:4 Display Related Items in Lists

Relative Importance:
① ② ③ ④ ○

Strength of Evidence:
① ② ③ ④ ○

Guideline: Display a series of related items in a vertical list rather than as continuous text.

Comments: A well-organized list format tends to facilitate rapid and accurate scanning. One study indicated that users scan vertical lists more rapidly than horizontal lists. Scanning a horizontal list takes users twenty percent longer than scanning a vertical list.

Sources: Mayhew, 1992; Nygren and Allard, 1996; Smith and Mosier, 1986; Tullis, 1984; Wright, 1977.

Example:

The Office of Data makes available for download:
- <u>Annual Production Statistics</u>
- <u>Monthly Production Statistics</u>
- <u>Weekly Production Statistics</u>
- <u>Quarterly Consumption Projections</u>

Bulleted lists are easier to scan and understand.

The Office of Data makes available for download <u>Annual Production Statistics</u>, <u>Monthly Production Statistics</u>, <u>Weekly Production Statistics</u>, and <u>Quarterly Consumption Projections</u>.

Horizontal lists are more difficult to scan and understand.

See page xxii for detailed descriptions of the rating scales
① ② ③ ④ ○

12:5 Introduce Each List

Relative Importance:
①②③○○

Strength of Evidence:
①②③④○

Guideline: Provide an introductory heading (i.e., word or phrase) at the top of each list.

Comments: Providing a descriptive heading allows users to readily understand the reason for having a list of items, and how the items relate to each other. The heading helps to inform users how items are categorized, or any prevailing principle or theme. Users are able to use lists better when they include headings.

Sources: Bransford and Johnson, 1972; Bransford and Johnson, 1973; Detweiler and Omanson, 1996; Engel and Granda, 1975; Levine, 1996; Redish, 1993; Smith and Goodman, 1984; Smith and Mosier, 1986.

Example:

In The News 2:23

- Live - 📷 Pentagon briefing on Iraq war
- Bloody street battles fought near Baghda
- Purported Saddam message calls for jihac
- U.S.: No proof of attack on 'human shields
- Rumsfeld war plan criticized on battlefield
- Basra civilians say pressured by Baath pa
- Jordan foils two alleged Iraqi terror plots
- Hong Kong to move SARS victims to cam
- PayPal accused of violating Patriot Act
- Markets: S&P 500 ⬆ 1.4% · Nasdaq -

News - Photos - Sports - Stocks -

Marketplace

- Save money at Dell!

Free CD-RW or DVD u
select Dell PCs. Expir
Details here

- Sephora J'Adore mini with purchase
- 1-800-Flowers - Get 20 Tulips free, when
Tulips - $29.99
- New Burberry at Neiman Marcus - Check
styles

Shopping - Gifts - Computers - Flow

Entertainment

- 50 Cent & Eminem Performance

Preview the forthcoming 5(
The New Breed, with Patie
performed live with Eminer

- Y! Sports Fantasy Baseball - Sign up now

ABOUT US

business opportunities
core values
employment
fbi in brief
field offices
headquarters & programs
legats

PRESS ROOM

congressional statements
fbi chats
fbi this week
field news
gotcha
press releases

LIBRARY & REFERENCE

freedom of information act
publications
uniform crime reports

MARKETS May 17; 2:45 p.m. ET

DJIA	11,195.05	▼	-224.84
NASDAQ	2,197.38	▼	-31.75
S&P 500	1,269.97	▼	-22.11

Quick
Quotes   Enter Sym   go

Your Portfolio | Stock Symbol Look Up

BUSINESS
- Asian-Owned Firms Booming
- Southwest May Assign Seats

📰 **ENRON TRIAL**
- Special Report » | Court Blog

NATION
- New Orleans's Changing Face
- Pentagon 9/11 Videos Released

POLITICS
- New Drug Plan Called Success
- Judge Sees Notes on Libby
- The Kingdom and the Power

WORLD
- E.U. Strains Evident in Debate
- Iraqis to Present Cabinet
- Indonesia's Mt. Merapi Erupts

HEALTH
- Abortion Foes Want Pill Pulled
- Group Studies Nanoparticles
- Sally Squires: Lean Plate Club

EDUCATION
- Group Seeks to Limit Closings
- From Hardships to Scholarships
- Special Ed. in Catholic School

RELIGION
- Archbishop Successor Named
- A Look at McCarrick's Tenure

12:6 Use Static Menus

Relative Importance:
❶❷❸○○

Strength of Evidence:
❶❷❸○○

Guideline: Use static menus to elicit the fastest possible speed when accessing menu items.

Comments: To elicit the fastest possible human performance, designers should put the most frequently used menus times in the first few positions of a menu. Designers should determine the location of items within a menu based on the frequency of use of each item. Adaptable menus, where users are allowed to change the order of menu items, elicits reasonably fast performance as well. The slowest performance is achieved when an adaptive menu, where the computer automatically changes the position of menu items, is used. One study found that users prefer having static menus, rather than adaptive menus.

Sources: Findlater and McGrenere, 2004; McGrenere, Baecker and Booth, 2002.

Example:

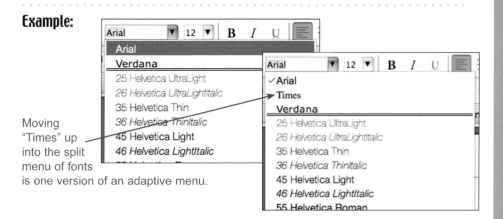

Moving "Times" up into the split menu of fonts is one version of an adaptive menu.

12:7 Start Numbered Items at One

Relative Importance:
❶❷○○○

Strength of Evidence:
❶❷○○○

Guideline: When items are numbered, start the numbering sequence at 'one' rather than 'zero.'

Comments: Do not start the numbering with a 'zero.' When counting, people start with 'one,' not 'zero.'

Sources: Engel and Granda, 1975; Smith and Mosier, 1986.

See page xxii for detailed descriptions of the rating scales
❶❷❸❹○

12:8 Use Appropriate List Style

Relative Importance:
❶❷○○○

Strength of Evidence:
❶❷❸❹○

Guideline: Use bullet lists to present items of equal status or value, and numbered lists if a particular order to the items is warranted.

Comments: Bullet lists work best when the items do not contain an inherent sequence, order, or rank. Numbered lists assign each item in the list an ascending number, making the numerical order readily apparent. Numbered lists are especially important when giving instructions.

Sources: Coney and Steehouder, 2000; Detweiler and Omanson, 1996; Lorch and Chen, 1986; Narveson, 2001; Spyridakis, 2000.

Example:

Use bullets if your list items are of equal value, or if they have no discernable order.

Agencies
- A-Z Index
- Federal Branches
- State, Local & Tribal
- International

Contact Government
- e-Mail
- Phone
- In-Person
- More

Reference
- News Releases
- Federal Forms
- Laws & Regulations
- Questions About Government?
- More

Zeitgeist This Week

Gaining Search Queries: Week Ending April 24, 2006

1. 420
2. nick lachey
3. silent hill
4. nepal
5. miss usa
6. chernobyl
7. gas prices
8. reggie bush
9. mothers day
10. denise richards
11. opie and anthony
12. pyramid head
13. david lee roth
14. aresanob
15. cinco de

Top Searches in 2005 - News

1. Janet Jackson
2. Hurricane Katrina
3. tsunami
4. xbox 360
5. Brad Pitt
6. Michael Jackson
7. American Idol
8. Britney Spears
9. Angelina Jolie
10. Harry Potter

Top Searches in 2005 - Products

1. ipod
2. digital camera
3. mp3 player
4. ipod mini
5. psp
6. laptop
7. xbox
8. ipod shuffle
9. computer desk
10. ipod nano

Using numbered lists is appropriate when items are in a proscribed order, such as this list of 'Top 10' searches.

Lists

Guideline: Capitalize the first letter of only the first word of a list item, a list box item, check box labels, and radio button labels.

Relative Importance:
❶○○○○

Strength of Evidence:
❶❷○○○

Comments: Only the first letter of the first word should be capitalized unless the item contains another word that would normally be capitalized.

Sources: Bailey, 1996; Fowler, 1998; Marcus, Smilonich and Thompson, 1995; Microsoft, 1992.

Example:

Information by Topic »

Services
- Email services
- Headline service
- Text alerts and PDA

Events & of
- Write topic
  win Pengu

Information
- Contact us
- Newsroom
- Style guide
- Advertising
- Privacy po
- Terms and
- The Guardian
- Guardian readers'
  editor
- The Observer
- Observer readers'
  editor

Smithsonian Research
→ Archives of American Art
→ Astrophysical Observatory (SAO)
→ Museum Conservation Institute (MCI)
→ Environmental Research Center (SERC)
→ Libraries
→ Tropical Research Institute (STRI)
→ More Research

- **Benefits and Grants**
  Loans, money, funding, financial aid...

- **Consumer Guides**
  Consumer credit, better business, recalls, fraud, debt, scams...

- **Defense and International**
  Military, international affairs, trade, embassies, visas, immigration...

- **Environment, Energy and Agriculture**
  Farms, food production, natural resources, conservation, weather...

- **Family, Home and Community**
  Housing, human services, community development...

- **Health and Nutrition**
  Medical, health care, insurance, diet, fitness, public health...

- **History, Arts, and Culture**
  Museums, libraries, genealogy, ethnic traditions...

13

Screen–Based Controls (Widgets)

In order to interact with a Web site, users

usually require the use of screen-based controls (sometimes known as 'widgets'). Besides the pervasive link, commonly used screen-based controls include pushbuttons, radio buttons, check boxes, drop-down lists and entry fields. Designers should ensure that they use familiar widgets in a conventional or commonly-used manner.

When pushbuttons are used, ensure that they look like pushbuttons and that they are clearly labeled. In some cases, the pushbuttons will need to be prioritized to facilitate their proper use.

Radio buttons are used to select from among two or more mutually-exclusive selections. Check boxes should be used to make binary choices, e.g., 'yes' or 'no.' Drop-down lists are generally used to select one item from among many. To speed user performance, show default values when appropriate, and do not limit the number of viewable list box options.

Entry fields are used when completing forms and entering text into search boxes. Designers should try to minimize the amount of information entered by users. Each entry field should be clearly and consistently labeled, with the labels placed close to the entry fields. Designers should also clearly distinguish between 'required' and 'optional' data entry fields, and attempt to minimize the use of the Shift key.

To facilitate fast entry of information, designers should automatically place the cursor in the first data entry field, provide labels for each field (e.g., pounds, miles, etc.), and provide auto-tabbing functionality. In order to increase accuracy of data entry, partition long data items into smaller units, enable the software to automatically detect errors, and do not require case-sensitive data entries. Showing users their data entries can increase accuracy. For experienced users, the fastest possible entry of information will come from allowing users to use entry fields instead of selecting from list boxes.

Guideline: Distinguish clearly and consistently between required and optional data entry fields.

Relative Importance:
①②③④⑤

Comments: Users should be able to easily determine which data entry fields are required and which are optional. Many Web sites are currently using an asterisk in front of the label for required fields. Other sites are adding the word 'required' near the label. One study found that bolded text is preferred when compared to the use of chevrons (>>>), checkmarks, or color to indicate required fields.

Strength of Evidence:
①②③○○

Sources: Bailey, 1996; Fowler, 1998; Morrell, et al., 2002; Tullis and Pons, 1997.

Example:

(required) First name:
(required) Last name:
Company/Organization:
(required) Mailing Address:

(required) City: State:
Zip Code
(required)Country:
(required) Phone(area code+number):
FAX (area code+number):
(required) E-mail:
Comments:

Asterisks (*) and labeling data entry field names with 'required' are two popular and effective methods of distinguishing between optional and required data entry fields.

A field with an asterisk (*) before it is a required field.

Prefix:
* First Name:
* Last Name:
* Address:

*City:
*State:
*Zip:
*Email Address:
*Phone Number:

13:2 Label Pushbuttons Clearly

Relative Importance:
① ② ③ ④ ⑤

Strength of Evidence:
① ② ○ ○ ○

Guideline: Ensure that a pushbutton's label clearly indicates its action.

Comments: The label of a pushbutton should clearly indicate the action that will be applied when the pushbutton is clicked. Common pushbutton labels include 'Update,' 'Go,' 'Submit,' 'Cancel,' 'Enter,' 'Home,' 'Next,' and 'Previous.'

Sources: Bailey, 1996; Fowler, 1998; Marcus, Smilonich and Thompson, 1995.

Example:

Effective use of short phrases leaves no doubt in the user's mind as to what will happen when the pushbutton is clicked.

◉ **Web** ○ **Directory** ○ **Photos**

[**Search**]

▨ **Yellow Pages** ▨ **White Pages** ▨ **Classifieds**

My Horoscope   edit — ✕

Get your daily horoscope!
Enter Your Birthday
(MM DD YYYY)

[**Get My Horoscope**]

Enter your search information:

Company name:
or CIK: *(Central Index Key)*
or File Number:
or State: *(two-letter abbreviation)*
and/or SIC: *(Standard Industrial Classification Code)*

(**Find Companies**)

Search by Business Entity Name: (**Find Business Entity ››**)

OR -

Search by Registered Agent Name: (**Find Agent ››**)

See page xxii for detailed descriptions of the rating scales
① ② ③ ④ ○

13:3 Label Data Entry Fields Consistently

Guideline: Ensure that data entry labels are worded consistently, so that the same data item is given the same label if it appears on different pages.

Relative Importance:
①②③④○

Strength of Evidence:
①②③○○

Comments: If possible, employ consistent labeling conventions. For example, do not use single words or phrases for some labels and short sentences for others, or use verbs for some and nouns for others.

Sources: Evans, 1998; Mahajan and Shneiderman, 1997; Smith and Mosier, 1986.

13:4 Do Not Make User-Entered Codes Case Sensitive

Guideline: Treat upper- and lowercase letters as equivalent when users are entering codes.

Relative Importance:
①②③④○

Strength of Evidence:
①②○○○

Comments: Do not make user-entered codes case sensitive unless there is a valid reason for doing so (such as increased security of passwords). If required, clearly inform users if they must enter codes in a case specific manner. When retaining data entered by users, show the data as it was entered by the user.

Sources: Ahlstrom and Longo, 2001; Smith and Mosier, 1986.

Example:

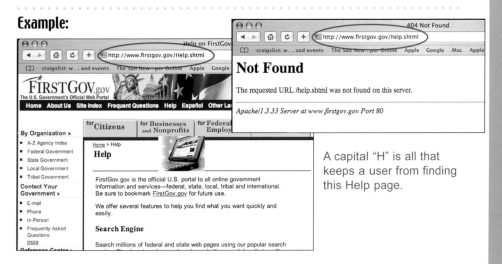

A capital "H" is all that keeps a user from finding this Help page.

13:5 Label Data Entry Fields Clearly

Relative Importance:
①②③④○

Strength of Evidence:
①②③○○

Guideline: Display an associated label for each data entry field to help users understand what entries are desired.

Comments: Employ descriptive labels that clearly, concisely, and unambiguously define the required entry. Make labels distinct enough so that readers do not confuse them with the data entries themselves. This can be done by bolding the labels or providing other visual cues, such as an asterisk.

Do not create new jargon when labeling data entry fields. Use common terms (e.g., male, female) rather than arbitrary labels (e.g., Group 1, Group 2). If the meaning of a proposed label is in doubt, conduct usability testing with an appropriate sample of qualified users.

Sources: Pew and Rollins, 1975; Smith and Mosier, 1986.

Example:

Date Flag Needed by:

Prefix:

Firstname:

Lastname:

Flag flown for:

Address:

City:

State:

Zipcode:

Home Phone:

Business Phone:

Fax:

E-mail Address:

A good design:
Each data entry field has an associated descriptive label.

Enter your account information

First name:

Last name:

Gender: ○ Male ○ Female

Birth date: [Month ▲] [Day ▲]

State: [Select One ▲]

ZIP code:

Time zone: [Select One ▲]

☐ I own or work with a small business

See page xxii
for detailed descriptions
of the rating scales
①②③④○

Relative Importance:

Strength of Evidence:

Guideline: Do not require users to enter the same information more than once.

Comments: Requiring re-entry of data imposes an additional task on users, and increases the possibility of entry errors. When entries made by users on one page are required on another page, the computer should retrieve the original entries, rather than requiring re-entry of the same information. In general, require users to make as few entries as possible.

Sources: Czaja and Sharit, 1997; Smith and Mosier, 1986; Zimmerman, et al., 2002.

Example: Clicking this button will prompt the server to copy information from the 'Billing Address' column to the 'Shipping Address' column, thus eliminating the need for users to re-input the data (if it is the same).

Step 1 of 4

BILLING ADDRESS	SHIPPING ADDRESS
* E-mail:	Copy from Billing Clear
* First Name:	* First Name:
* Last Name:	* Last Name:
Company:	Company:
* Address:	* Address:
Address2:	Address2:
* City:	* City:
* State & Zip: USA only	* State & Zip: USA only
* Phone:	* Phone:
* Country: Including US territories USA	* Country: Including US territories USA
Foreign Postal Code:	Foreign Postal Code:
Foreign Province/ Territory:	Foreign Province/

This Web site minimizes user data entry by remembering IDs.

Enter your ID and password to sign in

ID:

Password:

☑ Remember my ID on this computer

Sign In

Mode: Standard | Secure

Sign-in help   Password lookup

Screen–Based Controls (Widgets)

13:7 Put Labels Close to Data Entry Fields

Guideline: Ensure that labels are close enough to their associated data entry fields so that users will recognize the label as describing the data entry field.

Relative Importance:
①②③○○

Strength of Evidence:
①②○○○

Comments: All labels and related information should be close to the data entry field to enable users to easily relate the label and entries required.

Sources: Engel and Granda, 1975; Evans, 1998; Galitz, 2002; Smith and Mosier, 1986.

Example:

Placing labels very close to the data entry fields allows users to rapidly relate the label and the required entries.

Contact Information
* First Name
Enter First Name
*Last Name
Enter Last Name
*Address:
Enter Street
*City   *State   *Zip Code
Enter City   IL ⬍   Enter Zip
Phone Number
Enter Phone
*Email Address
Enter your Email
Email Format:

Placing labels away from the data entry field slows users' entry rates.

Please answer the questions and select **Next** at the bottom of the page.

What is your Social Security Number?
Please enter this number without the dashes. For example, 123456789.

What is your last name?

What is your first name?

What is your middle initial?

What is your date of birth?
Please enter this date in "mmddyyyy" format. For example, 08171975 for August 17, 1975.

Guideline: Create data entry fields that are large enough to show all of the entered data without scrolling.

Relative Importance:
❶❷❸○○

Strength of Evidence:
❶❷❸○○

Comments: Users should be able to see their entire entry at one time. There always will be some users who will enter more data than can be seen without scrolling; however, try to minimize the need to scroll or move the cursor to see all the data for that field. If there is a character limit for a particular field, state that near the entry field.

Designers should be particularly aware of the length of data entry fields used for entering search terms. One study found that this entry field should be at least 35-40 characters long to accommodate ninety-five percent of search terms being used.

Sources: Bailey, 1996; Bailey and Wolfson, 2005; Czaja and Sharit, 1997; Fowler, 1998.

Example:

The text expands vertically so that a user can see even very long entries without having to scroll horizontally.

Data entry fields should be wide enough so that the user can see their entire entry without scrolling.

Please select one of the following feedback categories: (required)

FirstGov website comments ⬍

E-mail Address: (required only if you would like a response)
usabilityguy@scrolling_is_ok.com

Feedback Message: (required)
I find the new layout much improved ...

However, there are still some problems that you might want to address. First off, your use of fonts (and an apparent need to

Submit Feedback

* 1. Establishment Name: tute's Communication Technologies Branch

Search the Internet

UK Search Only

Search News Sites

Screen-Based Controls (Widgets)

13:9 Use Radio Buttons for Mutually Exclusive Selections

Guideline: Provide radio buttons when users need to choose one response from a list of mutually exclusive options.

Relative Importance:
①②③○○

Strength of Evidence:
①②③④○

Comments: Radio buttons should be used when there is a need to select from among mutually exclusive items. Users should be able to click on the button or its text label to make their selection. Assign one of the radio button choices as the default when appropriate. One study reported that for making mutually exclusive selections, radio buttons elicit reliably better performance than drop-down lists. Radio buttons are also preferred over both open lists and drop-down lists.

Sources: Bailey, 1983; Bailey, 1996; Fowler, 1998; Galitz, 2002; Johnsgard, et al., 1995; Marcus, Smilonich and Thompson, 1995; Tullis and Kodimer, 1992.

Example:

If a user must be constrained to selecting one item in a list, employ radio buttons rather than check boxes.

> **When you use the U.S. Department of Education's (ED) I**
> *(Please check only one)*
>
> ○ Student
> ◉ Teacher
> ○ Education administrator or manager
> ○ Parent or family member
> ○ Researcher or analyst
> ○ Policy maker or legislator
> ○ Librarian
> ○ Writer or reporter
> ○ Other *(please specify)* [   ]

Only one option is clickable for each individual task below.

2. Communicate with and educate your staff, members, and persons in the communities that you serve:			
Task	**Not Started**	**In Progress**	**Completed**
• Find up-to-date, reliable pandemic information and other public health advisories from state and local health departments, emergency management agencies, and CDC. Make this information available to your organization and others.	◉	○	○
• Distribute materials with basic information about pandemic influenza: signs and symptoms, how it is spread, ways to protect yourself and your family (e.g., respiratory hygiene and cough etiquette), family preparedness plans, and how to care for ill persons at home.	◉	○	○
• When appropriate, include basic information about pandemic influenza in public meetings (e.g. sermons, classes, trainings, small group meetings and announcements).	○	◉	○

See page xxii for detailed descriptions of the rating scales
①②③④○

Relative Importance:
①②③○○

Strength of Evidence:
①②③○○

Guideline: Use widgets that are familiar to your users, and employ them in their commonly used manner.

Comments: Do not assume that all users are familiar with all available widgets. Unfamiliar widgets will slow some users, and cause others not to use the widget because they do not know how to make it work properly. For instance, one study showed that some users, particularly older users, do not know how to use a drop-down list.

In choosing widgets, designers typically consider such issues as the amount of available screen 'real estate,' reducing the number of user clicks, and whether the user will be choosing one from among many items, or several items at once. Usability test the performance and acceptability of widgets to ensure they do not confuse or slow users.

Sources: Bailey, Koyani and Nall, 2000; Nall, Koyani and Lafond, 2001.

Example: The circled widget is used in an unconventional manner. Users might expect this widget to be a text entry box. However, when a user places their cursor in the entry area, it invokes the linked text in the box at left from which the user must select the car type. A drop-down box would be a more suitable widget.

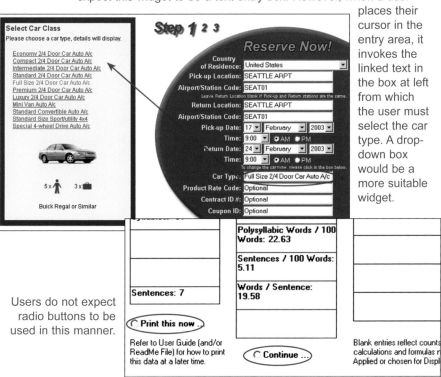

Users do not expect radio buttons to be used in this manner.

Screen-Based Controls (Widgets)

13:11 Anticipate Typical User Errors

Relative Importance:
①②❸○○

Strength of Evidence:
①❷○○○

Guideline: Use the computer to detect errors made by users.

Comments: Do not expect that users always will make correct entries. Anticipate possible user errors, and when possible, allocate responsibility to the computer to identify these mistakes and suggest corrections. For example, if a date is entered as 'February 31,' the computer should generate an error message asking for a revised entry.

Design the site's search engine (and other places where users enter data) to accommodate common misspellings and certain other errors.

Sources: Bailey and Koyani, 2004; Bailey, 1983; Pew and Rollins, 1975; Smith and Mosier, 1986.

Example:

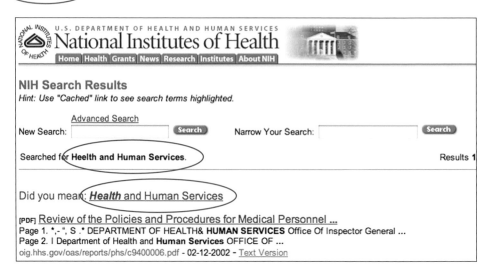

See page xxii
for detailed descriptions
of the rating scales
①②❸❹○

13:12 Partition Long Data Items

Relative Importance:
①②③○○

Strength of Evidence:
①②○○○

Guideline: Partition long data items into shorter sections for both data entry and data display.

Comments: Partitioning long data items can aid users in detecting entry errors, and can reduce erroneous entries. For example, it is easier to enter and verify a ten digit telephone number when entered as three groups, NNN-NNN-NNNN. Similarly, ZIP+4 codes and Social Security numbers are best partitioned.

Sources: Mayhew, 1992; Smith and Mosier, 1986.

Example: The 'Phone Number' entry field is partitioned correctly. However, the 'ZIP+4' field should be broken out into two fields (one five digits long, and one four digits long, separated by a hyphen).

...er copies of Labor Organization Reports (LM-1, LM-2, LM-3, LM-4, and Constitutions/Bylaws) via the Internet. Copies of reports are available to the ...er page; requests for 30 or fewer pages are provided free of charge. A bill listing any charges will be sent to you with the reports.

First Name:

Last Name:

Title:

Register of Reporting Labor Organizations ...eded for ordering reports: Affiliation's Short ...etc.), 6-digit File Number, Designation Name ...2-46583-GG, etc.), and Unit Name (Chicago

Your organization (if applicable):

Street Address:

City: State: Zip+4:

Phone Number:
( )- - ext

...labor organizations using this form. If you want to order additional reports, please submit a new form.

For example: Jane Smith

For example: 123456789

Please enter your PERSONAL IDENTIFICATION NUMBER (PIN)

In this example, the first and last names, along with the social security number, should be partitioned.

13:13 Use a Single Data Entry Method

Relative Importance:
❶❷❸〇〇

Strength of Evidence:
❶❷❸❹〇

Guideline: Design data entry transactions so that users can stay with one entry method as long as possible.

Comments: Do not have users shift back and forth between data entry methods. Requiring users to make numerous shifts from keyboard to mouse to keyboard can substantially slow their entry speed.

Sources: Czaja and Sharit, 1997; Engel and Granda, 1975; Foley and Wallace, 1974; Smith and Mosier, 1986.

Example: In this example, data entry methods are used consistently so that users do not have to shift back and forth between mouse entry and keyboard entry.

➕ **Quick Flight Search**   (Click here for advanced search and booking)

This service is currently available from [Australia ⬍] in [English ⬍] only.

Departure Airport [⬍]   Departure Date [⬍][⬍]

Arrival Airport [⬍]   Return Date [⬍][⬍]

Number of Passengers [1 ⬍]   **Check Availability**

This design forces users to switch between keyboard entry and mouse entry methods, and will slow the user's data entry task.

Title: [Ms ⬍]

First Name:(required) [_____]   Middle Initial: [_____]

Last Name:(required) [_____]   Maiden Name: [_____]

Degree: ⚪ BS – GC   ⚪ BS – InEd   GC Organization Member:
⚪ Master – GC   ⚪ Master – InEd   [None ⬍]

Year Graduated: (required)   **Month:** (required)

[2001 ⬍]   [May ⬍]

Home Address: [_____]   City: [_____]

State: [_____]   Zip Code: [_____]

Home Telephone Number: [_____]   **Email address:** (required) [_____]

For multi email addresses separate

Personal Website: (Optional) [_____]

See page xxii for detailed descriptions of the rating scales
❶❷❸❹〇

13:14 Prioritize Pushbuttons

Relative Importance:
①②③○○

Strength of Evidence:
①②③○○

Guideline: Use location and highlighting to prioritize pushbuttons.

Comments: If one pushbutton in a group of pushbuttons is used more frequently than the others, put that button in the first position. Also make the most frequently used button the default action, i.e., that which is activated when users press the Enter key.

One study reported that designers should place the button most likely to be clicked on the left side of a two-button set of buttons. This button arrangement allows the user to read the first button label, and since it is the most likely selection, click on that button immediately. Some users look at the left and then right button before making a selection, preferring to be fully informed before submitting a response.

Sources: Bailey, 1996; Fowler, 1998; Marcus, Smilonich and Thompson, 1995; Walker and Stanley, 2004.

Example: The 'Search' button is placed in the first position.

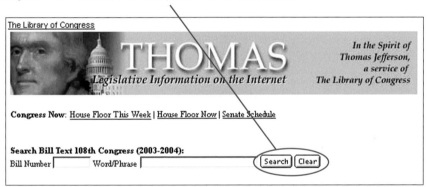

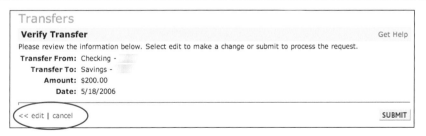

13:15 Use Check Boxes to Enable Multiple Selections

Guideline: Use a check box control to allow users to select one or more items from a list of possible choices.

Relative Importance:
①②❸○○

Strength of Evidence:
①②❸○○

Comments: Each check box should be able to be selected independently of all other check boxes. One study showed that for making multiple selections from a list of non-mutually exclusive items, check boxes elicit the fastest performance and are preferred over all other widgets. Users should be able to click on either the box or the text label.

Sources: Bailey, 1996; Fowler, 1998; Galitz, 2002; Johnsgard, et al., 1995; Marcus, Smilonich and Thompson, 1995.

Example: Check boxes are most appropriately used in these examples because users may wish to order more than one product or select more than one file format. Convention dictates that check boxes be used when more than one item in a list may be selected.

Media Type: ☑ DVD
☐ CD-ROM 1
☐ CD-ROM 2
☑ CD-ROM 3
☐ CD-ROM 4
☑ CD-ROM 5
☐ 8mm high density tar tape

Total cost of selections: $

We want to provide information in formats you ca[n]
us understand how you prefer to use information a[nd]

a. Short documents

How do you prefer to use short documents? *(Please check all that apply)*
☐ View/read online
☐ Download to view offline
☐ Download to print
☐ Download to edit or manipula[te]
What file format(s) do you prefer? *(Pl[ease]*
☐ Hypertext markup language (
☐ Plain ASCII text (.txt)
☐ Adobe Acrobat (.pdf)
☐ Compressed file (.zip)
☐ Other *(please specify)*

In my free time I'm interested in

☐ Arts
☐ Community Service
☐ Dancing
☐ Dining
☐ Family
☐ Movies
☐ Listening to Music
☐ Outdoor Activities
☐ Photography
☐ Reading
☐ Religion / Spirituality
☐ Watching Sports

☐ Theater
☐ Travel
☐ Cooking
☑ Computers / Internet
☐ Gaming
☐ Television
☐ Gardening
☐ Crafts
☐ Playing Music
☐ Playing Sports
☐ Health/Fitness

13:16 Label Units of Measurement

Relative Importance:
❶❷❸○○

Strength of Evidence:
❶❷❸○○

Screen-Based Controls (Widgets)

Guideline: When using data entry fields, specify the desired measurement units with the field labels rather than requiring users to enter them.

Comments: Designers should include units such as minutes, ounces, or centimeters, etc. as part of the data entry field label. This will reduce the number of keystrokes required of users (speeding the data entry process), and reduce the chance of errors.

Sources: Pew and Rollins, 1975; Smith and Mosier, 1986.

Example:

International Calculator

1. To which country are you mailing?

Select a Country

Tip: Typing the first letter of the country you want will jump the lis first country that starts with that letter.

2. How much does it weigh?

Pounds: 0   **Ounces:** 1

BODY MASS INDEX

Weight [ ] lbs.

Height [ ] feet [ ] inches

[Calculate] [Reset]

U.S. Values Calculator		
Female Required Data Entry		
Your Height In Feet 5 And Inches 5		
(Calculate) (Reset Values)		
Calculated Female Results		
Ideal Body Weight + or - 10% 125		Pounds
Ideal Body Weight + or - 10% 56.81818181818181		Kilograms
Calculated Height 1.6514227642276422	Meters	

See page xxii
for detailed descriptions
of the rating scales
❶❷❸❹○

13:17 Do Not Limit Viewable List Box Options

Guideline: When using open lists, show as many options as possible.

Relative Importance:
①②③○○

Comments: Scrolling to find an item in a list box can take extra time. In one study, an open list that showed only three (of five) options was used. To see the hidden two items, users had to scroll. The need

Strength of Evidence:
①②③○○

to scroll was not obvious to users who were not familiar with list boxes, and slowed down those that did know to scroll.

Sources: Bailey, Koyani and Nall, 2000; Zimmerman, et al., 2002.

Example:

This open list shows as many options as possible given the amount of available screen real estate.

Federal Register, Volume 60 (1995)
Federal Register, Volume 61 (1996)
Federal Register, Volume 62 (1997)
Federal Register, Volume 63 (1998)
Federal Register, Volume 64 (1999)
Federal Register, Volume 65 (2000)
Federal Register, Volume 66 (2001)
Federal Register, Volume 67 (2002)
Federal Register, Volume 68 (2003)
GAO Comptroller General Decisions
GAO Reports
GILS Records
Government Manual, 1995/1996
Government Manual, 1996/1997
Government Manual, 1997/1998

Despite plenty of screen real estate, only four of the six items in this list box are visible.

This site, even though the product is available in only four states, lists all 50, including the U.S. Virgin Islands. Only those four states provide counties, which are necessary before the "Submit" button can be chosen. This could be potentially confusing to users.

13:18 Display Default Values

Relative Importance:
❶❷❸○○

Strength of Evidence:
❶❷○○○

Guideline: Display default values whenever a likely default choice can be defined.

Comments: When likely default values can be defined, offer those values to speed data entry. The initial or default item could be the most frequently selected item or the last item selected by that user. In general, do not use the default position to display a heading or label for that widget.

Sources: Ahlstrom and Longo, 2001; Bailey, 1996; Fowler, 1998; Marcus, Smilonich and Thompson, 1995; Smith and Mosier, 1986.

Example:

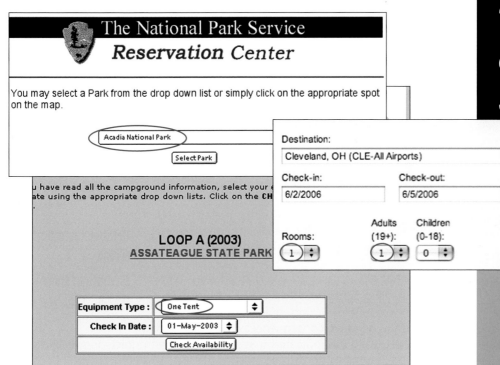

See page xxii
for detailed descriptions
of the rating scales
❶❷❸❹○

Screen-Based Controls (Widgets)

13:19 Place Cursor in First Data Entry Field

Guideline: Place (automatically) a blinking cursor at the beginning of the first data entry field when a data entry form is displayed on a page.

Relative Importance:
①②◯◯◯

Strength of Evidence:
①②◯◯◯

Comments: Users should not be required to move the mouse pointer to the first data entry field and click on the mouse button to activate the field. Designers should consider, however, that programming this automatic cursor placement might negatively impact the performance of screen reader software.

Sources: Ahlstrom and Longo, 2001; Smith and Mosier, 1986.

Example:

These two Web sites automatically place the cursor in the first data entry field.

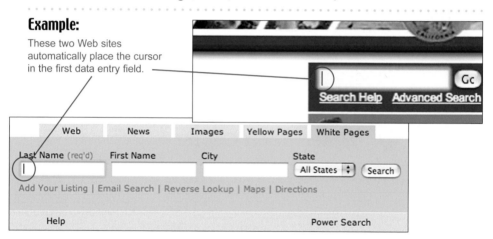

13:20 Ensure that Double–Clicking Will Not Cause Problems

Guideline: Ensure that double-clicking on a link will not cause undesirable or confusing results.

Relative Importance:
①②◯◯◯

Strength of Evidence:
①②◯◯◯

Comments: Many users double-click on a link when only one click is needed. Developers cannot stop users from double-clicking, but they should try to reduce the negative consequences of this behavior. Usability testing has indicated that if users start with quick double-clicks, they tend to continue to do this for most of the test. Sometimes, when both clicks are detected by the computer, the first click selects one link and the second click selects a second link, causing unexpected (i.e., puzzling) results.

Sources: Bailey, Koyani and Nall, 2000; Fakun and Greenough, 2002.

Screen–Based Controls (Widgets)

Guideline: Use open lists rather than drop-down lists to select one from many.

Relative Importance:

Comments: Generally, the more items users can see in a list (without scrolling), the faster their responses will be, and the fewer omission errors they will make. Ideally, users should be able to see all available items without scrolling.

Strength of Evidence:

When compared with drop-down lists, open lists tend to elicit faster performance primarily because drop-down lists require an extra click to open. However, if a list is extremely long, a drop-down list may be better. The available research does not indicate the upper number limit of items that should be displayed in a list.

Sources: Bailey, 1996; Fowler, 1998; Marcus, Smilonich and Thompson, 1995.

Example:

In this example, the designers opted to use a drop-down list to conserve screen real estate. This is a trade-off, however, as a drop-down list will slow users when compared with an open list.

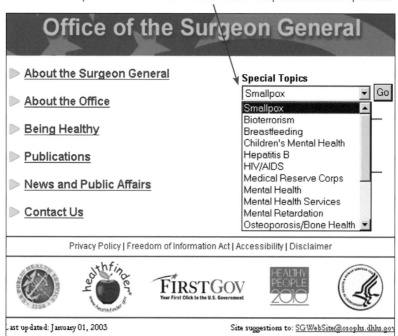

See page xxii
for detailed descriptions
of the rating scales

13:22 Use Data Entry Fields to Speed Performance

Guideline: Require users to enter information using data entry fields (instead of selecting from list boxes) if you are designing to speed human performance.

Relative Importance:
①②○○○

Strength of Evidence:
①②③④⑤

Comments: At least two studies have compared the effectiveness of text entry versus selection (list boxes) for entering dates and making airline reservations. Both studies found text entry methods were faster and preferred over all other methods. However, use of text entry fields tends to elicit more errors.

Sources: Bailey, 1996; Czaja and Sharit, 1997; Fowler, 1998; Gould, et al., 1988; Gould, et al., 1989; Greene, et al., 1988; Greene, et al., 1992; Marcus, Smilonich and Thompson, 1995; Tullis and Kodimer, 1992.

Example:

If users' entries cannot be easily defined or constrained (for example, their street address or a particular search term), use entry fields. However, if entries can be defined and errors reduced (state or country of residence) use list boxes. Be aware that alternating between these two entry methods will slow the user.

13:23 Use a Minimum of Two Radio Buttons

Guideline: Never use one radio button alone.

Relative Importance:
①②○○○

Strength of Evidence:
①②○○○

Comments: Use at least two radio buttons together. If users can choose not to activate any of the radio button choices, provide a choice labeled 'None.'

Sources: Bailey, 1996; Fowler, 1998; Marcus, Smilonich and Thompson, 1995.

Guideline: Provide auto-tabbing functionality for frequent users with advanced Web interaction skills.

Comments: Auto-tabbing can significantly reduce data entry times for frequent users by not requiring them to manually tab from field to field.

Relative Importance:

Strength of Evidence:

Sources: Ahlstrom and Longo, 2001; Pew and Rollins, 1975; Smith and Mosier, 1986.

13:25 Minimize Use of the Shift Key

Relative Importance:

Guideline: Design data entry transactions to minimize use of the Shift key.

Strength of Evidence:

Comments: If possible, designers should not require users to enter characters that require the use the Shift key. Using the Shift key imposes a demand for extra user attention and time. For example, the designer can include symbols such as the dollar or percent sign near data entry fields rather than requiring users to enter those characters. Designers also can treat upper- and lowercases as equivalent when entered by users.

Sources: Card, Moran and Newell, 1980b; John, 1996; Smith and Mosier, 1986.

Screen-Based Controls (Widgets)

14

Graphics, Images, and Multimedia

Graphics are used on many, if not most, Web

pages. When used appropriately, graphics can facilitate learning. An important image to show on most pages of a site is the organization's logo. When used appropriately, images, animation, video, and audio can add tremendous value to a Web site. When animation is used appropriately, it is a good idea to introduce the animation before it begins.

Many images require a large number of bytes that can take a long time to download, especially at slower connection speeds. When images must be used, designers should ensure that the graphics do not substantially slow page download times. Thumbnail versions of larger images allow users to preview images without having to download them.

Sometimes it is necessary to label images to help users understand them. Usability testing should be used to help ensure that Web site images convey the intended message. In many cases, the actual data should be included with charts and graphs to facilitate fast and accurate understanding.

It is usually not a good idea to use images as the entire background of a page. Complex background images tend to slow down page loading, and can interfere with reading the foreground text.

Experienced users tend to ignore graphics that they consider to be advertising. Designers should ensure that they do not create images that look like banner ads. Also, they should be careful about placing images in locations that are generally used for advertisements.

Relative Importance:
①②③④○

Strength of Evidence:
①②③④⑤

Guideline: Use background images sparingly and make sure they are simple, especially if they are used behind text.

Comments: Background images can make it difficult for users to read foreground text. A single, large, complex background image (including a picture) can substantially slow page download rates. If background images must be employed, use small, simple images with 'tiling,' and/or keep the image resolution as low as possible.

Sources: Boyntoin and Bush, 1956; Cole and Jenkins, 1984; Detweiler and Omanson, 1996; Hackman and Tinker, 1957; Jenkins and Cole, 1982; Levine, 1996; Levy, et al., 1996; Spencer, Reynolds and Coe, 1977a; Spencer, Reynolds and Coe, 1977b; Tinker and Paterson, 1931; Tinker, 1963.

Example: Complex graphics can obscure text, making it very difficult for users to read the site's content.

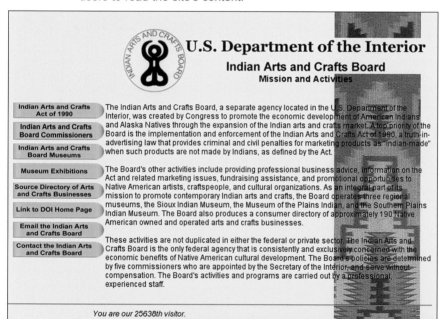

Graphics, Images, and Multimedia

14:2 Label Clickable Images

Guideline: Ensure that all clickable images are either labeled or readily understood by typical users.

Comments: Occasional or infrequent users may not use an image enough to understand or remember its meaning. Ensure that images and their associated text are close together so that users can integrate and effectively use them together. Additionally, alt text should accompany every clickable image.

Sources: Booher, 1975; Evans, 1998; Hackman and Tinker, 1957; Spool, et al., 1997; Tinker and Paterson, 1931; Vaughan, 1998; Williams, 2000.

Example:

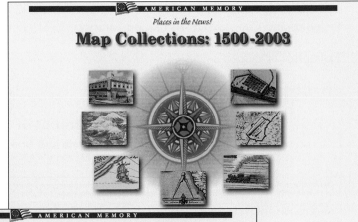

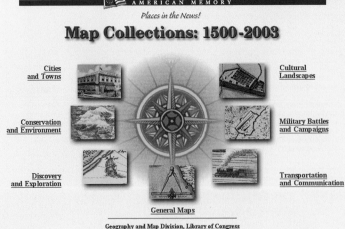

The addition of labels is essential for a user to understand the clickable image links.

See page xxii for detailed descriptions of the rating scales
①②③④○

Graphics, Images, and Multimedia

Guideline: Take steps to ensure that images on the Web site do not slow page download times unnecessarily.

Relative Importance: ①②③④○

Strength of Evidence: ①②③④○

Comments: User frustration increases as the length of time spent interacting with a system increases. Users tolerate less delay if they believe the task should be easy for the computer. One study reported that users rated latencies of up to five seconds as 'good.' Delays over ten seconds were rated as 'poor.' Users rate pages with long delays as being less interesting and more difficult to scan. One study reported no relationship between slow page download times and users giving up.

To speed download times, use several small images rather than a single large image on a page; use interlacing or progressive images; and use several of the same images. Designers should also minimize the number of different colors used in an image and put HEIGHT and WIDTH pixel dimension tags in an image reference. To achieve faster response time for users with dial-up modems, limit page size to less than 30,000 bytes.

Sources: Bouch, Kuchinsky and Bhatti, 2000; Farkas and Farkas, 2000; Marchionini, 1995; Martin and Corl, 1986; Nielsen, 1996a; Nielsen, 1997a; Nielsen, 1999c; Nielsen, 2000; Perfetti, 2001; Ramsay, Barbesi and Preece, 1998; Schroeder, 2003; Sears, Jacko and Borella, 1997; Selvidge, Chaparro and Bender, 2001; Shneiderman, 1984; Tullis, 2001.

Example:

The entire main content area - the background, text and photo is one large image. The page would load much quicker if normal html had been used here.

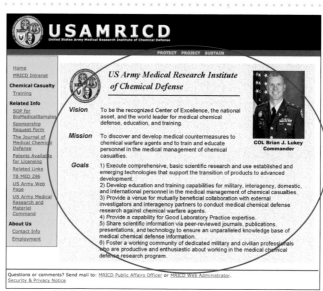

Graphics, Images, and Multimedia

14:4 Use Video, Animation, and Audio Meaningfully

Guideline: Use video, animation, and audio only when they help to convey, or are supportive of, the Web site's message or other content.

Relative Importance:
①②③④○

Strength of Evidence:
①②③④⑤

Comments: Multimedia elements (such as video, animation, and audio) can easily capture the attention of users; therefore, it is important to have clear and useful reasons for using multimedia to avoid unnecessarily distracting users. Some multimedia elements may take a long time to download, so it is important that they be worth the wait.

Used productively, multimedia can add great value to a site's content and help direct users' attention to the most important information and in the order that it is most useful.

Sources: Campbell and Maglio, 1999; Chen and Yu, 2000; Faraday and Sutcliffe, 1997; Faraday, 2000; Faraday, 2001; Harrison, 1995; Nielsen, 2000; Park and Hannafin, 1993; Reeves and Rickenberg, 2000; Spinillo and Dyson, 2000/2001; Sundar, Edgar and Mayer, 2000.

14:5 Include Logos

Guideline: Place your organization's logo in a consistent place on every page.

Relative Importance:
①②③④○

Strength of Evidence:
①②③④○

Comments: Users are frequently unaware when they click through to a different Web site. Having a logo on each page provides a frame of reference throughout a Web site so that users can easily confirm that they have not left the site. Ideally, the logo should be in the same location on each page: many designers place the logo in the top left corner.

Sources: Adkisson, 2002; Farkas and Farkas, 2000; Marchionini, 1995; Nall, Koyani and Lafond, 2001; Nielsen, 1999d; Omanson, Cline and Nordhielm, 2001; Omanson, et al., 1998; Osborn and Elliott, 2002; Spool, et al., 1997.

Example:

Guideline: Do not make important images look like banner advertisements or gratuitous decorations.

Relative Importance:
①②③④○

Strength of Evidence:
①②③④○

Comments: In a recent study, a graphic developed to inform users about access to live help was not clicked because many users thought it was an advertisement. Even though the graphic was larger than most other graphics on the page, some users missed the item completely because the graphic looked too much like a decoration or a banner advertisement.

Sources: Ahmadi, 2000; Badre, 2002; Bayles, 2002; Benway, 1998; Ellis and Kurniawan, 2000.

Example: This graphic, which contains three major, linked headers, looks like a banner advertisement. Consequently, users may skip over this design element, thus missing the headers.

NEWS!

PCPFS Mourns Longtime Physical Activity Advocate

COUNCIL CHAIRMAN TESTIFIES "It's Never Too Late to Move for Health"

REMARKS OF CHAIRMAN LYNN SWANN AT THE NATIONAL PRESS CLUB

COUNCIL ANNOUNCES NEW FITNESS AWARD TO
ENCOURAGE PHYSICAL ACTIVITY

COUNCIL MEMBERS SHARE FITNESS TIPS

**FAST FACTS ABOUT
THE PRESIDENT'S COUNCIL**

Click on the links below for more information:

- New Executive Order for the President's Council.
- Biographies of the Council members.
- President's Council Fact Sheet.
- Physical Activity Fact Sheet.
- History of the President's Council.
- Report "Physical Activity Fundamental to Preventing Disease" available online.
- Obesity Still On The Rise, New Data Show

See page xxii
for detailed descriptions
of the rating scales
①②③④○

Research-Based Web Design & Usability Guidelines

14:7 Limit Large Images Above the Fold

Relative Importance:
❶❷❸❹○

Strength of Evidence:
❶❷❸○○

Guideline: Do not fill the entire first screenful with one image if there are screensful of text information below the fold.

Comments: Large graphics that cover most of the screen at the top of the page suggest to users that there is no more information below the graphic. In one study, because a graphic filled the screen, some users did not use the scrollbar to scroll down to more content. In fact, some users did not even suspect that more information might be located below the fold.

Sources: Bailey, Koyani and Nall, 2000; Chen and Yu, 2000; Golovchinsky and Chignell, 1993; Nielsen and Tahir, 2002.

Example: As the scroll bar shows, there are several additional screenfuls of information below this large navigation graphic. Users may not look at the scroll bar, thus missing that information.

Graphics, Images, and Multimedia

Guideline: Ensure that Web site images convey the intended message to users, not just to designers.

Relative Importance:
①②③④○

Strength of Evidence:
①②③○○

Comments: Users and designers tend to differ in what they think is appropriate to convey a message. When attempting to select the best graphic from a set of graphics, users tend to select those that most other users would have selected (i.e., those that look familiar), while most developers favor graphics that look more artistic. One study found that seventy-five percent of users are able to find information on a content and link-rich site, whereas only seventeen percent could find the same information on a graphic-intensive site.

Sources: Ahmadi, 2000; Evans, 1998; Nielsen and Tahir, 2002; Spool, et al., 1997.

Example:

The new IRS site (left) is content and link-rich, allowing users to find information much faster than the old, graphic-heavy IRS site (right).

See page xxii for detailed descriptions of the rating scales
①②③④○

14:9 Limit the Use of Images

Relative Importance:
①②❸○○

Strength of Evidence:
①❷○○○

Guideline: Use images only when they are critical to the success of a Web site.

Comments: Ensure that a Web site's graphics add value and increase the clarity of the information on the site. Certain graphics can make some Web sites much more interesting for users, and users may be willing to wait a few extra seconds for them to load. Users tend to be most frustrated if they wait several seconds for a graphic to download, and then find that the image does not add any value. Some decorative graphics are acceptable when they do not distract the user.

Sources: Badre, 2002; Evans, 1998; Nielsen, 1997e; Nielsen, 1999b; Nielsen, 2000; Nielsen, 2003; Spool, et al., 1997; Wen and Beaton, 1996; Williams, 2000.

Example: The placement of this image disrupts the left justification of the other page elements and it is visually distracting, drawing the user's attention from the site's content.

This image is unrelated to the accompanying content.

See page xxii for detailed descriptions of the rating scales ①②❸❹○

Graphics, Images, and Multimedia

Guideline: Include actual data values with graphical displays of data when precise reading of the data is required.

Relative Importance:
①②③○○

Strength of Evidence:
①②③④○

Comments: Adjacent numeric annotation might be added to the ends of displayed bars on a bar graph, or to mark the points of a plotted curve. Some displays may require complete data annotation while others may require annotation only for selected data elements.

Sources: Pagulayan and Stoffregen, 2000; Powers, et al., 1961; Smith and Mosier, 1986; Spool, et al., 1997; Tufte, 1983.

Example:

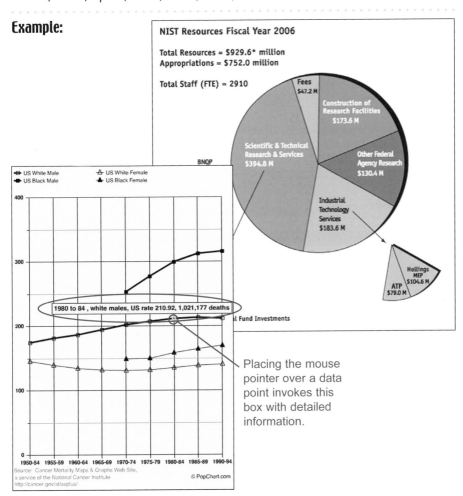

NIST Resources Fiscal Year 2006

Total Resources = $929.6* million
Appropriations = $752.0 million

Total Staff (FTE) = 2910

Fees
$47.2 M

Construction of
Research Facilities
$173.6 M

Scientific & Technical
Research & Services
$394.8 M

Other Federal
Agency Research
$130.4 M

Industrial
Technology
Services
$183.6 M

Hollings
MEP
$104.6 M

ATP
$79.0 M

BNQP

US White Male   US White Female
US Black Male   US Black Female

400

300

1980 to 84 , white males, US rate 210.92, 1,021,177 deaths

200

100

0
1950-54 1955-59 1960-64 1965-69 1970-74 1975-79 1980-84 1985-89 1990-94

Source: Cancer Mortality Maps & Graphs Web Site,
a service of the National Cancer Institute
http://cancer.gov/atlasplus/   © PopChart.com

Placing the mouse pointer over a data point invokes this box with detailed information.

Graphics, Images, and Multimedia

14:11 Display Monitoring Information Graphically

Graphics, Images, and Multimedia

Guideline: Use a graphic format to display data when users must monitor changing data.

Relative Importance:
① ② ③ ○ ○

Comments: Whenever possible, the computer should handle data monitoring and should call abnormalities to the users' attention. When that is not possible, and a user must monitor data changes, graphic displays will make it easier for users to detect critical changes and/or values outside the normal range.

Strength of Evidence:
① ② ③ ④ ○

Sources: Hanson, et al., 1981; Kosslyn, 1994; Powers, et al., 1961; Smith and Mosier, 1986; Tullis, 1981.

Example:

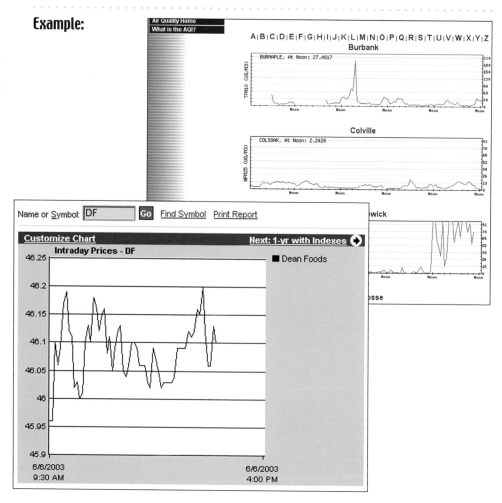

See page xxii for detailed descriptions of the rating scales
① ② ③ ④ ○

14:12 Introduce Animation

Relative Importance:
❶❷○○○

Strength of Evidence:
❶❷❸○○

Guideline: Provide an introductory explanation for animation prior to it being viewed.

Comments: Providing an explanation of animation before it begins will help users better integrate the animation and associated content. In other words, briefly explain to users what they are about to see before they see it. Also, allow animation to be user-controlled. The user should be able to pause, stop, replay, or ignore animation or other multimedia elements.

Sources: Evans, 1998; Faraday and Sutcliffe, 1999.

Example:

Each video clip is accompanied by text that explains to the user what they are about to view. In addition, this Web site allows the user to control when to start the video clip.

A Life Unfolds Inside the Womb

During the first 26 weeks of pregnancy, when the mother may only be beginning to appear to others to be pregnant, the sperm and egg cells have developed into a recognizable human fetus that can hear the sound of its mother's voice. Watch the videos below to follow the astonishing process of development.

When Two Cells Become One
What happens at the moment of conception? Embryologist Ian Gallicano, M.D., describes the delicate cellular choreography that creates a new life. **Watch the video animation.**

At Four Weeks
At four weeks from gestation, the human embryo could easily be mistaken for that of another animal, but its bond with its mother is already complex, and becoming more so with each passing day. **Watch the video animation.**

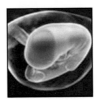

At Five Weeks
Barely more than a month old, the embryo's heart is beating and, as in a perfectly timed orchestral composition, the other organs develop in turn. **Watch the video animation.**

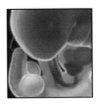

14:13 Emulate Real-World Objects

Relative Importance:
①②○○○

Strength of Evidence:
①②③④○

Graphics, Images, and Multimedia

Guideline: Use images that look like real-world items when appropriate.

Comments: Images (e.g., pushbuttons and navigation tabs) are likely to be considered as links when they are designed to emulate their real-world analogues. If a designer cannot make such images emulate real-world objects, the image may require at least one additional clickability cue, such as a descriptive label (like 'Home' or 'Next') or placement on the page. A text label can help inform users about a link's destination, but in one study some users missed this type of image link, even those that contained words, because the words were not underlined.

Sources: Ahmadi, 2000; Bailey, 2000b; Galitz, 2002; Nolan, 1989.

Example:

These control items are designed to look like real-world items. The buttons below, for example, look like the buttons you might find on an Automated Teller Machine. The control item image to the right controls video on a Web site, and thus is designed to look like a control on a VCR or DVD player.

Guideline: When viewing full-size images is not critical, first provide a thumbnail of the image.

Relative Importance:
①②◯◯◯

Strength of Evidence:
①②◯◯◯

Comments: By providing thumbnails of larger images, users can decide whether they want to wait for the full image to load. By using thumbnails, those who do not need or want to see the full image are not slowed down by large image downloads. Link the thumbnail image to the full-size copy.

Sources: Levine, 1996; Nielsen and Tahir, 2002.

Example: When one of the thumbnail images is clicked on the left, a new window pops up with a larger image and a brief description. This also offers a high resolution jpg file of the same image.

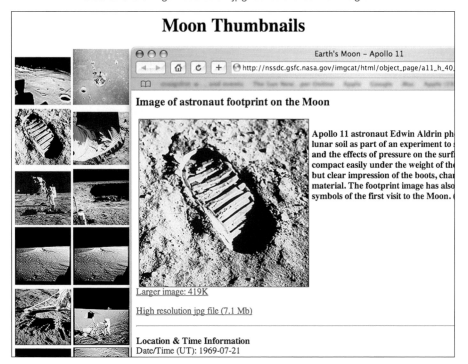

See page xxii for detailed descriptions of the rating scales
①②③④◯

14:15 Use Images to Facilitate Learning

Relative Importance:

Strength of Evidence:

Guideline: To facilitate learning, use images rather than text whenever possible.

Comments: The superiority of pictures over text in a learning situation appears to be strong. For example, pictures of common objects are recognized and recalled better than their textual names. Exceptions seem to occur when the items are conceptually very similar (e.g., all animals or tools), or when items are presented so quickly that learners cannot create verbal labels.

Sources: Golovchinsky and Chignell, 1993; Krull and Watson, 2002; Levy, et al., 1996; Lieberman and Culpepper, 1965; Nelson, Reed and Walling, 1976; Paivio and Csapo, 1969; Paivio, Rogers and Smythe, 1968; Rodden, et al., 2001; Williams, 1993.

Example:

These illustrations facilitate faster learning of key concepts.

If There Is Fire

« previous | next »   Download PDF

1. Exit the building as quickly as possible.
2. Crawl low in smoke.
3. Use a wet cloth to cover your nose and mouth.

If You Are Trapped

« previous | next »

1. If possible, use a flashlight to signal
2. Avoid unnecessary movement so that
3. Cover your mouth and nose with anything you have in hand. Dense weave cotton material can create a good filter. Try to breathe through the material.

If There Is An Explosion

« previous | next » Download PDF

1. Take shelter against your desk or a sturdy table.
2. Exit the building as quickly as possible.
3. Do not use elevators.

See page xxii for detailed descriptions of the rating scales

14:16 Using Photographs of People

Relative Importance:
❶○○○○

Strength of Evidence:
❶❷○○○

Guideline: Photographs of people may or may not help build trust in Web sites.

Comments: In one e-commerce study, having a labeled photograph on the Web site was perceived as more trustworthy than having a photograph with no label. Further, having a photograph with no label was perceived as more trustworthy than having no photograph at all. Highly experienced users showed the same degree of trust as users that were moderately experienced or inexperienced.

However, another study recommended that photos not be used to increase the trustworthiness of a Web site. They found that the presence of a photo did not affect the trust of a site, or user preferences for a site.

Sources: Riegelsberger, Sasse and McCarthy, 2003; Steinbrück, et al., 2002.

Example:

Photographs of people are used widely and very differently throughout the Federal government.

Graphics, Images, and Multimedia

15

Writing Web Content

"Vigorous writing is concise. A sentence should contain no unnecessary words, a paragraph no unnecessary sentences, for the same reason that a drawing should have no unnecessary lines and a machine no unnecessary parts."– William Strunk Jr., in Elements of Style

Content is the most important part of a Web site.

If the content does not provide the information needed by users, the Web site will provide little value no matter how easy it is to use the site.

When preparing prose content for a Web site, use familiar words and avoid the use of jargon. If acronyms and abbreviations must be used, ensure that they are clearly understood by typical users and defined on the page.

Minimize the number of words in a sentence and sentences in a paragraph. Make the first sentence (the topic sentence) of each paragraph descriptive of the remainder of the paragraph. Clearly state the temporal sequence of instructions. Also, use upper- and lowercase letters appropriately, write in an affirmative, active voice, and limit prose text on navigation pages.

15:1 Make Action Sequences Clear

Relative Importance:
①②③④⑤

Strength of Evidence:
①②③④○

Guideline: When describing an action or task that has a natural order or sequence (assembly instructions, troubleshooting, etc.), structure the content so that the sequence is obvious and consistent.

Comments: Time-based sequences are easily understood by users. Do not force users to perform or learn tasks in a sequence that is unusual or awkward.

Sources: Czaja and Sharit, 1997; Farkas, 1999; Krull and Watson, 2002; Morkes and Nielsen, 1998; Nielsen, 2000; Smith and Mosier, 1986; Wright, 1977.

Example:

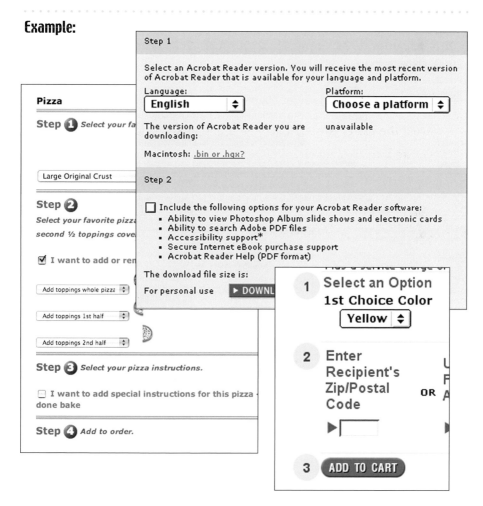

15:2 Avoid Jargon

Writing Web Content

Relative Importance:
①②③④○

Strength of Evidence:
①②③④○

Guideline: Do not use words that typical users may not understand.

Comments: Terminology plays a large role in the user's ability to find and understand information. Many terms are familiar to designers and content writers, but not to users. In one study, some users did not understand the term 'cancer screening.' Changing the text to 'testing for cancer' substantially improved users' understanding.

To improve understanding among users who are accustomed to using the jargon term, it may be helpful to put that term in parentheses. A dictionary or glossary may be helpful to users who are new to a topic, but should not be considered a license to frequently use terms typical users do not understand.

Sources: Cockburn and Jones, 1996; Evans, 1998; Horton, 1990; Mayhew, 1992; Morkes and Nielsen, 1997; Morkes and Nielsen, 1998; Nall, Koyani and Lafond, 2001; Schramm, 1973; Spyridakis, 2000; Tullis, 2001; Zimmerman and Prickett, 2000; Zimmerman, et al., 2002.

Example: These Web pages, often visited by the public, do not use language that is accessible and free of jargon.

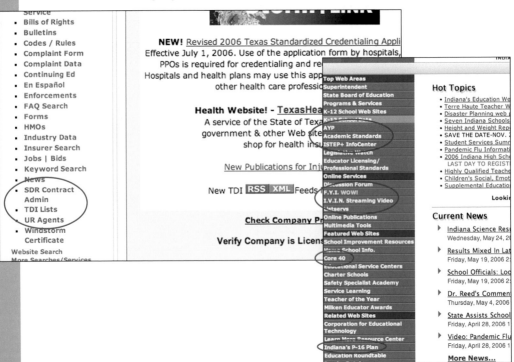

See page xxii for detailed descriptions of the rating scales
①②③④○

15:3 Use Familiar Words

Writing Web Content

Relative Importance:
①②③④○

Strength of Evidence:
①②③○○

Guideline: Use words that are frequently seen and heard.

Comments: Use words that are familiar to, and used frequently by, typical users. Words that are more frequently seen and heard are better and more quickly recognized. There are several sources of commonly used words (see Kucera and Francis, 1967 and Leech et al., 2001 in the Sources section).

Familiar words can be collected using open-ended surveys, by viewing search terms entered by users on your site or related sites, and through other forms of market research.

Sources: Furnas, et al., 1987; Kucera and Francis, 1967; Leech, Rayson and Wilson, 2001; Spyridakis, 2000; Whissell, 1998.

Example:

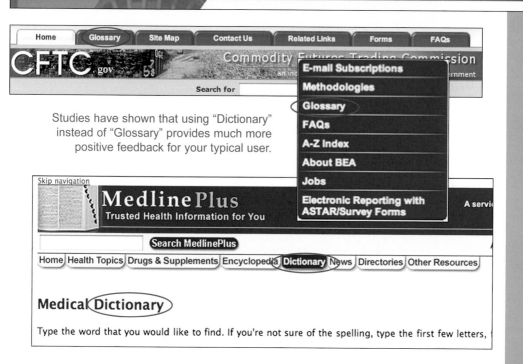

Studies have shown that using "Dictionary" instead of "Glossary" provides much more positive feedback for your typical user.

15:4 Define Acronyms and Abbreviations

Guideline: Do not use unfamiliar or undefined acronyms or abbreviations on Web sites.

Relative Importance:
①②③④○

Comments: Acronyms and abbreviations should be used sparingly and must be defined in order to be understood by all users. It is important to remember that users who are new to a topic are likely to be unfamiliar with the topic's related acronyms and abbreviations. Use the following format when defining acronyms or abbreviations: Physician Data Query (PDQ). Acronyms and abbreviations are typically defined on first mention, but remember that users may easily miss the definition if they scroll past it or enter the page below where the acronym or abbreviation is defined.

Strength of Evidence:
①②○○○

Sources: Ahlstrom and Longo, 2001; Evans, 1998; Morrell, et al., 2002; Nall, Koyani and Lafond, 2001; Nielsen and Tahir, 2002; Tullis, 2001.

Example: Undefined acronyms on a homepage may leave users confused regarding the site's contents or purpose.

This detailed, highly-technical content page is designed for experts and not novice users. However, the designer has still defined each acronym and abbreviation on the page.

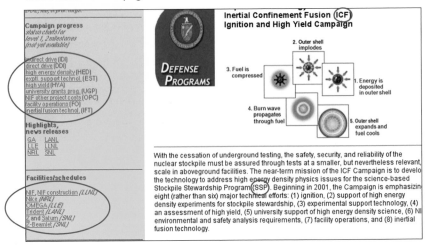

15:5 Use Abbreviations Sparingly

Relative Importance:
①②③④○

Strength of Evidence:
①②○○○

Guideline: Show complete words rather than abbreviations whenever possible.

Comments: The only times to use abbreviations are when they are significantly shorter, save needed space, and will be readily understood by typical users. If users must read abbreviations, choose only common abbreviations.

Sources: Ahlstrom and Longo, 2001; Engel and Granda, 1975; Evans, 1998; Smith and Mosier, 1986.

Example:

If abbreviations are in common usage (DoD) then it is acceptable to use them. However, if an abbreviation is not in common usage (DARS, DFARS, AKSS), the complete title should be used.

Site Menu
About DPAP
DPAP Directorates
(DARS)
PAIC
Policy
PDI
Resources
(DFARS)
PGI
DoD 5000 Series
Policy Vault
Business Transformatio
Common Supplier Engn
DPAP Archives

Items of Interest
(DFARS) Transformation
Interagency Acquisition
Purchase Card
Unique Identification
Outreach and Comm
AcqDemo
International Contracting
Doing Business w/ DoD
Ethics
Education
AcqDemo Training
Defense Acq. University
Systems
(AKSS)
ACC
Defense Acq. Guidebook

See page xxii for detailed descriptions of the rating scales
①②③④○

15:6 Use Mixed Case with Prose

Writing Web Content

Relative Importance:
①②③④○

Strength of Evidence:
①②③④⑤

Guideline: Display continuous (prose) text using mixed upper- and lowercase letters.

Comments: Reading text is easier when capitalization is used conventionally to start sentences and to indicate proper nouns and acronyms. If an item is intended to attract the user's attention, display the item in all uppercase, bold, or italics. Do not use these methods for showing emphasis for more than one or two words or a short phrase because they slow reading performance when used for extended prose.

Sources: Breland and Breland, 1944; Engel and Granda, 1975; Mills and Weldon, 1987; Moskel, Erno and Shneiderman, 1984; Poulton and Brown, 1968; Smith and Mosier, 1986; Spyridakis, 2000; Tinker and Paterson, 1928; Tinker, 1955; Tinker, 1963; Vartabedian, 1971; Wright, 1977.

Example:

Reading text is easier when capitalization is used conventionally to start sentences and to indicate proper nouns and acronyms. If an item is intended to attract the user's attention, display the item in all UPPERCASE, **bold**, or *italics*. Do not use these methods for showing emphasis for more than one or two words or a short phrase because they slow reading performance when used for extended prose.

READING TEXT IS EASIER WHEN CAPITALIZATION IS USED CONVENTIONALLY TO START SENTENCES AND TO INDICATE PROPER NOUNS AND ACRONYMS. IF AN ITEM IS INTENDED TO ATTRACT THE USER'S ATTENTION, DISPLAY THE ITEM IN ALL UPPERCASE, **BOLD**, OR *ITALICS*. DO NOT USE THESE METHODS FOR SHOWING EMPHASIS FOR MORE THAN ONE OR TWO WORDS OR A SHORT PHRASE BECAUSE THEY SLOW READING PERFORMANCE WHEN USED FOR EXTENDED PROSE.

See page xxii for detailed descriptions of the rating scales
①②③④○

Guideline: To optimize reading comprehension, minimize the number of words in sentences, and the number of sentences in paragraphs.

Relative Importance:
① ② ③ ④ ○

Strength of Evidence:
① ② ③ ④ ○

Comments: To enhance the readability of prose text, a sentence should not contain more than twenty words. A paragraph should not contain more than six sentences.

Sources: Bailey, 1996; Bailey, Koyani and Nall, 2000; Bouma, 1980; Chervak, Drury and Ouellette, 1996; Evans, 1998; Kincaid, et al., 1990; Marcus, 1992; Mills and Caldwell, 1997; Nielsen, 1997c; Palmquist and Zimmerman, 1999; Rehe, 1979; Spyridakis, 2000; Zimmerman and Clark, 1987.

Example: This example shows how to optimize reading comprehension. The number of words in a sentence is minimized, and there are few sentences in each paragraph.

What's Happening Now?

A pandemic is a global disease outbreak. A flu pandemic occurs when a new influenza virus emerges for which people have little or no immunity, and for which there is no vaccine. The disease spreads easily person-to-person, causes serious illness, and can sweep across the country and around the world in very short time.

It is difficult to predict when the next influenza pandemic will occur or how severe it will be. Wherever and whenever a pandemic starts, everyone around the world is at risk. Countries might, through measures such as border closures and travel restrictions, delay arrival of the virus, but cannot stop it.

Health professionals are concerned that the continued spread of a highly pathogenic avian H5N1 virus across eastern Asia and other countries represents a significant threat to human health. The H5N1 virus has raised concerns about a potential human pandemic because:

- It is especially virulent
- It is being spread by migratory birds
- It can be transmitted from birds to mammals and in some limited circumstances to humans, and
- Like other influenza viruses, it continues to evolve.

Since 2003, a growing number of human H5N1 cases have been reported in Azerbaijan, Cambodia, China, Djibouti, Egypt, Indonesia, Iraq, Thailand, Turkey, and Vietnam. More than half of the people infected with the H5N1 virus have died. Most of these cases are all believed to have been caused by exposure to infected poultry. There has been no sustained human-to-human transmission of the disease, but the concern is that H5N1 will evolve into a virus capable of human-to-human transmission.

▲ top of page

Avian Influenza Viruses

Avian (bird) flu is caused by influenza A viruses that occur naturally among birds. There are different subtypes of these viruses because of changes in certain proteins (hemagglutinin [HA] and neuraminidase [NA]) on the surface of the influenza A virus and the way the proteins combine.

Each combination represents a different subtype. All known subtypes of influenza A viruses can be found in birds. The avian flu currently of concern is the H5N1 subtype.

▲ top of page

Guideline: Do not put a lot of prose text on navigation pages.

Relative Importance:

①②❸○○

Comments: When there are many words on navigation pages, users tend to rapidly scan for specific words or begin clicking on many different links, rather than reading the text associated with the links.

Strength of Evidence:

①②❸○○

Sources: Bailey, Koyani and Nall, 2000; Evans, 1998; Morkes and Nielsen, 1998; Nielsen, 2000; Spyridakis, 2000.

Example: The lack of prose text allows navigation elements to take center stage on this navigation page.

Citizen Gateway February 6, 2003

Online Transactions and e-Services for Citizens
Conduct your business with government from the convenience of your home or office.

Auctions and Sales | Benefits | Citizenship | Consumer |
Forms and Applications | Health | Homes and Communities | Jobs | Postal Service |
Publications and Subscriptions | Taxes and Money | Travel and Recreation

Government Auctions and Sales
Shop Online
Auctions
Cars and Other Vehicles for Sale
Loans and Investments for Sale
Real Estate for Sale
Souvenirs, Books and Gifts for Sale
Supplies and Equipment for Sale
For Government and Non-Profit Buyers
Find Sales by Agency

Benefits
Determine Eligibility for Federal Programs
Social Security Online
Veterans Pension and Benefit Applications

Citizenship and Government
Participate Online in Federal Rulemaking
Register for the Military Draft

Jobs
America's Job Bank: an online service for employers and jobseekers
Foreign Service Exam
Government Jobs
Presidential Appointments Application
Resume Builder
Security Clearance and Background Investigation Application (Federal Employment)

Postal Service
Certified Mail and Personal Services
Hold Mail Authorization Form (.pdf form | requires Adobe Acrobat Reader)
Hold Mail
Schedule Redelivery of Mail
Stamps Online
Zip Code Look-Up

Skip Navigation
United States Department of Agriculture

USDA **National Food and Agriculture Council**

NFAC Links:
Home
FAC Leadership
About
News & Info
News
Directives
Minutes
Community Development
Strategic Plan
Contacts
Related Links:
Service Center Modernization
CCE
AIST
Data
Telecom.
ITWG
State Office Locator
Privacy
Agencies

NFAC Main Menu

Welcome to the Food and Agriculture Council Homepage.

The Food and Agriculture Council (FAC) at the national, state, and local levels are the vehicles used to coordinate the U.S. Department of Agriculture's programs, initiatives, and activities requiring cooperative involvement across mission area and agency lines. FACs were instituted by the Secretary of Agriculture in order to provide a policy level, cross agency, decision making and communication medium as needed to achieve the USDAs goals and objectives.

The National FAC (NFAC) is the management entity designated by the Secretary of Agriculture to carry out USDA's field restructuring and modernization effort. The NFAC is comprised of the Administrators of all USDA agencies that are active at the State level. The Chair of the NFAC rotates annually between the Administrators of the Farm Service Agency, the Chief of the Natural Resources Conservation Service, and the Deputy Under Secretary for Operations and Management of the Rural Development agencies.

The NFAC is supported by an Executive Officer who also heads USDAs Service Center Implementation Team (SCIT). The SCIT is an interagency staff that supports the activities of the NFAC, and initiates activities and projects on behalf of the partner agencies to ensure the successful implementation of the USDAs Service Center Initiative.

The large volume of prose text forces navigation links (the primary purpose of the page) into the left panel.

See page xxii for detailed descriptions of the rating scales
①②❸❹○

15:9 Use Active Voice

Relative Importance:
①②③〇〇

Strength of Evidence:
①②③④〇

Guideline: Compose sentences in active rather than passive voice.

Comments: Users benefit from simple, direct language. Sentences in active voice are typically more concise than sentences in passive voice. Strong verbs help the user know who is acting and what is being acted upon. In one study, people who had to interpret federal regulation language spontaneously translated passive sentences into active sentences in order to form an understanding of the passages.

Sources: Flower, Hayes and Swarts, 1983; Horton, 1990; Palermo and Bourne, 1978; Palmquist and Zimmerman, 1999; Redish, Felker and Rose, 1981; Smith and Mosier, 1986; Spinillo and Dyson, 2000/2001; Spyridakis, 2000; Wright, 1977; Zimmerman and Clark, 1987.

Example: Active voice example   Passive voice example

John hit the baseball.   The baseball was hit by John.

15:10 Write Instructions in the Affirmative

Guideline: As a general rule, write instructions in affirmative statements rather than negative statements.

Relative Importance:
①②③〇〇

Strength of Evidence:
①②〇〇〇

Comments: When giving instructions, strive to tell users what to do (see a dentist if you have a toothache), rather than what to avoid doing (avoid skipping your dentist appointment if you have a toothache). If the likelihood of making a wrong step is high or the consequences are dire, negative voice may be clearer to the user.

Sources: Greene, 1972; Herriot, 1970; Krull and Watson, 2002; Palmquist and Zimmerman, 1999; Smith and Mosier, 1986; Wright, 1977; Zimmerman and Clark, 1987.

Example: An example of negative voice pointing out consequences to the user.

Message successfully posted by: **156.40.129.142** (Logged!).

IMPORTANT: Do **NOT** press BACK - If you come back to this page, your message will be posted a second time!

15:11 Make First Sentences Descriptive

Guideline: Include the primary theme of a paragraph, and the scope of what it covers, in the first sentence of each paragraph.

Relative Importance:
①②③○○

Strength of Evidence:
①②③④○

Comments: Users tend to skim the first one or two sentences of each paragraph when scanning text.

Sources: Bailey, Koyani and Nall, 2000; Lynch and Horton, 2002; Morkes and Nielsen, 1997; Morkes and Nielsen, 1998; Spyridakis, 2000.

Example: Descriptive first sentences set the tone for each of these paragraphs, and provide users with an understanding of the topic of each section of text.

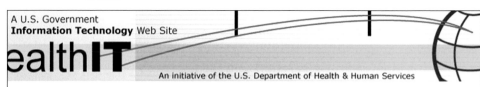

A U.S. Government
Information Technology Web Site

ealth**IT**

An initiative of the U.S. Department of Health & Human Services

Home

nformation

fforts

r Awareness

eas

Consumer Awareness

Documents in PDF format require the Adobe Acrobat Reader®. If you experience problems with PDF documents, please download the latest version of the Reader®.

Ending the Document Game, Full Report from The Commission on Systemic Interoperability

Addressing Healthcare Connectivity as a Matter of Life and Death

Executive Summary
Americans need a connected system of electronic healthcare information available to all doctors and patients whenever and wherever necessary.

In 2000, the Institute of Medicine (IoM) estimated that between 44,000 and 98,000 Americans die each year from preventable medical errors. Subsequent studies have estimated that the number may be twice as high. Medical errors are killing more people per year, in America, than breast cancer, AIDS, or motor vehicle accidents. This pain and suffering is compounded by the knowledge that many of these errors could have been avoided.

The lack of immediate access to patient healthcare information is the source of one-fifth of these errors.

One of every seven primary care visits is affected by missing medical information. In a recent study, 80 percent of errors were initiated by miscommunication, including missed communication between physicians, misinformation in medical records, mishandling of patient requests and messages, inaccessible records, mislabeled specimens, misfiled or missing charts, and inadequate reminder systems.

Under the current paper-based system, patients and their doctors lack instant, constant access to medical information. As a result,

Mission S

"We will make wid records and other technology to help reduce dangerous
-- President Bush

"..to link all health an interoperable s privacy as it conne providers and pay fewer medical mis lower costs and be
-- HHS Se

Ne

05/17/2006 - Ar Information Comm First Set of Recom

01/17/2006 - HH Project Launched t Electronic Prescrib

11/17/2005 - CM Enters Into Agreer Digital Health Reco Case

Spee

See page xxii for detailed descriptions of the rating scales
①②③④○

16

Content Organization

After ensuring that content is useful, well-written,

and in a format that is suitable for the Web, it is important to ensure that the information is clearly organized. In some cases, the content on a site can be organized in multiple ways to accommodate multiple audiences.

Organizing content includes putting critical information near the top of the site, grouping related elements, and ensuring that all necessary information is available without slowing the user with unneeded information. Content should be formatted to facilitate scanning, and to enable quick understanding.

16:1 Organize Information Clearly

Relative Importance:
①②③④⑤

Strength of Evidence:
①②③④○

Guideline: Organize information at each level of the Web site so that it shows a clear and logical structure to typical users.

Comments: Designers should present information in a structure that reflects user needs and the site's goals. Information should be well-organized at the Web site level, page level, and paragraph or list level.

Good Web site and page design enables users to understand the nature of the site's organizational relationships and will support users in locating information efficiently. A clear, logical structure will reduce the chances of users becoming bored, disinterested, or frustrated

Sources: Benson, 1985; Clark and Haviland, 1975; Detweiler and Omanson, 1996; Dixon, 1987; Evans, 1998; Farkas and Farkas, 2000; Keyes, 1993; Keyes, Sykes and Lewis, 1988; Lynch and Horton, 2002; Nielsen and Tahir, 2002; Redish, 1993; Redish, Felker and Rose, 1981; Schroeder, 1999; Spyridakis, 2000; Tiller and Green, 1999; Wright, 1987; Zimmerman and Akerelrea, 2002; Zimmerman, et al., 2002.

Example: This design clearly illustrates to the user the logical structure of the Web site. The structure is built on the user's needs—namely, completing a form in ten steps.

See page xxii for detailed descriptions of the rating scales
①②③④○

16:2 Facilitate Scanning

Relative Importance:
①②③④⑤

Strength of Evidence:
①②③④○

Guideline: Structure each content page to facilitate scanning: use clear, well-located headings; short phrases and sentences; and small readable paragraphs.

Comments: Web sites that are optimized for scanning can help users find desired information. Users that scan generally read headings, but do not read full text prose–this results in users missing information when a page contains dense text.

Studies report that about eighty percent of users scan any new page. Only sixteen percent read each word. Users spend about twelve percent of their time trying to locate desired information on a page.

To facilitate the finding of information, place important headings high in the center section of a page. Users tend to scan until they find something interesting and then they read. Designers should help users ignore large chunks of the page in a single glance. Keep in mind that older users (70 and over) will tend to scan much more slowly through a web page than will younger users (ages 39 and younger).

Sources: Bailey, Koyani and Nall, 2000; Byrne, et al., 1999; Evans, 1998; Koyani and Bailey, 2005; Koyani, et al., 2002; Morkes and Nielsen, 1997; Morkes and Nielsen, 1998; Nielsen, 1997e; Nielsen, 2000; Schriver, 1997; Spool, et al., 1997; Spyridakis, 2000; Sticht, 1985; Sullivan and Flower, 1986; Toms, 2000; Zimmerman, et al., 1996.

Example: This page facilitates scanning.

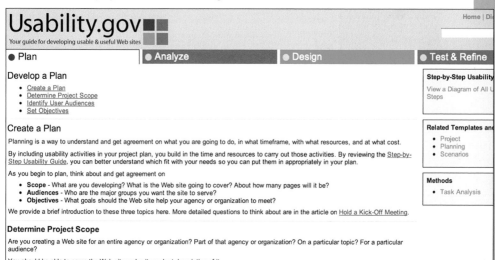

16:3 Ensure that Necessary Information is Displayed

Guideline: Ensure that all needed information is available and displayed on the page where and when it is needed.

Relative Importance:
①②③④⑤

Strength of Evidence:
①②○○○

Comments: Users should not have to remember data from one page to the next or when scrolling from one screenful to the next. Heading information should be retained when users scroll data tables, or repeated often enough so that header information can be seen on each screenful.

Sources: Engel and Granda, 1975; Smith and Mosier, 1986; Spyridakis, 2000; Stewart, 1980; Tullis, 1983.

Example: This header row disappears as users scroll down the table. This can negatively effect users' performance on the site by exceeding their 'working memory' capacity.

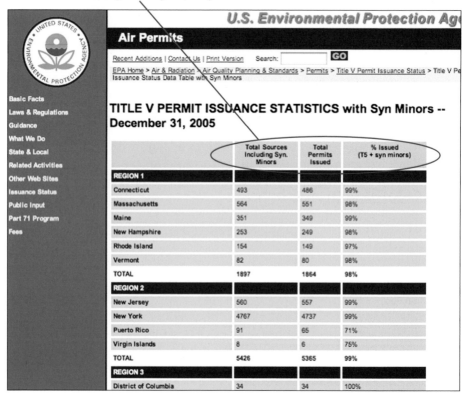

See page xxii
for detailed descriptions
of the rating scales
①②③④○

16:4 Group Related Elements

Relative Importance:
①②③④〇

Strength of Evidence:
①②③④⑤

Guideline: Group all related information and functions in order to decrease time spent searching or scanning.

Comments: All information related to one topic should be grouped together. This minimizes the need for users to search or scan the site for related information. Users will consider items that are placed in close spatial proximity to belong together conceptually. Text items that share the same background color typically will be seen as being related to each other.

Sources: Ahlstrom and Longo, 2001; Cakir, Hart and Stewart, 1980; Faraday, 2000; Gerhardt-Powals, 1996; Kahn, Tan and Beaton, 1990; Kim and Yoo, 2000; Nall, Koyani and Lafond, 2001; Niemela and Saarinen, 2000; Nygren and Allard, 1996; Spyridakis, 2000.

Example: This site organizes information well by grouping core navigation elements and key topic areas. These features allow users to search and scan for information faster.

Content Organization

Guideline: To allow users to efficiently find what they want, design so that the most common tasks can be successfully completed in the fewest number of clicks.

Relative Importance:
①②③④○

Strength of Evidence:
①②③○○

Comments: Critical information should be provided as close to the homepage as possible. This reduces the need for users to click deep into the site and make additional decisions on intervening pages. The more steps (or clicks) users must take to find the desired information, the greater the likelihood they will make an incorrect choice. Important information should be available within two or three clicks of the homepage.

One study found that the time to complete a task was closely related to the number of clicks made by users. It appears that users will keep clicking as long as they feel like they are getting closer to their goal. Another study showed that when users were trying to find a target, they were no more likely to quit after three clicks than after 12 clicks.

Sources: Evans, 1998; Levine, 1996; Nall, Koyani and Lafond, 2001; Nielsen and Tahir, 2002; Porter, 2003; Spyridakis, 2000; Zimmerman, et al., 2002; Zimmerman, et al., 1996.

Example: A topic such as Lung Cancer, one of the most common cancer types, is one click off of the homepage of this cancer site.

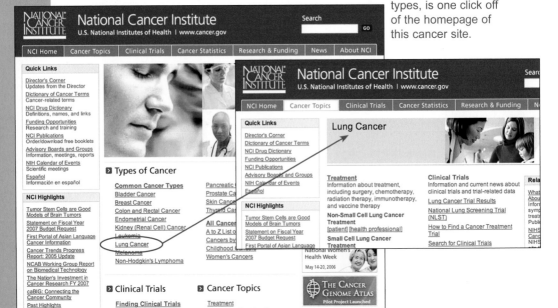

See page xxii for detailed descriptions of the rating scales
①②③④○

Guideline: Design quantitative information to reduce the time required to understand it.

Relative Importance:
①②③○○

Comments: Make appropriate use of tables, graphics, and visualization techniques to hasten the understanding of information. Presenting quantitative information in a table (rather than a graph) generally elicits the best performance; however, there are situations where visualizations will elicit even better performance. Usability testing can help to determine when users will benefit from using tabular data, graphics, tables, or visualizations.

Strength of Evidence:
①②③○○

Sources: Chen and Yu, 2000; Galitz, 2002; Gerhardt-Powals, 1996; Kosslyn, 1994; Meyer, 1997; Meyer, Shamo and Gopher, 1999; Meyer, Shinar and Leiser, 1997; Tufte, 1983.

Example:

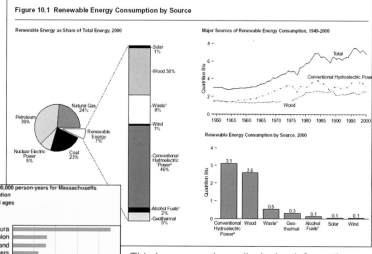

Figure 10.1 Renewable Energy Consumption by Source

This is a case where displaying information using graphs and bars allows users to discern the importance of data much more quickly than when it is presented in a table format.

Presenting numerical data as bar charts may speed up the user's understanding of data.

Content Organization

Guideline: Limit page information only to that which is needed by users while on that page.

Relative Importance:
①②③○○

Strength of Evidence:
①②③④○

Comments: Do not overload pages or interactions with extraneous information. Displaying too much information may confuse users and hinder assimilation of needed information. Allow users to remain focused on the desired task by excluding information that task analysis and usability testing indicates is not relevant to their current task. When user information requirements cannot be precisely anticipated by the designer, allow users to tailor displays online.

Sources: Ahlstrom and Longo, 2001; Engel and Granda, 1975; Gerhardt-Powals, 1996; Mayhew, 1992; Morkes and Nielsen, 1998; Powers, et al., 1961; Smith and Mosier, 1986; Spyridakis, 2000; Stewart, 1980; Tullis, 1981; Tullis, 2001; Zhang and Seo, 2001.

Example: An example of extraneous information. In this case, the user is looking for a weather forecast for Manchester, United Kingdom. The site provides this information, but also indicates tonight's vacation weather for Prague—this information is extraneous to the user's original task.

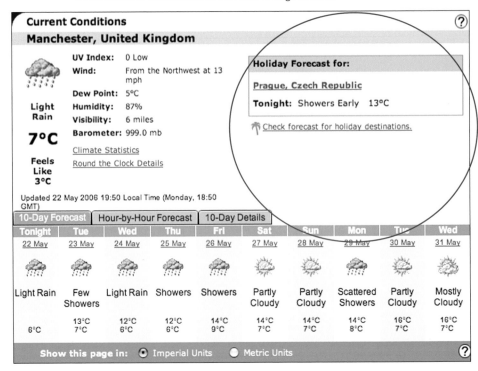

Guideline: Design search engines to search the entire site, or clearly communicate which part of the site will be searched.

Relative Importance:
①②③④⑤

Strength of Evidence:
①②③○○

Comments: Designers may want to allow users to control the range of their searches. However, users tend to believe that a search engine will search the entire Web site. Do not have search engines search only a portion of the site without clearly informing users which parts of the site are being searched.

Keep in mind that what a designer may consider to be the entirety of a site may not be the same as what the user thinks is the 'whole' site. For example, many large sites have various subsections that are maintained by different designers, so the user may think of a site as something that designers think of as several sites. Make sure it is clear to users what part(s) of the Web site are being searched. Provide a means for users to narrow the scope of searches on large Web sites by providing easy access to specific subsites when searching.

Sources: Bailey and Koyani, 2004; Spool, et al., 1997.

Example:

This design allows users to easily bound their search to a selected subsection of the Web site, or to run an unbounded search by selecting the 'All of SSA' menu choice.

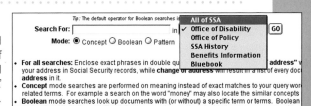

17:3 Make Upper- and Lowercase Search Terms Equivalent

Guideline: Treat user-entered upper- and lowercase letters as equivalent when entered as search terms.

Relative Importance:
①②③④○

Strength of Evidence:
①②○○○

Comments: For example, 'STRING,' 'String,' and 'string' should be recognized and accepted equally by the Web site. When searching, users will generally be indifferent to any distinction between upper- and lowercase. The site should not compel a distinction that users do not care or know about, or that the user may find difficult to make. In situations when case actually is important, allow users to specify case as a selectable option in the string search.

Sources: Smith and Mosier, 1986.

Search

17:4 Provide a Search Option on Each Page

Guideline: Provide a search option on each page of a content-rich Web site.

Relative Importance:
①②③④○

Comments: A search option should be provided on all pages where it may be useful–users should not have to return to the homepage to conduct a search. Search engines can be helpful on content-rich Web sites, but do not add value on other types of sites.

Strength of Evidence:
①②○○○

Designers should be careful not to rely too heavily on search engines. They are not a substitute for good content organization, and do not always improve users' search performance. Designers should carefully consider the advantages and disadvantages of including a search engine, and whether their Web site lends itself to automated searches.

Sources: Detweiler and Omanson, 1996; Farkas and Farkas, 2000; Levine, 1996; Nielsen, 1996a; Nielsen, 1997e; Nielsen, 1999d; Spool, et al., 1997.

Example: As users delve deeper into the site's content, the search capability remains immediately available.

See page xxii for detailed descriptions of the rating scales
①②③④○

Guideline: Construct a Web site's search engine to respond to users' terminology.

Relative Importance:
①②③④〇

Strength of Evidence:
①②③〇〇

Comments: Users seem to rely on certain preferred keywords when searching. They will generally conduct one or two searches before trying another site or search engine (or abandoning the search altogether). Therefore, it is important that users succeed on their first try.

Determining the keywords users are using may require considerable data collection. Designers should make use of search engine logs, surveys, and other techniques to determine the preferred search words for their site, and make information relevant to those terms easy to find through the site's search engine. Keep in mind that designers' preferred keywords may not match users' preferred keywords, and content writers may overestimate the specialized vocabulary of their audience. For the most common searches, provide a 'best bets' set of results. Ensure that the 'best bets' do not appear as advertising or paid links.

In addition to responding to users' keywords, try to design the site's search engine to accommodate common misspellings, extra spaces, alternative punctuation, misused plurals, and other common user search errors.

Sources: Bailey and Koyani, 2004; Dumais, Cutrell and Chen, 2001; Egan, et al., 1989; Evans, 1998; Hooke, DeLeo and Slaughter, 1979; Koyani and Nall, 1999; Schiano, Stone and Bectarte, 2001; Spyridakis, 2000.

Example:

A search for "tongue cancer" also returns results on Oral Cancer, Head and Neck Cancer, and Lip and Oral Cavity Cancer.

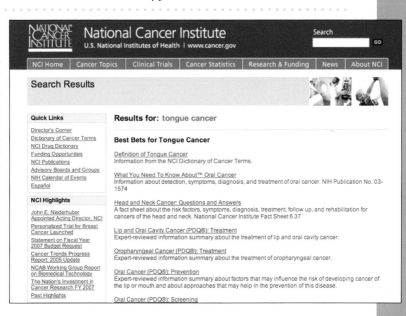

17:6 Allow Simple Searches

Relative Importance:
①②❸○○

Strength of Evidence:
❶❷○○○

Guideline: Structure the search engine to accommodate users who enter a small number of words.

Comments: The search function should be easy to use and allow for users to be successful when searching. Most users tend to employ simple search strategies. They rarely use advanced search features (such as Boolean operators), so it is important not to rely on those to improve the effectiveness of the site's search engine. If most of the site's users are inexperienced Web searchers, provide simple instructions and examples to help guide users' searching and use of the search results.

Provide a box (entry field) for entering search terms that is at least 35 to 40 characters wide. Users will self-detect more errors when they see what they have entered.

Sources: Bailey and Koyani, 2004; Bayles and Bernard, 1999; Koyani and Nall, 1999; Nielsen, 2001a; Nielsen, et al., 2000; Pollock and Hockley, 1996; Spink, Bateman and Jansen, 1999; Spool, Schroeder and Ojakaar, 2001.

Example:

Simple search engines will accommodate most users' search strategies.

To search the GPO Web Site, enter terms in the box above. (Present configuration confin search to only the files resident on this site. It does not search GPO Access databases resident on other GPO servers.)

This search page is far too complex for the average user. Such advanced search capabilities are best presented on a page dedicated to advanced searches.

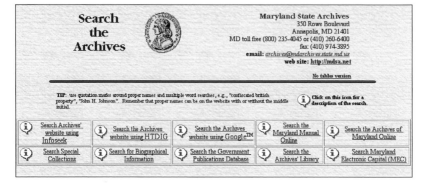

Guideline: If more than one type of search option is provided, ensure that users are aware of all the different types of search options and how each is best used.

Relative Importance:
①②③○○

Strength of Evidence:
①②③○○

Comments: Most users assume that a Web site has only one type of search. In one study, when there were multiple search types available, users tended to miss some of the search capabilities.

Sources: Bailey, Koyani and Nall, 2000; Levy, et al., 1996.

Example:
These sites all offer multiple ways of searching.

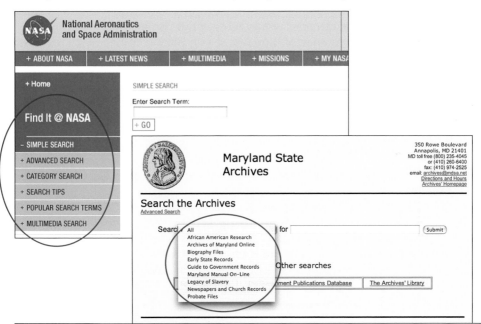

See page xxii
for detailed descriptions
of the rating scales
①②③④○

17:8 Include Hints to Improve Search Performance

Search

Guideline: Include specific hints to improve search performance.

Relative Importance:
①②③○○

Comments: A major tradeoff that must be considered in the design of a search input interface is related to the need to provide sufficient instructions for users to take advantage of the power of the search engine, while keeping in mind the reluctance of users to read instructions.

Strength of Evidence:
①②③○○

One study found a direct link between the content of search hints and task effectiveness. When syntactic information was included in the search hint, participants achieved significantly greater syntactic performance. When semantic information was included in the search hint, participants achieved significantly greater semantic performance. In addition, participants' confidence that their queries would retrieve the correct answer was reliably enhanced by the presence of semantic search hints (but not syntactic hints). The presence of examples improved semantic performance, but had no effect on syntactic performance. When hints contained more than one type of information (syntactic, semantic, or examples), performance was generally lower than when only one hint type was presented. Also, participants were able to complete the search tasks faster when only one hint was presented.

Sources: Bandos and Resnick, (2004).

Example: This site provides search hints to assist the user.

Searching Hints

What you type	Documents will be listed if their index entries contain:
netscape browser netscape and browser netscape <and> browser	The two words *netscape* and *browser*. Those two words (regardless of capitalization) must occur somewhere in the index but not necessarily together or in any order. (Words separated by spaces are treated as if the space was an implied <and> operator.)
"netscape browser"	The words *netscape browser* together in that order anywhere in the entry, regardless of capitalization. (Multiple words enclosed by quotation marks are treated as a single search phrase.)
netscape or browser netscape <or> browser	Either the word *netscape* or the word *browser* anywhere in the entry, including together, regardless of capitalization.
"Netscape browser" Compass	Documents containing both the phrase *Netscape browser* and the word *Compass*.

See page xxii for detailed descriptions of the rating scales
①②③④○

17:9 Provide Search Templates

Relative Importance:
①②◯◯◯

Strength of Evidence:
①②③◯◯

Guideline: Provide templates to facilitate the use of search engines.

Comments: Search templates assist users in formulating better search queries. A template consists of predefined keywords that help users select their search terms. The keywords can be used directly, or can help users formulate their own queries. Each template should be organized as a hierarchy of predefined keywords that could help to restrict the users' initial search sets, and improve the relevance of the returned 'hits.' One study reported that people using templates find seventy percent more target Web sites than those not using templates.

Sources: Fang and Salvendy, 1999.

Example: Some 'search template' examples include:

To find information on 'human error' use

errors	fault	miscalculation
slips	blunder	slip-up
mistakes	inaccuracy	

To find information on 'usability testing' use

user interface testing	cognitive walkthroughs
performance testing	automatic tests
heuristics evaluations	remote testing

To get more specific search results, try using the following tips:

Check <u>spelling</u>

Use <u>multiple words</u>
    Example: `our free product`
Use <u>similar words</u>
    Example: `safe secure privacy security`
Use appropriate <u>capitalization</u>
    Example: `Search Template Reference`
Use <u>quotation marks</u>
    Example: `"our pledge to you"`
Use <u>plus (+) or minus (-)</u>
    Example: `+"template language"`

Use <u>field searches</u>
    Examples:
    `title:about`
    `desc:"Our Team"`
    `keys:membership`
    `body:security`
    `alt:"try now"`
    `url:help`
    `target:Atomz`
Use <u>wildcards</u>
    Examples:
    `wh*`
    `"wh* are"`
    `415-*-*`

18

Usability Testing

There are two major considerations when

conducting usability testing. The first is to ensure that the best possible method for testing is used. Generally, the best method is to conduct a test where representative participants interact with representative scenarios. The tester collects data on the participant's success, speed of performance, and satisfaction. The findings, including both quantitative data and qualitative observations information, are provided to designers in a test report. Using 'inspection evaluations,' in place of well-controlled usability tests, must be done with caution. Inspection methods, such as heuristic evaluations or expert reviews, tend to generate large numbers of potential usability 'problems' that never turn out to be actual usability problems.

The second major consideration is to ensure that an iterative approach is used. After the first test results are provided to designers, they should make changes and then have the Web site tested again. Generally, the more iterations, the better the Web site.

Guideline: Develop and test prototypes through an iterative design approach to create the most useful and usable Web site.

Relative Importance:
①②③④○

Strength of Evidence:
①②③④⑤

Comments: Iterative design consists of creating paper or computer prototypes, testing the prototypes, and then making changes based on the test results. The 'test and make changes' process is repeated until the Web site meets performance benchmarks (usability goals). When these goals are met, the iterative process ends.

The iterative design process helps to substantially improve the usability of Web sites. One recent study found that the improvements made between the original Web site and the redesigned Web site resulted in thirty percent more task completions, twenty-five percent less time to complete the tasks, and sixty-seven percent greater user satisfaction. A second study reported that eight of ten tasks were performed faster on the Web site that had been iteratively designed. Finally, a third study found that forty-six percent of the original set of issues were resolved by making design changes to the interface.

Sources: Badre, 2002; Bailey, 1993; Bailey and Wolfson, 2005; Bradley and Johnk, 1995; Egan, et al., 1989; Hong, et al., 2001; Jeffries, et al., 1991; Karat, Campbell, and Fiegel, 1992; LeDoux, Connor and Tullis, 2005; Norman and Murphy, 2004; Redish and Dumas, 1993; Tan, et al., 2001.

See page xxii
for detailed descriptions
of the rating scales
①②③④○

18:2 Solicit Test Participants' Comments

Guideline: Solicit usability testing participants' comments either during or after the performance of tasks.

Relative Importance:
①②③○○

Strength of Evidence:
①②③④○

Comments: Participants may be asked to give their comments either while performing each task ('think aloud') or after finishing all tasks (retrospectively). When using the 'think aloud' method, participants report on incidents as soon as they happen. When using the retrospective approach, participants perform all tasks uninterrupted, and then watch their session video and report any observations (critical incidents).

Studies have reported no significant difference between the 'think aloud' versus retrospective approaches in terms of the number of useful incident reports given by participants. However, the reports (with both approaches) tended to be positively biased and 'think aloud' participants may complete fewer tasks. Participants tend not to voice negative reports. In one study, when using the 'think aloud' approach, users tended to read text on the screen and verbalize more of what they were doing rather than what they were thinking.

Sources: Bailey, 2003; Bowers and Snyder, 1990; Capra, 2002; Hoc and Leplat, 1983; Ohnemus and Biers, 1993; Page and Rahimi, 1995; Van Den Haak, De Jong, and Schellens, 2003; Wright and Converse, 1992.

18:3 Evaluate Web Sites Before and After Making Changes

Guideline: Conduct 'before and after' studies when revising a Web site to determine changes in usability.

Relative Importance:
①②③○○

Strength of Evidence:
①②③○○

Comments: Conducting usability studies prior to and after a redesign will help designers determine if changes actually made a difference in the usability of the site. One study reported that only twenty-two percent of users were able to buy items on an original Web site. After a major redesign effort, eighty-eight percent of users successfully purchased products on that site.

Sources: John and Marks, 1997; Karat, 1994a; Ramey, 2000; Rehman, 2000; Williams, 2000; Wixon and Jones, 1996.

18:4 Prioritize Tasks

Relative Importance:
①②❸○○

Strength of Evidence:
①❷○○○

Guideline: Give high priority to usability issues preventing 'easy' tasks from being easy.

Comments: When deciding which usability issues to fix first, address the tasks that users believe to be easy but are actually difficult. The Usability Magnitude Estimation (UME) is a measure that can be used to assess user expectations of the difficulty of each task. Participants judge how difficult or easy a task will be before trying to do it, and then make a second judgment after trying to complete the task. Each task is eventually put into one of four categories based on these expected versus actual ratings:

- Tasks that were expected to be easy, but were actually difficult;
- Tasks that were expected to be difficult, but were actually easy;
- Tasks that were expected to be easy and were actually easy; and
- Tasks that were expected to be difficult and were difficult to complete.

Sources: Rich and McGee, 2004.

18:5 Distinguish Between Frequency and Severity

Guideline: Distinguish between frequency and severity when reporting on usability issues and problems.

Relative Importance:
①②❸○○

Strength of Evidence:
①②❸○○

Comments: The number of users affected determines the frequency of a problem. To be most useful, the severity of a problem should be defined by analyzing difficulties encountered by individual users. Both frequency and severity data can be used to prioritize usability issues that need to be changed. For example, designers should focus first on fixing those usability issues that were shown to be most severe. Those usability issues that were encountered by many participants, but had a severity rating of 'nuisance,' should be given much less priority.

Sources: Woolrych and Cockton, 2001.

See page xxii for detailed descriptions of the rating scales
①②❸❹○

18:6 Select the Right Number of Participants

Guideline: Select the right number of participants when using different usability techniques. Using too few may reduce the usability of a Web site; using too many wastes valuable resources.

Relative Importance:
①②③○○

Strength of Evidence:
①②③④○

Comments: Selecting the number of participants to use when conducting usability evaluations depends on the method being used:

- Inspection evaluation by usability specialists:
  - The typical goal of an inspection evaluation is to have usability experts separately inspect a user interface by applying a set of broad usability guidelines. This is usually done with two to five people.
  - The research shows that as more experts are involved in evaluating the usability of the product, the greater the number of usability issues will be identified. However, for every true usability problem identified, there will be at least one usability issue that is not a real problem. Having more evaluators does decrease the number of misses, but is also increases the number of false positives. Generally, the more expert the usability specialists, the more useful the results.

- Performance usability testing with users:
  - Early in the design process, usability testing with a small number of users (approximately six) is sufficient to identify problems with the information architecture (navigation) and overall design issues. If the Web site has very different types of users (e.g., novices and experts), it is important to test with six or more of each type of user. Another critical factor in this preliminary testing is having trained usability specialists as the usability test facilitator and primary observers.
  - Once the navigation, basic content, and display features are in place, quantitative performance testing (measuring times, wrong pathways, failure to find content, etc.) can be conducted to ensure that usability objectives are being met. To measure each usability objective to a particular confidence level, such as ninety-five percent, requires a larger number of users in the usability tests.
  - When the performance of two sites is compared (i.e., an original site and a revised site), quantitative usability testing should be employed. Depending on how confident the usability specialist wants to be in the results, the tests could require a larger number of participants.

– It is best to perform iterative cycles of usability testing over the course of the Web site's development. This enables usability specialists and designers to observe and listen to many users.

Sources: Bailey, 1996; Bailey, 2000c; Bailey, 2000d; Brinck and Hofer, 2002; Chin, 2001; Dumas, 2001; Gray and Salzman, 1998; Lewis, 1993; Lewis, 1994; Nielsen and Landauer, 1993; Perfetti and Landesman, 2001; Virzi, 1990; Virzi, 1992.

18:7 Use the Appropriate Prototyping Technology

Guideline: Create prototypes using the most appropriate technology for the phase of the design, the required fidelity of the prototype, and skill of the person creating the prototype.

Relative Importance:
①②○○○

Strength of Evidence:
①②③○○

Comments: Designers can use either paper-based or computer-based prototypes. Paper-based prototyping appears to be as effective as computer-based prototyping when trying to identify most usability issues. Several studies have shown that there was no reliable difference in the number of usability issues detected between computer and paper prototypes. However, usability test participants usually prefer interacting with computer-based prototypes. Paper prototypes can be used when it is necessary to view and evaluate many different (usually early) design ideas, or when computer-based prototyping does not support the ideas the designer wants to implement, or when all members of the design team need to be included–even those that do not know how to create computer-based prototypes.

Software tools that are available to assist in the rapid development of prototypes include PowerPoint, Visio, including other HTML base tools. PowerPoint can be used to create medium fidelity prototypes. These prototypes can be both interactive and dynamic, and are useful when the design requires more than a 'pencil-and-paper' prototype.

Sources: Sefelin, Tscheligi and Giller, 2003; Silvers, Voorheis and Anders, 2004; Walker, Takayama and Landay, 2002.

See page xxii for detailed descriptions of the rating scales
①②③④○

18:8 Use Inspection Evaluation Results Cautiously

Guideline: Use inspection evaluation results with caution.

Relative Importance:
①②◯◯◯

Comments: Inspection evaluations include heuristic evaluations, expert reviews, and cognitive walkthroughs. It is a common practice to conduct an inspection evaluation to try to detect and resolve obvious problems before conducting usability tests. Inspection evaluations should be used cautiously because several studies have shown that they appear to detect far more potential problems than actually exist, and they also tend to miss some real problems. On average, for every hit there will be about 1.3 false positives and .5 misses.

Strength of Evidence:
①②③④◯

Another recent study concluded that the low effectiveness of heuristic evaluations as a whole was worrisome because of the low problem detection rate ($p=.09$), and the large number of evaluators required (16) to uncover seventy-five percent of the potential usability issues.

Another difficulty when conducting heuristic evaluations is that evaluators frequently apply the wrong heuristic, which can mislead designers that are trying to fix the problem. One study reported that only thirty-nine percent of the heuristics were appropriately applied.

Evaluators seem to have the most success identifying usability issues that can be seen by merely looking at the display, and the least success finding issues that require users to take several steps (clicks) to a target.

Heuristic evaluations and expert reviews may best be used to identify potential usability issues to evaluate during usability testing. To improve somewhat on the performance of heuristic evaluations, evaluators can use the 'usability problem inspector' (UPI) method or the 'Discovery and Analysis Resource' (DARe) method.

Sources: Andre, Hartson and Williges, 2003; Bailey, Allen and Raiello, 1992; Catani and Biers, 1998; Cockton and Woolrych 2001; Cockton and Woolrych, 2002; Cockton, et al., 2003; Fu, Salvendy and Turley, 1998; Fu, Salvendy and Turley, 2002; Law and Hvannberg, 2002; Law and Hvannberg, 2004; Nielsen and Landauer, 1993; Nielsen and Mack, 1994; Rooden, Green and Kanis, 1999; Stanton and Stevenage, 1998; Virzi, Sorce and Herbert, 1993; Wang and Caldwell, 2002.

See page xxii
for detailed descriptions
of the rating scales
①②③④◯

18:9 Recognize the 'Evaluator Effect'

Relative Importance:
①②〇〇〇

Guideline: Beware of the 'evaluator effect' when conducting inspection evaluations.

Strength of Evidence:
①②③④〇

Comments: The 'evaluator effect' occurs when multiple evaluators evaluating the same interface detect markedly different sets of problems. The evaluators may be doing an expert review, heuristic evaluation, or cognitive walkthrough.

The evaluator effect exists for evaluators who are novice or experienced, while detecting cosmetic and severe problems, and when evaluating simple or complex Web sites. In fact, when using multiple evaluators, any one evaluator is unlikely to detect the majority of the 'severe' problems that will be detected collectively by all evaluators. Evaluators also tend to perceive the problems they detected as more severe than the problems detected by others.

The main cause of the 'evaluator effect' seems to be that usability evaluation is a complex cognitive activity that requires evaluators to exercise difficult judgments.

Sources: Hertzum and Jacobsen, 2001; Jacobsen, Hertzum and John, 1998; Molich, et al., 1998; Molich, et al., 1999; Nielsen and Molich, 1990; Nielsen, 1992; Nielsen, 1993; Redish and Dumas, 1993; Selvidge, 2000.

18:10 Apply Automatic Evaluation Methods

Guideline: Use appropriate automatic evaluation methods to conduct initial evaluations on Web sites.

Relative Importance:
①〇〇〇〇

Comments: An automatic evaluation method is one where software is used to evaluate a Web site. An automatic evaluation tool can help find certain types of design difficulties, such as pages

Strength of Evidence:
①②③〇〇

that will load slowly, missing links, use of jargon, potential accessibility problems, etc. While automatic evaluation methods are useful, they should not be used as a substitute for evaluations or usability testing with typical users. There are many commercially available automatic evaluation methods available for checking on a variety of Web site parameters.

Sources: Brajnik, 2000; Campbell and Stanley, 1963; Gray and Salzman, 1998; Holleran, 1991; Ivory and Hearst, 2002; Ramey, 2000; Scholtz, 1998; World Wide Web Consortium, 2001.

18:11 Use Cognitive Walkthroughs Cautiously

Guideline: Use cognitive walkthroughs with caution.

Comments: Cognitive walkthroughs are often conducted to resolve obvious problems before conducting performance tests. The cognitive walkthrough appears to detect far more potential problems than actually exist, when compared with performance usability testing results. Several studies have shown that only about twenty-five percent of the potential problems predicted by the cognitive walkthrough were found to be actual problems in a performance test. About thirteen percent of actual problems in the performance test were missed altogether in the cognitive walkthrough. Cognitive walkthroughs may best be used to identify potential usability issues to evaluate during usability testing.

Relative Importance:
❶⭘⭘⭘⭘

Strength of Evidence:
❶❷❸❹⭘

Sources: Blackmon, et al., 2002; Desurvire, Kondziela and Atwood, 1992; Hassenzahl, 2000; Jacobsen and John, 2000; Jeffries and Desurvire, 1992; John and Mashyna, 1997; Karat, 1994b; Karat, Campbell and Fiegel, 1992; Spencer, 2000.

18:12 Choosing Laboratory vs. Remote Testing

Guideline: Testers can use either laboratory or remote usability testing because they both elicit similar results.

Relative Importance:
❶⭘⭘⭘⭘

Strength of Evidence:
❶❷❸❹⭘

Comments: In laboratory-based testing, the participant and the tester are in the same physical location. In remote testing, the tester and the participant are in different physical locations. Remote testing provides the opportunity for participants to take a test in their home or office. It is convenient for participants because it requires no travel to a test facility.

Studies have evaluated whether remote testing is as effective as traditional, lab-based testing. To date, they have found no reliable differences between lab-based and remote testing in terms of the number of types of usability issues identified. Also, they report no reliable differences in task completion rate, time to complete the tasks, or satisfaction scores.

Sources: Brush, Ames and Davis, 2004; Hartson, et al., 1996; Thompson, Rozanski and Rochester, 2004; Tullis, et al., 2002.

Usability Testing

Guideline: Use severity ratings with caution.

Relative Importance:
①○○○○

Strength of Evidence:
①②③④○

Comments: Most designers would like usability specialists to prioritize design problems that they found either by inspection evaluations or expert reviews. So that they can decide which issues to fix first, designers would like the list of potential usability problems ranked by each one's 'severity level'. The research literature is fairly clear that even highly experienced usability specialists cannot agree on which usability issues will have the greatest impact on usability.

One study had 17 expert review and usability test teams evaluate and test the same Web page. The teams had one week to do an expert review, or two weeks to do a usability test. Each team classified each usability issue as a minor problem, serious problem, or critical problem. There was considerable disagreement in which problems the teams judged as minor, serious or critical, and there was little agreement on which were the 'top five problems'. Another study reported that heuristic evaluators overestimated severity twenty-two percent of the time, and underestimated severity seventy-eight percent of the time when compared with usability testing results.

Sources: Bailey, 2005; Catani and Biers, 1998; Cockton and Woolrych, 2001; Dumas, Molich and Jeffries, 2004; Hertzum and Jacobsen, 2001; Jacobsen, Hertzum and John, 1998; Law and Hvannberg, 2004; Molich, 2005.

See page xxii
for detailed descriptions
of the rating scales
①②③④○

Glossary

Above the fold

The region of a Web page that is visible without scrolling. The area above the fold will vary according to a user's monitor size and their resolution settings. The region above the fold is called a screenful.

Active voice

Active voice makes subjects do something (to something). For example, in 'Jill selected the link,' the verb 'selected' is in the active voice.

Anchor links

Anchor links can be used on content pages that contain several (usually three or more) screenfuls of information. Anchor links allow users to skip through textual information, resulting in a more efficient information-finding process. Anchor links are best arranged as a table of contents for the page. See also 'Within-page links.'

Applet

A mini-software program that a Java- or Active X-enabled browser downloads and uses automatically.

Assistive technologies

Technologies (software or hardware) that increase, maintain, or improve the functional capabilities of individuals with disabilities when interacting with computers or computer-based systems.

Auto-tabbing

A Web site feature whereby the data entry cursor automatically moves from one entry field to the next as a user enters a pre-determined number of characters. For instance, when entering phone number data in three separate entry fields of three digits, three digits, four digits, the data entry cursor would auto-tab from the first field to the second field once the user has entered three digits, and again from the second field to the third field once the user has entered another three digits.

Banner

Banners are graphic images that commonly function as Web-based billboards. Banner ads generally appear toward the top-center of the screen, and are used as attention-grabbing links to other sites.

Breadcrumbs

Breadcrumbs are a navigation element that allows users to orient themselves within a Web site, or efficiently move to one of the intermediate pages. Breadcrumbs are usually placed near the top of the page (generally immediately beneath the browser's address bar). For example, if users are reading about the features and benefits of 'widget x,' breadcrumbs might show the following information:

> **Home > Products > Widget x > Features/Benefits**

Breadcrumbs allow users to find their way to the homepage and ensure that they won't easily become lost. Breadcrumbs should be designed so that users can click on any of the words in the breadcrumb string to jump to that section of the Web site.

Card sorting

A method used to identify categories that are inherent in a set of items. The goal of card sorting is to understand how a typical user views a given set of items. Card sorting can be done manually by writing items on individual paper cards, and then asking users to group together similar cards. This also can be done using many different software systems. The grouping information from all card sorters is then combined and analyzed using cluster analysis software.

Cascading menu

A menu structure where submenus open when the user selects a choice from a menu. Cascading menus are particularly useful in hierarchically-complex Web sites.

Check box
A control element that a user can click to turn an option on or off. When the option is on, an '**X**' or '**✓**' appears in the box. Check boxes are conventionally used when users may select one or more items from a list of items.

Clickability cues
A visual indication that a given word or item on a Web page is clickable. Cues that can be used to indicate the clickability of an item include color, underlining, bullets, and arrows.

Client-side
Occurring on the client side of a client-server system. JavaScript scripts are client-side because they are executed by the user's browser (the client). In contrast, CGI scripts are server-side because they run on the Web server.

Cognitive walkthrough
An inspection method for evaluating the design of a user interface, with special attention to how well the interface supports 'exploratory learning,' i.e., first-time use without formal training. The evaluation is done by having a group of evaluators go step-by-step through commonly used tasks. It can be performed by evaluators in the early stages of design, before performance testing is possible.

Connection speed
The maximum rate at which Web pages are downloaded to a user's computer. Connection speed is often quoted in bps (bits per second). Common connection speeds include dial-up (modem) at 56,000 bps, DSL/cable at 500,000 bps or higher, and T1 at 1,500,000 bps or higher.

Content page
A Web page designed to convey specific information to a user. Content pages are often found two or three clicks deep within a Web site. The defining characteristic of a content page is a reliance on text, graphics, and pictures that are designed to convey information on a given subject to users.

Continuous text
In a Web context, continuous text comprises sentences and paragraphs. See also '**Prose Text.**'

Data entry field
A visually well-defined location on a page where users may type data.

Density, page
A measure of the percentage of the screen that is filled with text and graphics. .

Destination page
The location in a Web site where a given user goes after clicking on a link. See also '**Target page.**'

Download time
The amount of time required for a requested page to fully appear on a user's screen.

Drop-down list
Screen-based controls in which one list item shows, and the remaining list items are hidden until users click on a downward-facing arrow. Drop-down lists allow designers to preserve screen real estate while maintaining the ability to present a full suite of options to users.

Embedded link
A link that is found in the middle of prose or continuous text. Embedded links are often used to provide users with the definitions of terms or to lead them to supporting or related information.

Entry field
The entry field, which is also known as a data or text entry field, is employed when users are required to make text or data entries, including keywords, commands, quantities, etc.

Expert evaluation or **Expert review**
See 'Heuristic evaluation.'

Fold
The fold is defined as the lowest point where a Web page is no longer visible on a computer monitor or screen. Where on a Web page the fold falls is a function of the monitor size, the screen resolution, and the font size selection. The information that is visible when a Web page first loads is considered to be 'above the fold.' Those regions of the same Web page that are visible only by scrolling are considered to be 'below the fold.'

Frame
A feature supported by most browsers that enables the designer to divide the display area into two or more sections (frames). The contents of each frame behave like different Web pages.

Gloss
An automated action that provides summary information on where a link will take a user prior to the user clicking on the link. Often, glosses appear as a small 'pop-up' text box adjacent to a link. The gloss appears as the user moves the mouse over the link that is programmed with the gloss.

Heading
The title, subtitle, or topic that stands at the top or beginning of a paragraph or section of text.

Heuristic evaluation
An inspection method for finding certain types of usability problems in a user interface design. Heuristic evaluation involves having one or more usability specialists individually examine the interface and judge its compliance with recognized usability principles. These usability principles are the 'heuristics' from which the method takes its name.

Image map
A graphic designed to assist users' navigation of a Web site. Regions of the graphic are designed to be clickable.

Index link
Index links function as a table of contents—they provide users a quick glance at the Web site organization, allows users to quickly ascertain where they want to go, and to navigate there directly from the homepage.

Keyword
A word that is used as a reference point for finding other words or information using a search capability in a Web site.

Masthead
The (usually) graphical banner at the top of a Web page that identifies the organization or group that hosts the Web site. The masthead typically contains the name of the organization and site (if different) and an organizational logo.

Minesweeping
An action designed to identify where on a page links are located. Minesweeping involves the user rapidly moving the cursor or pointer over a page, watching to see where the cursor or pointer changes to indicate the presence of a link. See also 'Mouseover.'

Mouseover
A Web interaction wherein some visually-apparent change occurs to an item when the user's cursor/pointer is placed over the item. Examples of visually-apparent change includes links highlighting (words, images, etc.), cursors/pointers changing shape, or menus opening. See also 'Minesweeping.'

Navigation page
A Web page that contains no content and that is designed solely to direct or redirect users. Navigation pages may be designed as homepages, site maps, site overviews, etc.

Open list
An open list is a screen-based control where either all of the list items are

immediately visible on the screen, or where several list items are immediately visible to the user, and the remaining list items can be viewed by scrolling the list.

Page title
Page titles refer to the text located in the browser title bar (this is the bar found at the very top of the screen of common browsers).

Paging
A Web site design methodology that requires users to follow a series of 'Next page' links to read an entire article. Moving from page-to-page is an alternative to scrolling through long pages.

Panels
Visually and thematically-defined sections of a Web page. Panels are frequently placed in the left and right margins of pages. Panels often contain navigation aids, including related links. Content is not usually placed in left or right panels.

Passive voice
Voice is a grammatical feature of English verbs. Passive voice permits subjects to have something done to them (by someone or something).
For example, 'The link was clicked by John.' Some argue that passive voice is more indirect and wordier than active voice.

Path
The route taken by a user as they move through a Web site. The path can be shown by breadcrumbs.

Performance objectives
The goals set for user behaviors on an individual Web page or a series of Web pages. These objectives usually are stated in terms of the time to correctly select a link, the overall accuracy of selecting links, the average time to select a target page, etc.

Performance test
A usability test that is characterized by having typical users perform a series of tasks where their speed, accuracy and success are closely monitored and measured.

Physical consistency
Physical consistency refers to the 'look and feel' of a Web site. Physically consistent Web pages will have logos, headers, and navigation elements all located in the same place. The pages also will use the same fonts and graphic elements across all pages in the site.

Plug-in
A software module that adds a specific feature or service to a larger system. For example, there is a number of plug-ins for common browsers that enable them to display different types of audio and video.

Point-and-click
A term used to describe conventional Web surfing behavior. When a user visually identifies a link they wish to follow, they place their mouse pointer over the link (point) and depress the appropriate button on the mouse (click). See also **'Mouseover.'**

Pop-under/Pop-up
A pop-under or pop-up is a window that is automatically invoked when a user loads a Web page. Pop-under appears 'below' the active browser window, whereas pop-ups appear 'above' the active window and can obscure screen contents.

Preference objectives
The goals set for user attitudes toward individual Web pages or an entire Web site. The objectives are usually set and measured using questionnaires. These objectives include information concerning user acceptance and user satisfaction.

Prose text
Ordinary writing, in a Web context, prose text comprises sentences and paragraphs. See also 'Continuous Text.'

Pushbutton
Pushbuttons are screen-based controls that contain a text label or an image (or both). Pushbuttons are used to provide quick and convenient access to frequently-used actions. The pushbutton control is always activated with a single click of a mouse button. Clicking on pushbuttons should cause the indicated action to take place, i.e., 'search.' Do not use pushbuttons to move from one location to another in a Web site.

Radio button
A screen-based control used to select one item from a list of mutually-exclusive items (i.e., use radio buttons when only one item in a list of several items can be selected).

Reveals
Information that automatically appears on the screen during a Web-based slideshow presentation, or while viewing a multimedia Web page.

Scanning
An information-retrieval method whereby users look quickly through a Web page looking for target information (headers, keywords, etc.). Scanning can be a quick and efficient information-retrieval method if Web pages are designed to accommodate scanning.

Screen reader
A software program used to allow reading of content and navigation of the screen using speech or Braille output. Used primarily by people who have difficulty seeing.

Screenful
A screenful is defined as that portion of a Web page that is visible on any given user's monitor or screen at any given point in time. The size of the screenful is determined by the user's monitor size, screen resolution settings, and the user's selected font size.

Scroll bar
The scroll bar is visible along the right edge of common browsers. It is defined by a movable box that runs on a vertical or horizontal axis.

Scroll stopper
A graphic or other page element that may visually impede a user from scrolling to the true top or bottom of a page. Misplaced headers, horizontal lines, or sections of text in very small fonts may act as scroll stoppers.

Scrolling
A method of traversing a Web page wherein users either roll the scroll wheel on their mouse, or manually move the scroll bar located on the right side of their browser's screen.

Section 508
Section 508 of the Rehabilitation Act was enacted to eliminate barriers in information technology, to make available new opportunities for people with disabilities, and to encourage development of technologies that will help achieve these goals. The law applies to all Federal agencies when they develop, procure, maintain, or use electronic and information technology. Under Section 508 (29 U.S.C. § 794d), agencies must give disabled employees and members of the public access to information that is comparable to the access available to others.

Semantics
Semantics is a term used to distinguish the meaning of an instruction from its format. A semantic error occurs when you enter a legal command that does not make sense in the current context. To reduce error, provide semantic hints. Example of a semantic hint: 'Use AND to retrieve a smaller set of records in which both of the search terms are present. Use

OR to retrieve a larger number of records; OR is commonly used to search for synonymous terms or concepts.'

Server-side (image map)
Occurring on the server side of a client-server system. For example, on the Web, CGI scripts are server-side applications because they run on the Web server. In contrast, JavaScript scripts are client-side because they are executed by the browser (the client). Java applets can be either server-side or client-side depending on which computer (the server or the client) executes them.

Simultaneous menus
Menus that simultaneously display choices from multiple levels in the menu hierarchy, providing users with the ability to make menu choices in any order.

Site map
A clickable, graphic- or text-based display of a Web site's hierarchy.

Style sheet
A set of statements that specify presentation of a document. Style sheets may have three different origins: they may be written by content providers, created by users, or built into browsers or plug-ins.

Syntax
The formatting rules that address the spelling of language components and the rules controlling how components should be combined. A syntax error occurs if you misspell a command, use inappropriate grammar, capitalization, etc. To reduce error, provide syntactic hints. Example of a syntactic hint: 'Enter search terms separated by AND, OR, NOT, and/or enclose terms in double quotes to specify your search.' 'All operators must be capitalized.'

Tab
A graphical navigation element that is most often placed at the top of a Web page. Effective tabs should be designed so that they resemble real-world file folder tabs.

Tagline
A phrase or short sentence placed directly below a Web page's masthead. The tagline functions to quickly identify the purpose of the Web site. It may be a subtitle, an organizational motto, or a vision or purpose statement.

Target page
The location in a site where a user will find the information they are seeking. See also '**Destination page.**'

Task analysis
A method used to identify and understand the activities to be performed by users when interacting with a Web site.

Thumbnail image
A small copy of a larger image.

Time out
When entering data that may be sensitive (e.g., credit card or social security numbers), many Web sites will disconnect ('time out') if a user has not interacted with the browser in a set amount of time.

URL
URL is an abbreviation for Uniform Resource Locator. Every Web page has a URL that is used to identify the page and the server on which the page resides.

Usability testing
Usability testing includes a range of test and evaluation methods that include automated evaluations, inspection evaluations, operational evaluations and human performance testing. In a typical performance test, users perform a variety of tasks with a prototype (or an operational system) while observers note what each user does and says while performance data are recorded. One of the main purposes of usability testing is to identify issues that keep users from meeting the usability goals of a Web site.

Widget
Screen-based controls that are used
to interact with a Web site and other
systems. Widgets include pushbuttons,
selection lists, radio buttons, sliders, etc.

Within-page links
Within-page links are used on content
pages that contain several (e.g., three or
more) screenfuls of information. Within-
page links are best arranged as a table
of contents for the page. Within-page
links allow users to skip through textual
information, resulting in a more efficient
information-finding process. See also
'Anchor links.'

Appendices

Guidelines Ranked by **Relative Importance**

Chapter: Guideline #	Guideline Heading	Relative Importance
1:1	Provide Useful Content	5
1:2	Establish User Requirements	5
1:3	Understand and Meet User's Expectations	5
1:4	Involve Users in Establishing User Requirements	5
2:1	Do Not Display Unsolicited Windows or Graphics	5
3:1	Comply with Section 508	5
3:2	Design Forms for Users Using Assistive Technology	5
3:3	Do Not Use Color Alone to Convey Information	5
5:1	Enable Access to the Homepage	5
5:2	Show All Major Options on the Homepage	5
5:3	Create a Positive First Impression of Your Site	5
6:1	Avoid Cluttered Displays	5
6:2	Place Important Items Consistently	5
6:3	Place Important Items at Top Center	5
8:1	Eliminate Horizontal Scrolling	5
9:1	Use Clear Category Labels	5
10:1	Use Meaningful Link Labels	5
13:1	Distinguish Required and Optional Data Entry Fields	5
13:2	Label Pushbuttons Clearly	5
15:1	Make Action Sequences Clear	5
16:1	Organize Information Clearly	5
16:2	Facilitate Scanning	5
16:3	Ensure that Necessary Information is Displayed	5
17:1	Ensure Usable Search Results	5
17:2	Design Search Engines to Search the Entire Site	5
1:5	Set and State Goals	4
1:6	Focus on Performance Before Preference	4
1:7	Consider Many User Interface Issues	4
1:8	Be Easily Found in the Top 30	4
2:2	Increase Web Site Credibility	4
2:3	Standardize Task Sequences	4
2:4	Reduce the User's Workload	4
2:5	Design For Working Memory Limitations	4
2:6	Minimize Page Download Time	4
2:7	Warn of 'Time Outs'	4
2:8	Display Information in a Directly Usable Format	4
2:9	Format Information for Reading and Printing	4
2:10	Provide Feedback when Users Must Wait	4
2:11	Inform Users of Long Download Times	4
2:12	Develop Pages that Will Print Properly	4
3:4	Enable Users to Skip Repetitive Navigation Links	4
3:5	Provide Text Equivalents for Non-Text Elements	4

Guidelines Ranked by **Relative Importance**

Chapter: Guideline #	Guideline Heading	Relative Importance
3:6	Test Plug-Ins and Applets for Accessibility	4
4:1	Design for Common Browsers	4
4:2	Account for Browser Differences	4
4:3	Design for Popular Operating Systems	4
4:4	Design for User's Typical Connection Speed	4
5:4	Communicate the Web Site's Value and Purpose	4
5:5	Limit Prose Text on the Homepage	4
5:6	Ensure the Homepage Looks like a Homepage	4
6:4	Structure for Easy Comparison	4
6:5	Establish Level of Importance	4
6:6	Optimize Display Density	4
6:7	Align Items on a Page	4
7:1	Provide Navigational Options	4
7:2	Differentiate and Group Navigation Elements	4
7:3	Use a Clickable 'List of Contents' on Long Pages	4
7:4	Provide Feedback on Users' Location	4
7:5	Place Primary Navigation Menus in the Left Panel	4
9:2	Provide Descriptive Page Titles	4
9:3	Use Descriptive Headings Liberally	4
9:4	Use Unique and Descriptive Headings	4
9:5	Highlight Critical Data	4
9:6	Use Descriptive Row and Column Headings	4
10:2	Link to Related Content	4
10:3	Match Link Names with Their Destination Pages	4
10:4	Avoid Misleading Cues to Click	4
10:5	Repeat Important Links	4
10:6	Use Text for Links	4
10:7	Designate Used Links	4
11:1	Use Black Text on Plain, High-Contrast Backgrounds	4
11:2	Format Common Items Consistently	4
11:3	Use Mixed-Case for Prose Text	4
11:4	Ensure Visual Consistency	4
12:1	Order Elements to Maximize User Performance	4
12:2	Place Important Items at Top of the List	4
12:3	Format Lists to Ease Scanning	4
12:4	Display Related Items in Lists	4
13:3	Label Data Entry Fields Consistently	4
13:4	Do Not Make User-Entered Codes Case Sensitive	4
13:5	Label Data Entry Fields Clearly	4
13:6	Minimize User Data Entry	4
14:1	Use Simple Background Images	4
14:2	Label Clickable Images	4

Guidelines Ranked by **Relative Importance**

Chapter: Guideline #	Guideline Heading	Relative Importance
14:3	Ensure that Images Do Not Slow Downloads	4
14:4	Use Video, Animation, and Audio Meaningfully	4
14:5	Include Logos	4
14:6	Graphics Should Not Look like Banner Ads	4
14:7	Limit Large Images Above the Fold	4
14:8	Ensure Web Site Images Convey Intended Messages	4
15:2	Avoid Jargon	4
15:3	Use Familiar Words	4
15:4	Define Acronyms and Abbreviations	4
15:5	Use Abbreviations Sparingly	4
15:6	Use Mixed Case with Prose	4
15:7	Limit the Number of Words and Sentences	4
16:4	Group Related Elements	4
16:5	Minimize the Number of Clicks or Pages	4
17:3	Make Upper- and Lowercase Search Terms Equivalent	4
17:4	Provide a Search Option on Each Page	4
17:5	Design Search Around Users' Terms	4
18:1	Use an Iterative Design Approach	4
1:9	Set Usability Goals	3
2:13	Do Not Require Users to Multitask While Reading	3
2:14	Use Users' Terminology in Help Documentation	3
2:15	Provide Printing Options	3
3:7	Ensure that Scripts Allow Accessibility	3
3:8	Provide Equivalent Pages	3
3:9	Provide Client-Side Image Maps	3
3:10	Synchronize Multimedia Elements	3
3:11	Do Not Require Style Sheets	3
4:5	Design for Commonly Used Screen Resolutions	3
5:7	Limit Homepage Length	3
6:8	Use Fluid Layouts	3
6:9	Avoid Scroll Stoppers	3
6:10	Set Appropriate Page Lengths	3
6:11	Use Moderate White Space	3
7:6	Use Descriptive Tab Labels	3
7:7	Present Tabs Effectively	3
9:7	Use Headings in the Appropriate HTML Order	3
10:8	Provide Consistent Clickability Cues	3
10:9	Ensure that Embedded Links are Descriptive	3
10:10	Use 'Pointing-and-Clicking'	3
10:11	Use Appropriate Text Link Lengths	3
10:12	Indicate Internal vs. External Links	3
10:13	Clarify Clickable Regions on Images	3

Guidelines Ranked by **Relative Importance**

Chapter: Guideline #	Guideline Heading	Relative Importance
10:14	Link to Supportive Information	3
11:5	Use Bold Text Sparingly	3
11:6	Use Attention-Attracting Features when Appropriate	3
11:7	Use Familiar Fonts	3
11:8	Use at Least a 12-Point Font	3
12:5	Introduce Each List	3
12:6	Use Static Menus	3
13:7	Put Labels Close to Data Entry Fields	3
13:8	Allow Users to See Their Entered Data	3
13:9	Use Radio Buttons for Mutually Exclusive Selections	3
13:10	Use Familiar Widgets	3
13:11	Anticipate Typical User Errors	3
13:12	Partition Long Data Items	3
13:13	Use a Single Data Entry Method	3
13:14	Prioritize Pushbuttons	3
13:15	Use Check Boxes to Enable Multiple Selections	3
13:16	Label Units of Measurement	3
13:17	Do Not Limit Viewable List Box Options	3
13:18	Display Default Values	3
14:9	Limit the Use of Images	3
14:10	Include Actual Data with Data Graphics	3
14:11	Display Monitoring Information Graphically	3
15:8	Limit Prose Text on Navigation pages	3
15:9	Use Active Voice	3
15:10	Write Instructions in the Affirmative	3
15:11	Make First Sentences Descriptive	3
16:6	Design Quantitative Content for Quick Understanding	3
16:7	Display Only Necessary Information	3
16:8	Format Information for Multiple Audiences	3
17:6	Allow Simple Searches	3
17:7	Notify Users when Multiple Search Options Exist	3
17:8	Include Hints to Improve Search Performance	3
18:2	Solicit Test Participants' Comments	3
18:3	Evaluate Web Sites Before and After Making Changes	3
18:4	Prioritize Tasks	3
18:5	Distinguish Between Frequency and Severity	3
18:6	Select the Right Number of Participants	3
1:10	Use Parallel Design	2
2:16	Provide Assistance to Users	2
3:12	Provide Frame Titles	2
3:13	Avoid Screen Flicker	2
5:8	Announce Changes to a Web Site	2

Guidelines Ranked by **Relative Importance**

Chapter: Guideline #	Guideline Heading	Relative Importance
5:9	Attend to Homepage Panel Width	2
6:12	Choose Appropriate Line Lengths	2
7:8	Keep Navigation-Only Pages Short	2
7:9	Use Appropriate Menu Types	2
7:10	Use Site Maps	2
8:2	Facilitate Rapid Scrolling While Reading	2
8:3	Use Scrolling Pages for Reading Comprehension	2
8:4	Use Paging Rather Than Scrolling	2
8:5	Scroll Fewer Screenfuls	2
9:8	Provide Users with Good Ways to Reduce Options	2
11:9	Color-Coding and Instructions	2
11:10	Emphasize Importance	2
11:11	Highlighting Information	2
12:7	Start Numbered Items at One	2
12:8	Use Appropriate List Style	2
13:19	Place Cursor in First Data Entry Field	2
13:20	Ensure that Double-Clicking Will Not Cause Problems	2
13:21	Use Open Lists to Select One from Many	2
13:22	Use Data Entry Fields to Speed Performance	2
13:23	Use a Minimum of Two Radio Buttons	2
13:24	Provide Auto-Tabbing Functionality	2
14:12	Introduce Animation	2
14:13	Emulate Real-World Objects	2
14:14	Use Thumbnail Images to Preview Larger Images	2
16:9	Use Color for Grouping	2
17:9	Provide Search Templates	2
18:7	Use the Appropriate Prototyping Technology	2
18:8	Use Inspection Evaluation Results Cautiously	2
18:9	Recognize the 'Evaluator Effect'	2
1:11	Use Personas	1
6:13	Use Frames When Functions Must Remain Accessible	1
7:11	Use 'Glosses' to Assist Navigation	1
7:12	Breadcrumb Navigation	1
12:9	Capitalize First Letter of First Word in Lists	1
13:25	Minimize Use of the Shift Key	1
14:15	Use Images to Facilitate Learning	1
14:16	Using Photographs of People	1
18:10	Apply Automatic Evaluation Methods	1
18:11	Use Cognitive Walkthroughs Cautiously	1
18:12	Choosing Laboratory vs. Remote Testing	1
18:13	Use Severity Ratings Cautiously	1

Appendices

Guidelines Ranked by **Strength of Evidence**

Chapter: Guideline #	Guideline Heading	Relative Importance
1:1	Provide Useful Content	5
2:3	Standardize Task Sequences	5
2:5	Design for Working Memory Limitations	5
6:7	Align Items on a Page	5
9:3	Use Descriptive Headings Liberally	5
11:1	Use Black Text on Plain, High-Contrast Backgrounds	5
11:6	Use Attention-Attracting Features when Appropriate	5
11:7	Use Familiar Fonts	5
11:10	Emphasize Importance	5
12:1	Order Elements to Maximize User Performance	5
13:22	Use Data Entry Fields to Speed Performance	5
14:1	Use Simple Background Images	5
14:4	Use Video, Animation, and Audio Meaningfully	5
14:15	Use Images to Facilitate Learning	5
15:6	Use Mixed Case with Prose	5
16:4	Group Related Elements	5
16:9	Use Color for Grouping	5
18:1	Use an Iterative Design Approach	5
1:2	Establish User Requirements	4
1:8	Be Easily Found in the Top 30	4
1:10	Use Parallel Design	4
2:6	Minimize Page Download Time	4
2:10	Provide Feedback When Users Must Wait	4
2:13	Do Not Require Users to Multitask While Reading	4
3:3	Do Not Use Color Alone to Convey Information	4
5:3	Create a Positive First Impression of Your Site	4
5:6	Ensure the Homepage Looks like a Homepage	4
6:2	Place Important Items Consistently	4
6:3	Place Important Items at Top Center	4
6:4	Structure for Easy Comparison	4
6:9	Avoid Scroll Stoppers	4
6:11	Use Moderate White Space	4
6:12	Choose Appropriate Line Lengths	4
6:13	Use Frames when Functions Must Remain Accessible	4
7:8	Keep Navigation-Only Pages Short	4
7:9	Use Appropriate Menu Types	4
7:10	Use Site Maps	4
8:1	Eliminate Horizontal Scrolling	4
8:2	Facilitate Rapid Scrolling While Reading	4
8:3	Use Scrolling Pages for Reading Comprehension	4
8:4	Use Paging Rather Than Scrolling	4
9:1	Use Clear Category Labels	4

Guidelines Ranked by **Strength of Evidence**

Chapter: Guideline #	Guideline Heading	Relative Importance
10:1	Use Meaningful Link Labels	4
10:3	Match Link Names with Their Destination Pages	4
10:5	Repeat Important Links	4
10:6	Use Text for Links	4
10:9	Ensure that Embedded Links are Descriptive	4
11:4	Ensure Visual Consistency	4
11:8	Use at Least 12-Point Font	4
11:9	Color-Coding and Instructions	4
12:2	Place Important Items at Top of the List	4
12:3	Format Lists to Ease Scanning	4
12:4	Display Related Items in Lists	4
12:5	Introduce Each List	4
12:8	Use Appropriate List Style	4
13:9	Use Radio Buttons for Mutually Exclusive Selections	4
13:13	Use a Single Data Entry Method	4
13:25	Minimize Use of the Shift Key	4
14:2	Label Clickable Images	4
14:3	Ensure that Images Do Not Slow Downloads	4
14:5	Include Logos	4
14:6	Graphics Should Not Look like Banner Ads	4
14:10	Include Actual Data with Data Graphics	4
14:11	Display Monitoring Information Graphically	4
14:13	Emulate Real-World Objects	4
15:1	Make Action Sequences Clear	4
15:2	Avoid Jargon	4
15:7	Limit the Number of Words and Sentences	4
15:9	Use Active Voice	4
15:11	Make First Sentences Descriptive	4
16:1	Organize Information Clearly	4
16:2	Facilitate Scanning	4
16:7	Display Only Necessary Information	4
18:2	Solicit Test Participants' Comments	4
18:6	Select the Right Number of Participants	4
18:8	Use Inspection Evaluation Results Cautiously	4
18:9	Recognize the 'Evaluator Effect'	4
18:11	Use Cognitive Walkthroughs Cautiously	4
18:12	Choosing Laboratory vs. Remote Testing	4
18:13	Use Severity Ratings Cautiously	4
1:3	Understand and Meet User's Expectations	3
1:4	Involve Users in Establishing User Requirements	3
1:6	Focus on Performance Before Preference	3
1:7	Consider Many User Interface Issues	3

Guidelines Ranked by **Strength of Evidence**

Chapter: Guideline #	Guideline Heading	Relative Importance
1:9	Set Usability Goals	3
2:1	Do Not Display Unsolicited Windows or Graphics	3
2:2	Increase Web Site Credibility	3
2:4	Reduce the User's Workload	3
2:7	Warn of 'Time Outs'	3
2:8	Display Information in a Directly Usable Format	3
2:9	Format Information for Reading and Printing	3
2:11	Inform Users of Long Download Times	3
2:14	Use Users' Terminology in Help Documentation	3
2:16	Provide Assistance to Users	3
3:9	Provide Client-Side Image Maps	3
5:1	Enable Access to the Homepage	3
5:4	Communicate the Web Site's Value and Purpose	3
5:5	Limit Prose Text on the Homepage	3
5:9	Attend to Homepage Panel Width	3
6:1	Avoid Cluttered Displays	3
6:5	Establish Level of Importance	3
6:6	Optimize Display Density	3
6:8	Use Fluid Layouts	3
6:10	Set Appropriate Page Lengths	3
7:2	Differentiate and Group Navigation Elements	3
7:3	Use a Clickable 'List of Contents' on Long Pages	3
7:5	Place Primary Navigation Menus in the Left Panel	3
7:6	Use Descriptive Tab Labels	3
7:7	Present Tabs Effectively	3
7:12	Breadcrumb Navigation	3
9:4	Use Unique and Descriptive Headings	3
9:5	Highlight Critical Data	3
9:6	Use Descriptive Row and Column Headings	3
10:10	Use 'Pointing-and-Clicking'	3
10:11	Use Appropriate Text Link Lengths	3
10:13	Clarify Clickable Regions of Images	3
11:3	Use Mixed-Case for Prose Text	3
11:5	Use Bold Text Sparingly	3
11:11	Highlighting Information	3
12:6	Use Static Menus	3
13:1	Distinguish Required and Optional Data Entry Fields	3
13:3	Label Data Entry Fields Consistently	3
13:5	Label Data Entry Fields Clearly	3
13:6	Minimize User Data Entry	3
13:8	Allow Users to See Their Entered Data	3
13:10	Use Familiar Widgets	3

Guidelines Ranked by **Strength of Evidence**

Chapter: Guideline #	Guideline Heading	Relative Importance
13:14	Prioritize Pushbuttons	3
13:15	Use Check Boxes to Enable Multiple Selections	3
13:16	Label Units of Measurement	3
13:17	Do Not Limit Viewable List Box Options	3
13:24	Provide Auto-Tabbing Functionality	3
14:7	Limit Large Images Above the Fold	3
14:8	Ensure Web Site Images Convey Intended Messages	3
14:12	Introduce Animation	3
15:3	Use Familiar Words	3
15:8	Limit Prose Text on Navigation Pages	3
16:5	Minimize the Number of Clicks or Pages	3
16:6	Design Quantitative Content for Quick Understanding	3
16:8	Format Information for Multiple Audiences	3
17:1	Ensure Usable Search Results	3
17:2	Design Search Engines to Search the Entire Site	3
17:5	Design Search Around Users' Terms	3
17:7	Notify Users When Multiple Search Options Exist	3
17:8	Include Hints to Improve Search Performance	3
17:9	Provide Search Templates	3
18:3	Evaluate Web Sites Before and After Making Changes	3
18:5	Distinguish Between Frequency and Severity	3
18:7	Use the Appropriate Prototyping Technology	3
18:10	Apply Automatic Evaluation Methods	3
1:5	Set and State Goals	2
1:11	Use Personas	2
2:12	Develop Pages that Will Print Properly	2
2:15	Provide Printing Options	2
3:1	Comply with Section 508	2
3:2	Design Forms for Users Using Assistive Technologies	2
3:4	Enable Users to Skip Repetitive Navigation Links	2
3:5	Provide Text Equivalents for Non-Text Elements	2
3:6	Test Plug-Ins and Applets for Accessibility	2
3:7	Ensure that Scripts Allow Accessibility	2
3:8	Provide Equivalent Pages	2
3:10	Synchronize Multimedia Elements	2
3:12	Provide Frame Titles	2
4:1	Design for Common Browsers	2
4:2	Account for Browser Differences	2
4:3	Design for Popular Operating Systems	2
4:4	Design for User's Typical Connection Speed	2
4:5	Design for Commonly Used Screen Resolutions	2
5:2	Show All Major Options on the Homepage	2

Guidelines Ranked by **Strength of Evidence**

Chapter: Guideline #	Guideline Heading	Relative Importance
5:7	Limit Homepage Length	2
5:8	Announce Changes to a Web Site	2
7:1	Provide Navigational Options	2
7:4	Provide Feedback on Users' Location	2
7:11	Use 'Glosses' to Assist Navigation	2
8:5	Scroll Fewer Screenfuls	2
9:2	Provide Descriptive Page Titles	2
9:7	Use Headings in the Appropriate HTML Order	2
9:8	Provide Users with Good Ways to Reduce Options	2
10:2	Link to Related Content	2
10:4	Avoid Misleading Cues to Click	2
10:7	Designate Used Links	2
10:8	Provide Consistent Clickability Cues	2
10:12	Indicate Internal vs. External Links	2
10:14	Link to Supportive Information	2
11:2	Format Common Items Consistently	2
12:7	Start Numbered Items at One	2
12:9	Capitalize First Letter of First Word in Lists	2
13:2	Label Pushbuttons Clearly	2
13:4	Do Not Make User-Entered Codes Case Sensitive	2
13:7	Put Labels Close to Data Entry Fields	2
13:11	Anticipate Typical User Errors	2
13:12	Partition Long Data Items	2
13:18	Display Default Values	2
13:19	Place Cursor in First Data Entry Field	2
13:20	Ensure that Double-Clicking Will Not Cause Problems	2
13:21	Use Open Lists to Select One from Many	2
13:23	Use a Minimum of Two Radio Buttons	2
14:9	Limit the Use of Images	2
14:14	Use Thumbnail Images to Preview Larger Images	2
14:16	Using Photographs of People	2
15:4	Define Acronyms and Abbreviations	2
15:5	Use Abbreviations Sparingly	2
15:10	Write Instructions in the Affirmative	2
16:3	Ensure that Necessary Information is Displayed	2
17:3	Make Upper- and Lowercase Search Terms Equivalent	2
17:4	Provide a Search Option on Each Page	2
17:6	Allow Simple Searches	2
18:4	Prioritize Tasks	2
3:11	Do Not Require Style Sheets	1
3:13	Avoid Screen Flicker	1

Sources

Adamson, P.J. & Wallace, F.L. (1997). *A comparison between consistent and inconsistent graphical user interfaces.* Jacksonville: University of Northern Florida, Department of Computer and Information Sciences.

Adkisson, H.P. (2002). Identifying de-facto standards for e-commerce Web sites. *Proceedings of the IEEE International Professional Communication Conference,* 22-45.

Ahlstrom, V. & Longo, K. (2001). *Human factors design guide update* (Report number DOT/FAA/CT-96/01): *A revision to chapter 8 - computer human interface guidelines.* Retrieved November 2005, from http://acb220.tc.faa.gov/technotes/dot_faa_ct-01_08.pdf.

Ahmadi, M. (2000, October). *An evaluation of an instant messaging pilot program.* National Cancer Institute, Communications Technologies Branch.

Allinson, L. & Hammond, N. (1999). A learning support environment: The hitch-hiker's guide. In R. McAleese (Ed.), *Hypertext: Theory into Practice* (pp. 53-63). Exeter, UK: Intellect Books.

Amento, B., Hill, W., Terveen, L., Hix, D., & Ju, P. (1999). An empirical evaluation of user interfaces for topic management of web sites. *Proceedings of CHI'99,* 552-559.

Andre, T., Hartson, R. & Williges, R. (2003). Determining the effectiveness of the Usability Problem Inspector. *Human Factors, 45*(3), 455-482.

Asher, S.R. (1980). Topic interest and children's reading comprehension. In R.J. Sprio, D.C. Bruce, & W.F. Brewer (Eds.), *Theoretical Issues in Reading Comprehension* (pp. 525-534). Hillsdale, NJ: Lawrence Erlbaum.

Ashworth, C.A. & Hamilton, D.B. (1997, June). A case for frames. *Proceedings of the 3rd Conference on Human Factors and the Web.*

Ausubel, D.D. (1968). *Educational Psychology: A Cognitive View.* New York: Holt, Rinehart and Winston.

Baca, B. & Cassidy, A. (1999). Intranet development and design that works. *Human Factors and Ergonomics Society Annual Meeting Proceedings,* 777-790.

Baddeley, A. (1986). *Working Memory.* Cambridge: Cambridge University Press.

Baddeley, A. (1986). Working Memory. *Science,* 255, 556-559.

Badre, A.N. (2002). *Shaping Web Usability:* Interaction Design in Context. Boston, MA: Addison Wesley Professional.

Bailey, G.D. (1993). Iterative methodology and designer training in human-computer interface design. *Proceedings of InterCHI'93,* 198-205.

Bailey, R.W. & Koyani, S.J. (2004). Searching vs. linking on the web: A summary of the research. Health and Human Services Technical Report.

Bailey, R.W. (1983). *Human Error in Computer Systems.* Englewood Cliffs, NJ: Prentice-Hall.

Bailey, R.W. (1993). Selecting items in a graphical user interface. *User Interface Update-*1993.

Bailey, R.W. (1996). *Human performance engineering: Designing high quality professional user interfaces for computer products, applications and systems* (3rd ed.). Englewood Cliffs, NJ: Prentice-Hall.

Bailey, R.W. (2000a, September). Reducing reliance on superstition. Retrieved November 2005, from http://www.webusability.com.

Bailey, R.W. (2000b, October). Link affordance. Retrieved November 2005, from http://www.webusability.com.

Bailey, R.W. (2000c, December). Calculating the number of test subjects. Retrieved May 2003, from http://www.webusability.com.

Bailey, R.W. (2000d). The usability of punched ballots. Retrieved November 2005, from http://www.webusability.com.

Bailey, R.W. (2001). Reading from small point sizes. *User Interface* Update-2001.

Bailey, R.W. (2002, December). Optimal line length: Research supporting how line length affects usability. Retrieved November 2005, from http://webusability.com.

Bailey, R.W. (2003, July). 'Concurrent' vs. 'retrospective' comments. Retrieved November 2005, from http://webusability.com.

Bailey, R.W. (2005, October). Judging the severity of usability issues on web sites: This doesn't work. Retrieved November 2005, from http://usability.gov/pubs/102005news.html.

Bailey, R.W., Allen, R.W., & Raiello, P. (1992, October). Usability testing vs. heuristic evaluation: A head-to-head comparison. *Human Factors and Ergonomics Society Annual Meeting Proceedings.*

Bailey, R.W., Koyani, S., & Nall, J. (2000, September 7). Usability testing of several health information Web sites, *National Cancer Institute Technical Report.* Bethesda, MD.

Bailey, R.W. and Wolfson, C. (2005), FirstGov usability test results, Computer Psychology Technical Report, May.

Baldwin, R.S., Peleg-Bruckner, Z., & McClintock, A. (1985). Effects of topic interest and prior knowledge on reading comprehension, *Reading Research Quarterly,* 220(4), 497-504.

Ball, L.J., Evans, J., & Dennis, I. (1994). Cognitive processes in engineering design: A longitudinal study. *Ergonomics,* 37(11), 1753-1786.

Bandos, J. & Resnick, M.L. (2004). The effects of semantic and syntactic instruction on users performance and satisfaction in search user interface design. *Proceedings of the Human Factors and Ergonomics Society Annual Meeting.*

Barber, R.E. & Lucas, H.C. (1983). System Response time, operator productivity, and job satisfaction. *CACM,* 26(11), 972-986.

Barki, H. & Hartwick, J. (1991). User participation and user involvement in information system development. *Proceedings of the 24th Annual Hawaii International Conference on System Sciences,* 487-492.

Baroudi, J.J., Olson, M.H., & Ives, B. (1986). An empirical study of the impact of user involvement on system usage and information satisfaction. *Communications of the ACM,* 29(3), 232-238.

Bayles, M. & Bernard, M. (1999). Searching the Web: Who Uses the Advanced Search Options? *Usability News*, 1.2. Retrieved November 2005, from http://psychology.wichita.edu/surl/usabilitynews/1s/searching.htm.

Bayles, M.E. (2002). Designing online banner advertisements: Should we animate? *Proceedings of CHI* 2002, 363-366.

Benson, P. (1985). Writing visually: Design considerations in technical publications. *Technical Communication*, 32(4), 35-39.

Benway, J.P. (1998). Banner blindness: The irony of attention grabbing on the World Wide Web. *Human Factors and Ergonomics Society Annual Meeting Proceedings*, 463-467.

Bernard, M. & Hull, S. (2002). Where should you put the links? Comparing embedded and framed/non-framed links. Proceedings of CybErg 2002, *The Third International Cyberspace Conference on Ergonomics.*

Bernard, M. & Larsen, L. (2001). What is the best layout for multiple-column Web pages? *Usability News*, 3.2.

Bernard, M. (2001). Developing schemas for the location of common Web objects. *Usability News*, 3.1. Retrieved November 2005, from http://psychology.wichita.edu/surl/usabilitynews/3W/web_object.htm.

Bernard, M. (2002). Examining User Expectations for the Location of Common E-Commerce Web Objects. *Usability News*, 4.1. Retrieved November 2005, from http://psychology.wichita.edu/surl/usabilitynews/41/web_object-ecom.htm.

Bernard, M., Baker, R., & Fernandez, M. (2002). Paging vs. scrolling: Looking for the best way to present search results. *Usability News*, 4.1. Retrieved November 2005, from http://psychology.wichita.edu/surl/usabilitynews/41/paging.htm.

Bernard, M., Hull, S., & Drake, D. (2001). Where should you put the links? A Comparison of Four Locations. *Usability News*, 3.2. Retrieved November 2005, from http://psychology.wichita.edu/surl/usabilitynews/3S/links.htm.

Bernard, M. & Larsen, L. (2001). What is the best layout for multiple-column Web pages? *Usability News*, 3.2. Retrieved November 2005, from http://psychology.wichita.edu/surl/usabilitynews/3S/layout.htm.

Bernard, M., Liao, C., & Mills, M. (2001a). Determining the best online font for older adults. *Usability News*, 3.1. Retrieved November 2005, from http://psychology.wichita.edu/surl/usabilitynews/3W/fontSR.htm.

Bernard, M., Liao, C.H., & Mills, M. (2001b). The effects of font type and size on the legibility and reading time of online text by older adults. *Proceedings of CHI* 2002, 175-176. Retrieved November 2005, from http://psychology.wichita.edu/hci/projects/elderly.pdf.

Bernard, M., Lida, B., Riley, S., Hackler, T., & Janzen, K. (2002). A comparison of popular online fonts: Which size and type is best? *Usability News*, 4.1. Retrieved November 2005, from http://psychology.wichita.edu/surl/usabilitynews/41/onlinetext.htm.

Bernard, M. & Mills, M. (2000). So, what size and type of font should I use on my Web site? *Usability News*, 2.2. Retrieved November 2005, from http://psychology.wichita.edu/surl/usabilitynews/2S/font.htm.

Bernard, M., Mills, M., Peterson, M., & Storrer, K. (2001). A comparison of popular online fonts: Which is best and when? *Usability News*, 3.2. Retrieved November 2005, from http://psychology.wichita.edu/surl/usabilitynews/3S/font.htm.

Bieber, M. (1997). Enhancing information comprehension through hypertext. In C. Nicholas & J. Mayfield (Eds), *Intelligent Hypertext: Advanced Techniques for the World Wide Web* (pp. 1-11). Berlin: Springer-Verlag.

Billingsley, P.A. (1982). Navigation through hierarchical menu structures: Does it help to have a map? *Human Factors and Ergonomics Society Annual Meeting Proceedings*, 103-107.

Blackmon, M.H., Polson, P.G., Kitajima, M., & Lewis, C. (2002, April). Cognitive walkthrough for the web. *Proceedings of CHI* 2002, 463-470.

Booher, H.R. (1975). Relative comprehensibility of pictorial information and printed words in proceduralized instructions. *Human Factors*, 17(3), 266-277.

Bouch, A., Kuchinsky, A., & Bhatti, N. (2000). Quality is in the eye of the beholder: Meeting users' requirements for internet quality of service. *Proceedings of CHI 2000*, 297-304.

Bouma, H. (1980). Visual reading processes and the quality of text displays. In E. Granjean & E. Viglinai (Eds.), *Ergonomic Aspects of Visual Display Terminals* (pp. 101-114). London: Taylor and Francis Ltd.

Bovair, S., Kieras, D.E., & Polson, P.G. (1990). The acquisition and performance of text-editing skill: A cognitive complexity analysis. *Human-Computer Interaction*, 5(1), 1-48.

Bowers, V.A. & Snyder, H.I. (1990). Concurrent versus retrospective verbal protocol for comparing window usability. *Proceedings of the Human Factors and Ergonomics Society 46th Annual Meeting*, 1270-1274.

Boyarski, D., Neuwirth, C., Forlizzi, J., & Regli, S.H. (1998). A study of fonts designed for screen display. *Proceedings of CHI'98*, 87-94.

Boyntoin, R.M., & Bush, W.R. (1956). Recognition of forms against a complex background. *Journal of the Optical Society of America*, 46, 759-764.

Bradley, R.F. & Johnk, L.D. (1995). Replacing a networking interface 'from hell.' *Proceedings of CHI'95*, 538-545.

Brajnik, G. (2000). Automatic web usability evaluation: What needs to be done? *Proceedings of the 6th Conference on Human Factors and the Web*. Retrieved November 2005, from http://www.tri.sbc.com/hfweb/brajnik/hfweb-brajnik.html.

Bransford, J. & Johnson, M. (1972). Contextual prerequisites for understanding: Some investigations of comprehension and recall. *Journal of Verbal Learning and Verbal Behavior*, 11, 717-726.

Bransford, J. & Johnson, M. (1973). Consideration of some problems of comprehension. In W. Chase (Ed.), *Visual Information Processing* (pp. 383-438). New York: Academic Press.

Breland, K. & Breland, M.K. (1944). Legibility of newspaper headlines printed in capitals and in lower case. *Journal of Applied Psychology*, 28, 117-120.

Brinck, T. & Hofer, E. (2002, April). Automatically evaluating the usability of web sites. *Proceedings of CHI* 2002, Extended Abstracts, 906-907.

Brinck, T., Gergle, D., & Wood, S.D. (2002). *Designing Web sites that work: Usability for the Web*. San Francisco: Morgan Kaufmann.

Broadbent, D.E. (1975). The magic number seven after fifteen years. In A. Kennedy & A. Wilkes (Eds.), *Studies in Long-Term Memory* (pp. 3-18). New York: Wiley.

Brown, J. (1958). Some tests of the decay theory of immediate memory. *Quarterly Journal of Experimental Psychology*, 10, 12-21.

Bruce, V., & Green, P.R. (1990). Visual Perception: *Physiology, Psychology and Ecology* (2nd ed.). Hillsdale, NJ: Lawrence Erlbaum.

Brush, A.J., Ames, M., & Davis, J. (2004). A comparison of synchronous remote and local usability studies for an expert interface. *CHI 2004 Proceedings*, 1179-1183. Retrieved November 2005, from http://research.microsoft.com/~ajbrush/papers/BrushRemoteUsabi

Buller, D.B., Woodall, W.G., Zimmerman, D.E., Heimendinger, J., Rogers, E.M., Slater, M.D., et al. (2001). Formative research activities to provide Web-based nutrition education to adults in the upper Rio Grande Valley. *Family and Community Health* 24(3), 1-12.

Byrne, M.D., Anderson, J.R., Douglass, S., & Matessa, M. (1999). Eye tracking the visual search of click-down menus. *Proceedings of CHI'99*, 402-409.

Byrne, M.D., John, B.E., Wehrle, N.S., & Crow, D.C. (1999). The tangled web we wove: A taskonomy of WWW use. *Proceedings of CHI'99*, 544-551.

Cakir, A., Hart, D.J., & Stewart, T.F.M. (1980). *Visual Display Terminals*, England: Wiley.

Campbell, C.S. & Maglio, P.P. (1999). Facilitating navigation in information spaces: Road signs on the World Wide Web. *International Journal of Human-Computer Studies*, 50, 309-327.

Campbell, D.T. & Stanley, J.C. (1963). *Experimental and Quasi-Experimental Design for Research*. Chicago: Rand McNally.

Capra, M.G. (2002). Contemporaneous versus retrospective user-reported critical incidents in usability evaluation. Proceedings of the *Human Factors and Ergonomics Society 46th Annual Meeting*, 1973-1977.

Card, S.K., Moran, T.P., & Newell, A. (1980a). Computer text editing: An information processing analysis of a routine cognitive skill. *Cognitive Psychology*, 12, 32-74.

Card, S.K., Moran, T.P., & Newell, A. (1980b). The keystroke-level model for user performance time with interactive systems. *Communications of the ACM*, 23(7), 396-410.

Card, S.K., Moran, T.P., & Newell, A. (1983). *The Psychology of Human-Computer Interaction*. Hillsdale, NJ: Erlbaum.

Card, S.K., Pirolli, P., Van Der Wege, M., Morrison, J., Reeder, R., Schraedley, P. et al. (2001). Information scent as a driver of web behavior graphs: Results of a protocol analysis method for web usability. *Proceedings of CHI 2001*, 498-505.

Carroll, J.M. (1990). *The Nurnberg Funnel: Designing Minimalist Instruction for Practical Computer Skill*. Cambridge, MA: MIT Press.

Carter, R. (1982). Visual search with color. *Journal of Experimental Psychology: Human Perception and Performance*, 8, 127-136.

Casner, S.M. & Larkin, J.H. (1989, August). Cognitive efficiency considerations for good graphic design. *Proceedings of the Eleventh Annual Conference of the Cognitive Science Society.* Ann Arbor, Michigan.

Catani, M.B. & Biers, D.W. (1998). Usability evaluation and prototype fidelity: Users and usability professionals. *Human Factors and Ergonomics Society Annual Meeting Proceedings,* 1331-1335.

Celsi, R. & Olson, J. (1988). The role of involvement in attention and comprehension processes. *Journal of Consumer Research,* 15(2), 210-224.

Chaparro, B.S. & Bernard, M.L. (2001). Finding information on the Web: Does the amount of whitespace really matter? Proceedings of the Tenth Annual Usability Professionals' Association Conference.

Chaparro, B.S., Minnaert, G., & Phipps, C. (2000). Limitations of using mouse-over with menu item selection. *Human Factors and Ergonomics Society Annual Meeting Proceedings.*

Chen, C. & Yu, Y. (2000). Empirical studies of information visualization: A meta-analysis. *International Journal of Human-Computer Studies,* 53, 851-866.

Chervak, S., Drury, C.G., & Ouellette, J.P. (1996). Simplified English for aircraft work cards. *Human Factors and Ergonomics Society Annual Meeting Proceedings,* 303-307.

Chi, E., Pirolli, P., & Pitkow, J. (2000). The scent of a site: A system for analyzing and predicting information scent, usage, and usability of a web site. *Proceedings of CHI 2000,* 161-168.

Chin, D.N. (2001). Empirical evaluation of user models and user-adapted systems. *User Modeling and User-Adapted Interaction,* 11, 181-194.

Chisholm, W., Vanderheiden, G., & Jacobs, I., Eds. (1999a). Web Content Accessibility Guidelines 1.0. Retrieved November 2005, from http://www.w3.org/TR/WCAG10/, Checkpoint 1.1.

Chisholm, W., Vanderheiden, G., & Jacobs, I., Eds. (1999b). Web Content Accessibility Guidelines 1.0. Retrieved November 2005, from http://www.w3.org/TR/WCAG10/, Checkpoint 1.4.

Chisholm, W., Vanderheiden, G., & Jacobs, I., Eds. (1999c). Web Content Accessibility Guidelines 1.0. Retrieved November 2005, from http://www.w3.org/TR/WCAG10/, Checkpoint 2.1.

Chisholm, W., Vanderheiden, G., & Jacobs, I., Eds. (1999d). Web Content Accessibility Guidelines 1.0. Retrieved November 2005, from http://www.w3.org/TR/WCAG10/, Checkpoint 5.1.

Chisholm, W., Vanderheiden, G., & Jacobs, I., Eds. (1999e). Web Content Accessibility Guidelines 1.0. Retrieved November 2005, from http://www.w3.org/TR/WCAG10/, Checkpoint 11.4.

Chisholm, W., Vanderheiden, G., & Jacobs, I., Eds. (1999f). Web Content Accessibility Guidelines 1.0. Retrieved November 2005, from http://www.w3.org/TR/WCAG10/, Checkpoint 12.1.

Christ, R.E. (1975). Review and analysis of color coding research for visual displays. *Human Factors,* 17(6), 542-570.

Clark, H. & Haviland, S. (1975). Comprehension and the given-new contract. In R. Freedle (Ed.), *Discourse Production and Comprehension* (pp. 1-40). Hillsdale, NJ: Erlbaum.

Coble, J.M., Karat, J., & Kahn, M.G. (1997, March). Maintaining a focus on user requirements throughout the development of clinical workstation software. *Proceedings of CHI'97*, 170-177.

Cockburn, A. & Jones, S. (1996). Which way now? Analysing and easing inadequacies in WWW navigation. *International Journal Human-Computer Studies, 45,* 105-129.

Cockton, G. & Woolrych, A. (2001). Understanding inspection methods: Lessons from an assessment of heuristic evaluation. In A. Blandford, J. Vanderdonckt & P.D. Gray (Eds.), *People and Computers XV: Interaction without Frontiers* (pp. 171-191). Heidelberg: Springer-Verlag.

Cockton, G. & Woolrych, A. (2002). Sale must end: Should discount methods be cleared off HCI's shelves? *Interactions, 9(5),* 13-18.

Cockton, G., Woolrych, A., Hall, L. & Hindmarch, M. (2003). Changing analysts' tunes: The surprising impact of a new instrument for usability inspection method assessment. People and Computers XVII, 145-162.

Cole, B.L. & Jenkins, S.E. (1984). The effect of variability of background elements on the conspicuity of objects. *Vision Research, 24,* 261-270.

Coney, M.B. & Steehouder, M. (2000). Role playing on the Web: Guidelines for designing and evaluating personas online. *Technical Communication, 47(3),* 327-340.

Cooper, A. (1999). *The inmates are running the asylum: Why high-tech products drive us crazy and how to restore the sanity.* Indianapolis: Sams.

Covi, L.M. & Ackerman, M.S. (1995, August). Such easy-to-use systems! How organizations shape the design and use of online help systems. *Proceedings of Conference on Organizational Computing Systems,* 280-288.

Curry, M.B., McDougall, S., & de Bruijn, O. (1998). The effects of the visual metaphor in determining icon efficacy. *Human Factors and Ergonomics Society Annual Meeting Proceedings,* 1590-1594.

Czaja, S.J., & Sharit, J. (1997). The influence of age and experience on the performance of a data entry task. *Human Factors and Ergonomics Society Annual Meeting Proceedings,* 144-147.

DeRouvray, C. & Couper, M.P. (2002). Designing a strategy for reducing 'no opinion' responses in web-based surveys. *Social Science Computer Review, 20(1),* 3-9.

Desurvire, H., Kondziela, J., & Atwood, M.E., (1992). What is gained and lost when using methods other than empirical testing: Striking a balance. *Proceedings of CHI'92,* 2, 125-126.

Detweiler, M.C. & Omanson, R.C. (1996). *Ameritech Web Page User Interface Standards and Design Guidelines.* Ameritech (now SBC).

Dias, P. & Sousa, A.P. (1997). Understanding navigation and disorientation in hypermedia learning environments. *Journal of Educational Multimedia and Hypermedia,* 6, 173-185.

Dixon, P. (1987). The processing of organizational and component step information in written directions. *Journal of Memory and Language, 26,* 24-35.

Duchnicky, R.L., & Kolers, P.A. (1983). Readability of text scrolled on visual display terminals as a function of window size. *Human Factors, 25,* 683-692.

Dumais, S., Cutrell, E., & Chen, H. (2001). Optimizing search by showing results in context. *Proceedings of CHI 2001, 277-283.*

Dumas, J. (2001). How many participants in a usability test are enough. In R.J. Branaghan (Ed.), *Design by People for People: Essays on Usability* (pp. 173-182). Chicago: Usability Professionals Association.

Dumas, J.S., Molich, R. & Jeffries, R. (2004). Describing usability problems: Are we sending the right message? *Interactions*, 11(4), 24-29.

Dyson, M.C. & Haselgrove, M. (2000). The effects of reading speed and reading patterns on our understanding of text read from screen. *Journal of Research in Reading*, 23(1), 210-233.

Dyson, M.C. & Kipping, G.J. (1998). The effects of line length and method of movement on patterns of reading from screen. *Visible Language*, 32(2), 150-180.

Eberts, R.E. & Schneider, W. (1985). Internalizing the system dynamics for a second-order system. *Human Factors*, 27, 371-393.

Egan, D.E., Remde, J.R., Gomez, L.M., Landauer, T.K., Eberhardt, J., & Lochbaum, C.C. (1989). Formative design-evaluation of SuperBook research contributions. *ACM Transactions on Information Systems*, 7(1), 30-57.

Egan, D.E., Remde, J.R., Landauer, T.K., Lochbaum, C.C. & Gomez, L.M. (1989). Behavioral evaluation and analysis of a hypertext browser. *Proceedings of CHI'89*, 205-210.

Ehret, B.D. (2002). Learning where to look: Location learning in graphical user interfaces. *CHI 2002 Conference Proceedings*, 211-218.

Ellis, R.D. & Kurniawan, S.H. (2000). Increasing the usability of online information for older users: A case study of participatory design. *International Journal of Human-Computer Interaction*, 12(2), 263-276.

Engel, S.E. & Granda, R.E. (1975). *Guidelines for Man/Display Interfaces* (Technical Report TR 00.2720). Poughkeepsie, NY: IBM.

Esperet, E. (1996). Notes on hypertext, cognition, and language. In J.F. Rouet, J.J. Levonen, A. Dillon, & R.J. Spiro (Eds.), *Hypertext and Cognition* (pp. 149-155). Mahwah, NJ: Lawrence Erlbaum.

Evans, M. (1998). *Web Design: An Empiricist's Guide.* Unpublished master's thesis. Seattle: University of Washington. Retrieved May 2003, from http://response. restoration.noaa.gov/webmastr/webdesgn.pdf.

Fakun, D. & Greenough, R.M. (2002). User-interface design heuristics for developing usable industrial hypermedia applications. *Human Factors and Ergonomics in Manufacturing*, 12(2), 127-149.

Fang, X. & Salvendy, G. (1999). Templates for search queries: A user-centered feature for improving web search tools. *International Journal of Human-Computer Interaction*, 11(4), 301-315.

Faraday, P. & Sutcliffe, A. (1997). Designing effective multimedia presentations. *Proceedings of CHI'97*, 272-278.

Faraday, P. & Sutcliffe, A. (1999). Authoring animated web pages using 'contact point.' *Proceedings of CHI'97*, 458-465.

Faraday, P. (2000). Visually critiquing web pages. *Proceedings of the 6th Conference on Human Factors and the Web*. Retrieved November 2005, from http://www.tri.sbc.com/hfweb/faraday/FARADAY.HTM.

Faraday, P. (2001). Attending to web pages. *Proceedings of CHI* 2001, 159-160.

Farkas, D.K. & Farkas, J.B. (2000). Guidelines for designing web navigation. *Technical Communication, 47*(3), 341-358.

Farkas, D.K. (1999). The logical and rhetorical construction of procedural discourse. *Technical Communication, 46*(1), 42-54.

Farris, J.S., Jones, K.S., & Elgin, P.D. (2001). Mental representations of hypermedia: An evaluation of the spatial assumption. *Human Factors and Ergonomics Society Annual Meeting Proceedings*, 1156-1160.

Findlater, M.L. & McGrenere, J. (2004). A comparison of static, adaptive, and adaptable menus. *CHI 2004 Conference Proceedings*, 89-96.

Flower, L., Hayes, J.R., & Swarts, H. (1983). Revising function documents: The scenario principle. In P. Anderson, J. Brockmann, & C. Miller (Eds.), *New Essays in Technical and Scientific Communication: Research, Theory, and Practice* (pp. 41-58). Farmingdale, NY: Baywood.

Fogg, B.J. (2002). Stanford guidelines for web credibility. A research summary from the Stanford Persuasive Technology Lab. Retrieved November 2005, from http://www.webcredibility.org/guidelines/.

Fogg, B.J. Marshall, J., Laraki, O., Osipovich, A., Varma, C., Fang, N., Paul, J., Rangnekar, A., Shon, J., Swani, P. and Treinen, M. (2001). What makes Web sites credible? A report on a large quantitative study. CHI 2001 Conference Proceedings, 3(1), 61-6.

Foley, J. & Wallace, V. (1974). The art of natural graphic man-machine conversation. *Proceedings of the IEEE, 62*(4), 62-79.

Foltz, P.W., Davies, S.E., Polson, P.G., & Kieras, D.E. (1988). Transfer between menu systems. *Proceedings of CHI'88*, 107-112.

Forrester Research (2001, July). Forrester Report. Retrieved November 2005, from http://www.forrester.com/.

Foster, J. & Coles, P. (1977). An experimental study of typographical cueing in printed text. *Ergonomics, 20*, 57-66.

Foster, S.T. & Franz, C.R. (1999). User involvement during information systems development: A comparison of analyst and user perceptions of system acceptance. *Journal of Engineering and Technology Management, 16*, 329-348.

Fowler, S. (1998). *GUI Design Handbook*. New York: McGraw-Hill.

Fu, L., Salvendy, G. & Turley, L. (1998). Who finds what in usability evaluation. *Proceedings of the Human Factors and Ergonomics Society 42nd Annual Meeting*, 1341-1345.

Fu, L., Salvendy, G. & Turley, L. (2002). Effectiveness of user testing and heuristic evaluation as a function of performance classification. *Behaviour and Information Technology*, 137-143.

Furnas, G.W., Landauer, T.K., Gomez, L.M., & Dumais, S.T. (1987). The vocabulary problem in human-system communication: An analysis and a solution, *Communications of the ACM, 30*(11), 964-971.

Galitz, W.O. (2002). *The Essential Guide to User Interface Design*. New York: John Wiley & Sons.

Gerhardt-Powals, J. (1996). Cognitive engineering principles for enhancing human-computer performance. *International Journal of Human-Computer Interaction*, 8(2), 189-211.

Goldsmith, E. (1987). The analysis of illustration in theory and practice. In H.A. Houghton & D.M. Willows (Eds.), *The Psychology of Illustration* (pp. 53-85). New York: Springer-Verlag.

Golovchinsky, G. & Chignell, M. (1993). Queries-R-Links: Graphical markup for text navigation. *Proceedings of INTERCHI'93, 24-29.*

Goodwin, K. (2001, July/August). Perfecting your personas. *Cooper Interaction Design Newsletter*. Retrieved November 2005, from http://www.cooper.com/newsletters/2001_07/perfecting_your_personas.htm.

Gould, J.D., Alfaro, L., Finn, R., Haupt, B., & Minuto, A. (1987a). Reading from CRT displays can be as fast as reading from paper. *Human Factors*, 29(5), 497-517.

Gould, J.D., Alfaro, L., Finn, R., Haupt, B., Minuto, A. & Salaun, J. (1987b). Why reading was slower from CRT displays than from paper. *Proceedings of CHI+GI'87,* 7-11.

Gould, J.D., Boies, S.J., Meluson, A., Rasamny, M., & Vosburgh, A.M. (1988). Empirical evaluation of entry and selection methods for specifying dates. *Human Factors and Ergonomics Society Annual Meeting Proceedings, 279-283.*

Gould, J.D., Boies, S.J., Meluson, A., Rasamny, M., & Vosburgh, A.M. (1989). Entry and selection methods for specifying dates. *Human Factors*, 31(2), 199-214.

Graham, M., Kennedy, J., & Benyon, D. (2000). Towards a methodology for developing visualizations. *International Journal of Human-Computer Studies, 53,* 789-807.

Gray, W.D. & Salzman, M.C. (1998). Damaged merchandise? A review of experiments that compare usability evaluation methods. *Human-Computer Interaction,* 13(3), 203-261.

Greene, J.M. (1972). *Psycholinguistics: Chomsky and Psychology*. Harmondsworth, Middlesex, U.K.: Penguin.

Greene, S.L., Gould, J.D., Boies, S.J., Meluson, A., & Rasamny, M. (1988). Entry-based versus selection-based interaction methods. *Human Factors and Ergonomics Society Annual Meeting Proceedings, 284-287.*

Greene, S.L., Gould, J.D., Boies, S.J., Rasamny, M., & Meluson, A. (1992). Entry and selection based methods of human-computer interaction. *Human Factors*, 34(1), 97-113.

Grose, E., Jean-Pierre, S., Miller, D., & Goff, R. (1999). Applying usability methods to a large intranet site. *Human Factors and Ergonomics Society Annual Meeting Proceedings, 762-766.*

Grudin, J. (1989). The case against user interface consistency. *Communications of the ACM, 32,* 1164-1173.

Georgia Institute of Technology (1998, October). GVU's WWW User Surveys. Retrieved November 2005, from http://www.cc.gatech.edu/gvu/user_surveys/survey-1998-10/graphs/graphs.html#general.

Haas, S.W. & Grams, E.S. (1998). A link taxonomy for Web pages. *Proceedings of the 61st Annual Meeting of the American Society for Information Science, 35,* 485-95.

Hackman, R.B. & Tinker, M.A. (1957). Effect of variations in color of print and background upon eye movements in reading. *American Journal of Optometry and Archives of the American Academy of Optometry, 34,* 354-359.

Halgren, S.L. & Cooke, N.J. (1993). Towards ecological validity in menu research. *International Journal of Man-Machine Studies, 39(1),* 51-70.

Halverson, T. & Hornof, A.J. (2004). Local density guides visual search: Sparse groups are first and faster. *Proceedings from the 48th Annual Human Factors and Ergonomics Meeting.*

Hanson, R.H., Payne, D.G., Shiveley, R.J., & Kantowitz, B.H. (1981). Process control simulation research in monitoring analog and digital displays. *Human Factors and Ergonomics Society Annual Meeting Proceedings,* 154-158.

Harrison, S.M. (1995). A comparison of still, animated, or nonillustrated on-line help with written or spoken instructions in a graphical user interface. *Proceedings of CHI'95,* 82-89.

Hartley, J. & Trueman, M. (1983). The effects of headings in text on recall, search, and retrieval. *British Journal of Educational Psychology, 53,* 205-214.

Hartson, H.R., Castillo, J.C., Kelso, J. & Neale, W.C. (1996). Remote evaluation: The network as an extension of the usability laboratory. *CHI96 Proceedings,* 228-235.

Hassenzahl, M. (2000). Prioritizing usability problems: Data-driven and judgment-driven severity estimates. *Behavior and Information Technology, 19(1),* 29-42.

Haubner, P. & Neumann, F. (1986, May). Structuring alpha-numerically coded information on visual display units. *Proceedings of the Conference on Work with Display Units, Stockholm,* 606-609.

Head, A. J. (2003). Personas: Setting the stage for building usable information sites. *Online, 27(4).* Retrieved November 2005, from http://www.infotoday.com/online/jul03/head.shtml.

Heinbokel, T., Sonnentag, S., Frese, M., Stolte, W. & Brodbeck, F.C. (1996). Don't underestimate the problems of user centredness in software development projects: There are many. Behaviour and Information Technology, 15(4), 226-236.

Herriot, P. (1970). *An Introduction to the Psychology of Language.* London: Methuen.

Hertzum, M. & Jacobsen, N.E. (2001). The evaluator effect: A chilling fact about usability evaluation methods. *International Journal of Human-Computer Interaction, 13,* 421-443.

Hertzum, M. & Jacobsen, N.E. (2001). The evaluator effect: A chilling fact about usability evaluation methods. *International Journal of Human-Computer Interaction, 13,* 421-443.

Hess, R. (2000, October). Can color-blind users see your site? Microsoft Corporation. Retrieved November 2005, from http://msdn.microsoft.com/library/default.asp?url=/library/en-us/dnhess/html/hess10092000.asp.

Hillstrom, A.P. & Yantis, S. (1994). Visual motion and attentional capture. *Perception and Psychophysics, 55(4),* 399-411.

Hoc, J-M & Leplat, J. (1983). Evaluation of different modalities of verbalization in a sorting task. *International Journal of Man-Machine Studies*, 18(3), 283-306.

Hochheiser, H. & Shneiderman, B. (2000). Performance benefits of simultaneous over sequential menus as task complexity increases. *International Journal of Human-Computer Interaction*, 12(2), 173-192.

Holleran, P.A. (1991). A methodological note on pitfalls in usability testing. *Behaviour and Information Technology*, 10(5), 345-57.

Hong, J.I., Li, F.C., Lin, J., & Landay, J.A. (2001). End-user perceptions of formal and informal representations of Web sites [Extended Abstracts]. *Proceedings of CHI 2000*, 385-386.

Hooke, L.R., DeLeo, P.J., & Slaughter, S.L. (1979). *Readability of Air Force publications: A criterion-referenced evaluation* (AFHRL-TR-79-21). Lowry AFB, Colorado: Technical Training Division, Air Force Human Resources Laboratory.

Hornof, A.J. & Halverson, T. (2003). Cognitive strategies and eye movements for searching hierarchical computer displays. *CHI 2003 Conference Proceedings*, 249-256.

Horton, W. (1990). *Designing and Writing Online Documentation*. Hoboken, NJ: Wiley.

Hull, S.S. (2004), Influence of training and exposure on the usage of breadcrumb navigation, Usability News, 6.1 (http://psychology.wichita.edu/surl/usabilitynews/61/breadcrumb.htm).

IBM (1999). *Web Design Guidelines Design in Action*. Retrieved May 2003, from www-3.ibm.com/ibm/easy/eou_ext.nsf/Publish/572.

Institute of Electrical and Electronics Engineers. *IEEE Web Publishing Guide.*

Isakson, C.S. & Spyridakis, J.H. (1999). The influence of semantics and syntax on what readers remember. *Technical Communication*, 46(3), 366-381.

Ives, B. & Olson, M. (1984). User involvement and MIS success: A review of the literature. *Management Science*, 30(5), 586-603.

Ivory, M.Y. & Hearst, M.A. (2002). Statistical profiles of highly-rated web site interfaces. Proceedings of CHI 2002, 367-374.

Ivory, M.Y., Sinha, R.R., & Hearst, M.A. (2000, June). Preliminary findings on quantitative measures for distinguishing highly rated information-centric web pages. *Proceedings of the 6th Conference on Human Factors and the Web*. Retrieved November 2005, from http://www.tri.sbc.com/hfweb/ivory/paper.html.

Ivory, M.Y., Sinha, R.R., & Hearst, M.A. (2001). Empirically validated Web page design metrics. *Proceedings of CHI 2001*, 53-60.

Jacobsen, N.E. & John, B.E. (2000). *Two case studies in using cognitive walkthroughs for interface evaluation* (CMU-CS-00-132). Carnegie Mellon University, School of Computer Science. Retrieved November 2005, from http://reports-archive.adm.cs.cmu.edu/cs2000.html.

Jacobsen, N.E., Hertzum, M., & John, B.E. (1998). The evaluator effect in usability studies: Problem detection and severity judgments. *Human Factors and Ergonomics Society Annual Meeting Proceedings.*

Jeffries, R. & Desurvire, H. (1992). Usability testing vs. heuristic evaluation: Was there a contest? *SIGCHI Bulletin*, 24(4), 39-41.

Jeffries, R., Miller, J.R., Wharton, C., & Uyeda, K.M. (1991). User interface evaluation in the real world: A comparison of four techniques. *Proceedings of CHI'91*, 119-124.

Jenkins, S.E. & Cole, B.L. (1982). The effect of the density of background elements on the conspicuity of objects. *Vision Research*, 22, 1241-1252.

John, B.E. & Marks, S.J. (1997). Tracking the effectiveness of usability evaluation methods. *Behaviour and Information Technology*, 16(4/5), 188-202.

John, B.E. & Mashyna, M.M. (1997). Evaluating a multimedia authoring tool with cognitive walkthrough and think-aloud user studies. *Journal of the American Society of Information Science*, 48(9), 1004-1022.

John, B.E. (1996). TYPIST: A theory of performance in skilled typing. *Human-Computer Interaction*, 11(4), 321-355.

Johnsgard, T.J., Page, S.R., Wilson, R.D., & Zeno, R.J. (1995). A comparison of graphical user interface widgets for various tasks. *Human Factors and Ergonomics Society Annual Meeting Proceedings*, 287-291.

Joseph, K.M., Knott, B.A. & Grier, R.A. (2002). The effects of bold text on visual search of form fields. *Proceedings of the Human Factors and Ergonomics Society 46th Annual Meeting*, 583-587.

Jupitermedia Corporation (2003). thecounter.com. Retrieved November 2005, from http://www.thecounter.com/.

Kahn, M.J., Tan, K.C., & Beaton, R.J. (1990). Reduction of cognitive workload through Information chunking. *Human Factors and Ergonomics Society Annual Meeting Proceedings*, 1509-1513.

Kalbach, J. & Bosenick, T. (2003). Web page layout: A comparison between left and right-justified site navigation menus. *Journal of Digital Information*, 4(1). Retrieved November 2005, from http://jodi.tamu.edu/Articles/v04/i01/Kalbach/.

Kandogan, E. & Shneiderman, B. (1997). Elastic windows: A hierarchical multi-window World-Wide Web browser. *Proceedings of the 10th Annual ACM Symposium on User Interface Software and Technology*, 169-177.

Karat, C-M. (1994a). A business case approach to usability cost justification. In R. G. Bias & D. J. Mayhew (Eds.), *Cost-Justifying Usability* (pp. 45-70). Boston: Academic Press.

Karat, C-M. (1994b). A comparison of user interface evaluation methods. In J. Nielsen & R. Mack (Eds.), *Usability Inspection Methods* (pp. 203-233). NY: John Wiley & Sons.

Karat, C-M. Campbell, R., & Fiegel, T. (1992). Comparison of empirical testing and walkthrough methods in user interface evaluation. *Proceedings of CHI'92*, 397-404.

Keil, M. & Carmel, E. (1995). Customer-developer links in software development. *Communications of the ACM*, 38(5), 33-43.

Kennedy, A. & Wilkes, A. (1975). *Studies in Long-Term Memory*. New York: John Wiley & Sons.

Keyes, E. (1993). Typography, color, and information structure. *Technical Communication*, 40(4), 638-654.

Keyes, E., Sykes, D., & Lewis, E. (1988). Technology + design + research = information design. In E. Barrett (Ed.), *Text, ConText, and HyperText: Writing With and For the Computer* (pp. 251-264). Cambridge, MA: MIT Press.

Kieras, D. (1997). A guide to GOMS model usability evaluation using NGOMSL (Chapter 31). In M. Helander, T.K. Landauer & P.V. Prabhu (Eds.), *Handbook of Human-Computer Interaction.* Amsterdam: North-Holland Elsevier Science Publishers.

Kim, H. & Hirtle, S.C. (1995). Spatial metaphors and orientation in hypertext browsing. *Behaviour and Information Technology,* 14, 239-250.

Kim, J. (1998). An empirical study of navigation aids in customer interfaces. *Behavior and Information Technology*, 18(3), 213-224.

Kim, J. & Yoo, B. (2000). Toward optimal link structure of the cyber shopping mall, *International Journal of Human-Computer Studies,* 52, 531-551.

Kincaid, J.P., Thomas, M., Strain, K., Couret, I., & Bryden, K. (1990). Controlled English for international technical communication, *Human Factors and Ergonomics Society Annual Meeting Proceedings*, 815-819.

Kingsburg, J.R. & Andre, A.D. (2004). A comparison of three-level web menus: Navigation structures. *Proceedings of the Human Factors and Ergonomics Society 48th Annual Meeting.*

Kosslyn, S.M. (1994). *Elements of Graphic Design.* New York: W.H. Freeman.

Koyani, S.J. (2001a, April). *Cancer mortality maps and graphs Web site.* National Cancer Institute, Communication Technologies Branch. Retrieved November 2005, from http://www3.cancer.gov/atlasplus/.

Koyani, S.J. (2001b, April). *WCCO/ACS findings.* National Cancer Institute, Communication Technologies Branch.

Koyani, S.J. & Bailey, R.W. (2005). Older users and the Web. *Proceedings of HCI International: 11th International Conference on Human-Computer Interaction.*

Koyani, S.J., Bailey, R.W., Ahmadi, M., Changkit, M. & Harley, K. (2002). Older users and the Web. *National Cancer Institute Technical Report.*

Koyani, S.J. & Nall, J. (1999, November). Web site design and usability guidelines. *National Cancer Institute, Communication Technologies Branch Technical Report.* Bethesda, MD.

Krull, R. & Watson, B. (2002). Beyond grammatical correctness in verbal instructions. *Proceedings of the IEEE International Professional Communication Conference,* 60-67.

Kucera, H. & Francis, W.N. (1967). *Computational Analysis of Present-day American English.* Providence, RI: Brown University Press.

Kujala, S. (2003). User involvement: A review of the benefits and challenges. *Behaviour and Information Technology,* 22(1), 1-16.

Landesman, L. & Schroeder, W. (2000). Report 5: Organizing links. In *Designing Information-Rich Web Sites.* Bradford, MA: User Interface Engineering.

Larson, K. & Czerwinski, M. (1998). Web page design: Implications of memory, structure and scent for information retrieval. *Proceedings of CHI'98,* 25-32.

Larson, K. (2004, July). The science of word recognition. Advanced Reading Technology Microsoft Corporation. Retrieved November 2005, from http://www.microsoft.com/typography/ctfonts/WordRecognition.aspx.

Law, E. L.-C. & Hvannberg, E.T. (2004). Analysis of strategies for improving and estimating the effectiveness of heuristic evaluation. *NordiCHI '04*, 241-250.

Law, L.-C. & Hvannberg, E.T. (2002). Complementarity and convergence of heuristic evaluation and usability testing. *Proceedings of the Second Nordic Conference on Human-Computer Interaction.*

Lawless, K.A. & Kulikowich, J.M. (1996). Understanding hypertext navigation through cluster analysis. *Journal of Educational Computing Research,* 14(4), 385-399.

LeCompte, D.C. (1999). Seven, plus or minus two, is too much to bear: Three (or fewer) is the real magic number. *Human Factors and Ergonomics Society Annual Meeting Proceedings,* 289-292.

LeCompte, D.C. (2000). 3.14159, 42, and 7 ± 2: Three numbers that (should) have nothing to do with user interface design. Retrieved November 2005, from http://www.internettg.org/newsletter/aug00/article_miller.html.

LeDoux, L.C., Connor, E. & Tullis, T. (2005). Extreme makeover: UI edition, measuring the benefits of user-centered design. *Proceedings of the Usability Professionals Association Conference.*

Leech, G. Rayson, P., & Wilson, A. (2001). *Word Frequencies in Written and Spoken English: based on the British National Corpus.* London: Longman. Retrieved November 2005, from http://www.comp.lancs.ac.uk/ucrel/bncfreq/.

Levine, R. (1996). *Guide to Web Style.* Sun Microsystems.

Levy, E., Zacks, J., Tversky, B., & Schiano, D. (1996). Gratuitous graphics? Putting preferences in perspective. *Proceedings of CHI'96,* 42-49.

Lewenstein, M., Edwards, G., Tatar, D., & Devigal, A. (2000). Where do users look first? Stanford Poynter Institute. Research excerpted in http://www.stanford.edu/dept/news/report/news/may10/eyetrack-55.html.

Lewis, C. & Walker, P. (1989). Typographic influences on reading. *Journal of Psychology,* 80, 241-257.

Lewis, J.R. (1993). Problem discovery in usability studies: A model based on the binomial probability formula. *Proceedings of the 5th International Conference on Human-Computer Interaction,* 666-671.

Lewis, J.R. (1994). Sample sizes for usability studies: Additional considerations. *Human Factors,* 36(2), 368-378.

Li, Q. & Henning R. (2003). Integrating usability into use cases: An empirical study of user-centered object orientation. *Proceedings of the Human Factors and Ergonomics Society 47th Annual Meeting,* 759-763.

Lichty, T. (1989). *Design Principles for Desktop Publishers.* Glenview, Il: Scott, Foresman.

Lieberman, L.R. & Culpepper, J.T. (1965). Words versus objects: Comparison of free verbal recall. *Psychological Reports,* 17, 983-988.

Lightner, N.J. (2003). What users want in e-commerce design: Effects of age, education and income. *Ergonomics,* 46(1-3), 153-168.

Lim, R.W. & Wogalter, M.S. (2000). The position of static and on-off banners in WWW displays on subsequent recognition. *Human Factors and Ergonomics Society Annual Meeting Proceedings*, 1071-1813.

Lorch, R.F. & Chen, A.H. (1986). Effects of number signals on reading and recall. *Journal of Educational Psychology*, 78(4), 263-270.

Lorch, R.F. Jr., & Lorch, E.P. (1995). Effects of organizational signals on text-processing strategies. *Journal of Educational Psychology*, 87(4), 537-544.

Lynch, P.J. & Horton, S. (2002). *Web Style Guide* (2nd Edition). New Haven, CO: Yale University Press. Retrieved November 2005, from http://www.webstyleguide.com/index.html?/contents.html.

Macbeth, S.A., Moroney, W.F., & Biers, D.W. (2000). Development and evaluation of symbols and icons: A comparison of the production and focus group methods. *Proceedings of the IEA 2000/HFES 2000 Congress*, 327-329.

MacGregor, J.N. (1987). Short-term memory capacity: Limitation or optimization? *Psychological Review*, 94(1), 107-108.

Mahajan, R. & Shneiderman, B. (1997). Visual and textual consistency checking tools for graphical user interfaces. *IEEE Transactions on Software Engineering*, 23, 722-735.

Mahlke, S. (2002). Factors influencing the experience of Web site usage [Extended Abstracts]. *Proceedings of CHI 2002*, 846-847.

Marchionini, G. (1995). *Information Seeking in Electronic Environments*. New York: Cambridge University Press.

Marcus, A. (1992). *Graphic Design for Electronic Documents and User Interfaces*. Reading, MA: Addison-Wesley.

Marcus, A., Smilonich, N., & Thompson, L. (1995). *The Cross-GUI Handbook*. Reading, MA: Addison-Wesley.

Marshall, S., Drapeau, T., & DiSciullo, M. (2001, June). Case study: Eye tracking the AT&T customer service site. *Proceedings of the IBM Make it Easy Conference*.

Martin, G.L. & Corl, K.G. (1986). System response time effects on user productivity. *Behaviour and Information Technology*, 5(1), 3-13.

Mayer, R.E., Dyck, J.L., & Cook, L.K. (1984). Techniques that help readers build mental models from scientific text: Definitions, pretraining, and signaling. *Journal of Educational Psychology*, 76, 1089-1105.

Mayes, D.K., Sims, V.K., & Koonce, J.M. (2000). Cognitive aspects of reading information from video display terminals. *Human Factors and Ergonomics Society Annual Meeting Proceedings*.

Mayhew, D. (1992). *Principles and Guidelines in User Interface Design*. Englewood Cliffs, NJ: Prentice-Hall.

McConkie, G. & Zola, D. (1982). Visual attention during eye fixations while reading. In M. Colheart (Ed.), *Attention and Performance XII*. London: Lawrence Erlbaum Associates.

McDonald, S. & Stevenson, R.J. (1998). Navigation in hyperspace: An evaluation of the effects of navigational tools and subject matter expertise on browsing and information retrieval in hypertext. *Interacting with Computers*, 10, 129-142.

McEneaney, J.E. (2001). Graphic and numerical methods to assess navigation in hypertext. *International Journal of Human-Computer Studies*, 55, 761-766.

McGee, M., Rich, A., & Dumas, J. (2004). Understanding the usability construct: User-perceived. *Proceedings of the Human Factors and Ergonomics Society 48th Annual Meeting.*

McGrenere, J., Baecker, R. & Booth, K. (2002). An evaluation of a multiple interface design solution for bloated software. *CHI letters*, 4(1), 163-170.

McGrew, J. (2001). Shortening the human computer interface design cycle: A parallel design process based on the genetic algorithm. *Human Factors and Ergonomics Society Annual Meeting Proceedings*, 603-606.

McKeen, J.D. & Guimaraes, T. (1997). Successful strategies for user participation in systems development. *Journal of Management Information Systems,* 14(2), 133-150.

Meyer, B.J.F. (1984). Text dimensions and cognitive processing. In H. Mandl, N.L. Stein & T. Trabasso (Eds.), *Learning and Comprehension of Text* (pp. 3-51). Hillsdale, NJ: Lawrence Erlbaum.

Meyer, J. (1997). A new look at an old study on information display: Washburne (1927) reconsidered. *Human Factors*, 39(3), 333-340.

Meyer, J., Shamo, M., & Gopher, D. (1999). Information structure and the relative efficacy of tables and graphs. *Human Factors*, 41(4), 570.

Meyer, J., Shinar, D., & Leiser, D. (1990). Time estimation of computer 'wait' message displays. *Human Factors and Ergonomics Society Annual Meeting Proceedings,* 130.

Meyer, J., Shinar, D., & Leiser, D. (1997). Multiple factors that determine performance with tables and graphs. *Human Factors*, 39(2), 268-286.

Microsoft Corporation (1992). *The Windows Interface: An Application Design Guide.* Redmond, WA: Microsoft Press.

Miller, C.S. & Remington, R.W. (2000). A computational model of web navigation: Exploring interactions between hierarchical depth and link ambiguity. *Proceedings of the 6th Conference on Human Factors and the Web.* Retrieved November 2005, from http://www.tri.sbc.com/hfweb/miller/article.html.

Miller, M.A. & Stimart, R.P. (1994). The user interface design process: The good, the bad and we did what we could in two weeks. *Human Factors and Ergonomics Society Annual Meeting Proceedings,* 305-309.

Mills, J.A. & Caldwell, B.S. (1997). Simplified English for computer displays. *Proceedings of the 7th International Conference on Human-Computer Interaction (HCI International '97)*, 2, 133-136.

Mills, C.B. & Weldon, L.J. (1987). Reading Text from Computer Screens. ACM Computing Surveys, 19(4), December.

Mobrand, K.A. & Spyridakis, J.H. (2002). A web-based study of user performance with enhanced local navigational cues. *Proceedings of the IEEE International Professional Communication Conference,* 500-508.

Molich, R. (2005). Comparative usability evaluation (CUE). Retrieved November 2005, from http://www.dialogdesign.dk/cue.html.

Molich, R., Bevan, N., Curson, I., Butler, S., Kindlund, E., Miller, D., et al. (1998). Comparative evaluation of usability tests. Proceedings of the Eighth Annual Usability Professionals' Association Conference.

Molich, R., Thomsen, A.D., Karyukina, B., Schmidt, L., Ede, M., Oel, W.V., et al. (1999). Comparative evaluation of usability tests. *Proceedings of CHI'99,* Extended Abstracts, 83-84.

Moray, N. & Butler, C. (2000). The effect of different styles of human-machine interaction on the nature of operator mental models. *Human Factors and Ergonomics Society Annual Meeting Proceedings,* 1-53-1-56.

Morkes, J. & Nielsen, J. (1997). Concise, SCANNABLE, and objective: How to write for the Web. Retrieved November 2005, from http://www.useit.com/papers/webwriting/writing.html.

Morkes, J. & Nielsen, J. (1998). Applying writing guidelines to Web pages. Retrieved November 2005, from http://www.useit.com/papers/webwriting/rewriting.html.

Morrell, R.W., Dailey, S.R., Feldman, C., Mayhorn, C.B., & Echt, K.V. (2002, April). Older adults and information technology: A compendium of scientific research and web site accessibility guidelines. *National Institute on Aging Report.* Bethesda, MD.

Moskel, S., Erno, J., & Shneiderman, B. (1984, June). *Proofreading and comprehension of text on screens and paper.* University of Maryland Computer Science Technical Report.

Murch, G.M. (1985, June). Colour graphics: Blessing or ballyhoo? Computer Graphics Forum, 4(2), 127-135.

Murphy, E.D. & Mitchell, C.M. (1986). Cognitive attributes: Implications for display design in supervisory control systems. *International Journal of Man-Machine Studies,* 25, 411-438.

Muter, P. (1996). Interface design and optimization of reading of continuous text. In H. van Oostendorp & S. de Mul (Eds), *Cognitive Aspects of Electronic Text Processing.* Norwood, NJ: Ablex.

Muter, P. & Maurutto, P. (1991). Reading and skimming from computer screens and books: The paperless office revisited? *Behaviour and Information Technology,* 10(4), 257-266.

Myers, B.A. (1985). The importance of percent-done progress indicators for computer-human interfaces. *Proceedings of CHI'85,* 11-17.

Nall, J., Koyani, S.J., & Lafond, C. (2001, January). *Lessons learned while usability testing the CancerNet Web site.* National Cancer Institute, Communication Technologies Branch Technical Report.

Narveson, R. (2001). Bulleted points and typographic cues: Effects on recall and recall order. *Dissertation Abstracts,* 62(3-A), 914.

Navai, M., Guo, X., Caird, J.K., & Dewar, R.E. (2001). Understanding of prescription medical labels as a function of age, culture, and language. *Human Factors and Ergonomics Society Annual Meeting Proceedings,* 1487-1491.

Navai, M., Guo, X., Caird, J.K., & Dewar, R.E. (2001). Understanding of prescription medical labels as a function of age, culture, and language. *Human Factors and Ergonomics Society Annual Meeting Proceedings,* 1487-1491.

Nelson, D.L., Reed, V.S., & Walling, J.R. (1976). Pictorial superiority effect. *Journal of Experimental Psychology: Human Learning and Memory*, 2, 523-528.

Nielsen, J. & Landauer, T.K. (1993). A mathematical model of the finding of usability problems. *Proceedings of INTERCHI'93*, 206-213.

Nielsen, J. & Mack, R.L. (1994). *Usability inspection methods.* New York: John Wiley & Sons.

Nielsen, J. (1990, March). The art of navigating through hypertext. *Communications of the ACM,* 33(3), 296-310.

Nielsen, J. (1992, May). Finding usability problems through heuristic evaluation. *Proceedings of CHI'92*, 373-380.

Nielsen, J. (1993). Heuristic evaluation. In J. Nielsen & R.I. Mack (Eds.), *Usability Inspection Methods.*

Nielsen, J. (1996a, May). Top ten mistakes in Web design. Retrieved November 2005, from http://www.useit.com/alertbox/9605.html.

Nielsen, J. (1996b, October). Accessible design for users with disabilities. Retrieved November 2005, from http://www.useit.com/alertbox/9610.html.

Nielsen, J. (1997a, March). The need for speed. Retrieved November 2005, from http://www.useit.com/alertbox/9703a.html.

Nielsen, J. (1997b, June). Top ten mistakes of Web management. Retrieved November 2005, from http://www.useit.com/alertbox/9706b.html.

Nielsen, J. (1997c, October). How users read on the Web. Retrieved November 2005, from http://www.useit.com/alertbox/9710a.html.

Nielsen, J. (1997d, November). The tyranny of the page: Continued lack of decent navigation support in Version 4 browsers. Retrieved November 2005, from http://www.useit.com/alertbox/9711a.html.

Nielsen, J. (1997e, December). Changes in Web usability since 1994. Retrieved November 2005, from http://www.useit.com/alertbox/9712a.html.

Nielsen, J. (1999a, April). Stuck with old browsers until 2003, April 18. Retrieved November 2005, from http://www.useit.com/alertbox/990418.html.

Nielsen, J. (1999b, May). 'Top ten mistakes' revisited three years later. Retrieved November 2005, from http://www.useit.com/alertbox/990502.html.

Nielsen, J. (1999c, May). The top ten new mistakes of Web design. Retrieved November 2005, from http://www.useit.com/alertbox/990530.html.

Nielsen, J. (1999d, October). Ten good deeds in Web design. Retrieved November 2005, from http://www.useit.com/alertbox/991003.html.

Nielsen, J. (2000). *Designing Web Usability.* Indianapolis, IN: New Riders.

Nielsen, J. (2001a, May). Search: Visible and simple. Retrieved November 2005, from http://www.useit.com/alertbox/20010513.html.

Nielsen, J. (2001b, July). Tagline blues: What's the site about? Retrieved November 2005, from http://www.useit.com/alertbox/20010722.html.

Nielsen, J. (2003, November 10). The ten most violated homepage design guidelines. *Alertbox.* Retrieved November 2005, from http://www.useit.com/alertbox/20031110.html.

Nielsen, J. & Molich, R. (1990, April). Heuristic evaluation of user interfaces. *Proceedings of CHI'90*, 249-256.

Nielsen, J., Molich, R., Snyder, C., & Farrell, S. (2000). E-commerce user experience: 207 guidelines for e-commerce sites. *Nielsen Norman Group Report.*

Nielsen, J. & Tahir, M. (2002). *Homepage Usability: 50 Sites Deconstructed.* Indianapolis, IN: New Riders Publishing.

Niemela, M. & Saarinen, J. (2000). Visual search for grouped versus ungrouped icons in a computer interface. *Human Factors, 42(4),* 630-635.

Nolan, P. (1989). Designing screen icons: Ranking and matching studies. *Human Factors and Ergonomics Society Annual Meeting Proceedings,* 380-384.

Nordby, K., Raanaas, R. & Magnussen, S. (2002). Keying briefly presented multiple-digit numbers. *Behaviour and Information Technology, 21(1),* 27-38.

Norman, K.L. & Murphy, E.D. (2004). Usability testing of an internet form for the 2004 overseas enumeration test. *Proceedings of the Human Factors and Ergonomics Society.*

Norman, M. (1993, December). What a task – Establishing user requirements! *ACM SIGOIS Bulletin,* 14(2), 23-26.

Nygren, E. & Allard, A. (1996). Between the clicks: Skilled users scanning of pages. *Proceedings of the 2nd Conference on Human Factors and the Web.* Retrieved November 2005, from http://www.microsoft.com/usability/webconf/nygren.rtf.

Ohnemus, K.R. & Biers, D.W. (1993). Retrospective versus concurrent thinking-out-loud in usability testing. *Proceedings of the Human Factors Society 37th Annual Meeting,* 1127-1131.

Omanson, R.C., Cline, J.A. & Nordhielm, C.L. (2001, May). Effects of visual consistency on the online brand experience. Presented at the 2001 Advertising and Consumer Psychology Conference.

Omanson, R.C., Cline, J.A., Kilpatrick, C.E. & Dunkerton, M.C. (1998). Dimensions affecting Web site identity. *Human Factors and Ergonomics Society Annual Meeting Proceedings,* 429-433.

Osborn, S. & Elliott, G. (2002). Standard creativity: Creating flexible web development standards. *Proceedings of the IEEE International Professional Communication Conference,* 1-21.

Ovaska, S. & Raiha, K.J. (1995). Parallel design in the classroom. *Proceedings of CHI'95,* 264-265.

Ozok, A.A. & Salvendy, G. (2000). Measuring consistency of web page design and its effects on performance and satisfaction. *Ergonomics, 43(4),* 443-460.

Ozok, A.A. & Salvendy, G. (2001). How consistent is your web design? *Behaviour and Information Technology, 20(6),* 433-447.

Page, C. & Rahimi, M. (1995). Concurrent and retrospective verbal protocols in usability testing: Is there value added in collecting both? *Proceedings of the Human Factors and Ergonomics Society 39th Annual Meeting,* 223-227.

Pagulayan, R.J. & Stoffregen, T.A. (2000). Content versus graphics in the ecological design of interfaces. *Human Factors and Ergonomics Society Annual Meeting Proceedings,* 291.

Paivio, A. & Csapo, K. (1969). Concrete image and verbal memory codes. *Journal of Experimental Psychology*, 80, 279-285.

Paivio, A., Rogers, T.B., & Smythe, P.C. (1968). Why are pictures easier to recall than words? *Psychonomic Science*, 11, 137-138.

Palermo, D.S. & Bourne, L.E. (1978). *Psychology of Language*. Glenview, IL: Scott, Foresman.

Palmquist, M. & Zimmerman, D.E. (1999). *Writing with a Computer*. Boston: Allyn and Bacon.

Park, I. & Hannafin, M.J. (1993). Empirically-based guidelines for the design of interactive multimedia. *Educational Technology Research and Development, 41*(3), 63-85.

Parush, A., Nadir, R., & Shtub, A. (1998). Evaluating the layout of graphical user interface screens: Validation of a numerical computerized model. *International Journal of Human-Computer Interaction*, 10(4), 343-360.

Paterson, D.G. & Tinker, M.A. (1940a). *How to Make Type Readable*. New York: Harper.

Paterson, D.G. & Tinker, M.A. (1940b). Influence of line width on eye movements. *Journal of Experimental Psychology, 27*, 572-577.

Perfetti, C. & Landesman, L. (2001, June). Eight is not enough. Retrieved November 2005, from http://www.uie.com/articles/eight_is_not_enough/.

Perfetti, C. (2001, January). The truth about download time. Retrieved November 2005, from http://www.uie.com/articles/download_time/.

Pew, R.W. & Rollins, A.M. (1975). *Dialog Specification Procedures* (Report 3129, revised). Cambridge, MA: Bolt Beranek and Newman.

Piolat, A., Roussey, J.Y., & Thunin, O. (1998). Effects of screen presentation on text reading and revising. *International Journal of Human Computer Studies, 47*, 565-589.

Plaisant, C., Marchionini, G., Bruns, T., Komlodi, A., & Campbell, L. (1997). Bringing treasures to the surface: Iterative design for the Library of Congress National Digital Library Program. *Proceedings of CHI'97*, 518-525.

Pollock, A. & Hockley, A. (1996). What's wrong with Internet searching. Proceedings of the 2nd Conference on Human Factors and the Web. Retrieved November 2005, from http://www.microsoft.com/usability/webconf/pollock.rtf.

Polson, P.G. & Kieras, D.E. (1985). A quantitative model of the learning and performance of text editing knowledge. *Proceedings of CHI'85*, 207-212.

Polson, P.G., Bovair, S., & Kieras, D. (1987). Transfer between text editors: Predictive cognitive modeling. *Proceedings of CHI+GI'87*, 27-32.

Polson, P.G., Muncher, E., & Engelbeck, G. (1986). A test of a common elements theory of transfer. *Proceedings of CHI'86*, 78-83.

Porter, J. (2003). Testing the 'three-click' rule. *User Interface Engineering Newsletter*. Retrieved November 2005, from http://uie.com/articles/three_click_rule/.

Poulton, E.C. & Brown, C.H. (1968). Rate of comprehension of existing teleprinter output and possible alternatives. *Journal of Applied Psychology, 52*, 16-21.

Powers, R., Sarbaugh, L.E., Culbertson, H., & Flores, T. (1961). *Comprehension of graphs* (Bulletin 31). Madison: Department of Agricultural Journalism, University of Wisconsin.

Raanaas, R., Nordby, K. & Magnussen, S. (2002). The expanding telephone number: Age variations in immediate memory. *Behaviour and Information Technology*, 21(1), 39-45.

Rajani, R. & Rosenberg, D. (1999, January). Usable? ...Or not? ...Factors affecting the usability of Web sites. *CMC Magazine*. Retrieved November 2005, from http://www.december.com/cmc/mag/1999/jan/rakros.html.

Ramey, J.A. (2000). Guidelines for Web data collection: Understanding and interacting with your users. *Technical Communication*, 47(3), 397-410.

Ramsay, J., Barbesi, A., & Preece, J. (1998). A psychological investigation of long retrieval times on the World Wide Web. *Interacting with Computers*, 10, 77-86.

Redish, J. & Dumas, J.S. (1993). *A Practical Guide to Usability Testing*. Norwood, NJ: Ablex.

Redish, J.C. (1993). Understanding readers. In C.M. Barnum & S. Carliner (Eds.), *Techniques for Technical Communicators* (pp. 14-41). NY: Prentice Hall.

Redish, J.C., Felker, D.B., & Rose, A.M. (1981). Evaluating the effects of document design principles. *Information Design Journal*, 236-243.

Reeves, B. & Rickenberg, R. (2000). The effects of animated characters on anxiety, task performance, and evaluations of user interfaces. *Proceedings of CHI 2000*, 49-56.

Rehe, R.F. (1979). *Typography: How to Make It More Legible*. Carmel, IN: Design Research International.

Rehman, A. (2000). *Holiday 2000 e-commerce*. Creative Good, Inc.

Resnick, M.L. & Fares, C. (2004). Visualizations to facilitate online tabular presentation of product data. *Proceedings of the Human Factors and Ergonomics Society Annual Meeting*.

Rich, A. & McGee, M. (2004). Expected usability magnitude estimation. *Proceedings of the Human Factors and Ergonomics Society Annual Meeting*.

Riegelsberger, J., Sasse, M.A. & McCarthy, J.D. (2003). Shiny happy people building trust? Photos on e-commerce Web sites and consumer trust. *CHI Proceedings*, 5(1), 121-128.

Rigden, C. (1999). Safe Web colours for colour-deficient vision. *British Telecommunications Engineering Journal*; also retrieved November 2005 from http://www.btplc.com/age_disability/ClearerInformation/Colours/othersites.htm.

Rodden, K., Basalaj, W., Sinclair, D., & Wood, K. (2001). Does organisation by similarity assist image browsing? *Proceedings of CHI 2001*, 190-197.

Rogers, L. & Chaparro, B. (2003). Breadcrumb navigation: Further investigation of usage. *Usability News*, 5.2. Retrieved November 2005, from http://psychology.wichita.edu/surl/usabilitynews/52/breadcrumb.htm.

Rooden, M.J., Green, W.S., & Kanis, H. (1999). Difficulties in usage of a coffeemaker predicted on the basis of design models. *Human Factors and Ergonomics Society Annual Meeting Proceedings*, 476-480.

Rosenfeld, L. & Morville, P. (2002). *Information Architecture for the World Wide Web* (second edition). Sebastopol, CA: O'Reilly.

Rosenholtz, R., Li, Y., Mansfield, J. & Jin, Z. (2005). Feature congestion: a measure of display. *CHI 2005 Proceedings*.

Sano, D. (1996). *Designing Large-scale Web Sites: A Visual Design Methodology.* New York: Wiley.

Sawyer, P. & Schroeder, W. (2000). Report 4: Links that give off scent. *In Designing Information-Rich Web Sites.* Bradford, MA: User Interface Engineering.

Scanlon, S. & Schroeder, W. (2000). Report 1: What people do with web sites. *In Designing Information-Rich Web Sites.* Bradford, MA: User Interface Engineering.

Scharff, L.F.V., Ahumada, A.J., & Hill, A.L. (1999). Discriminability measures for predicting readability. In B.E. Rogowitz & T.N. Pappas (Eds.) *Human Vision and Electronic Imaging I, SPIE Proc.,* 3644, paper 27.

Schiano, D., Stone, M., & Bectarte, R. (2001). Search and the subjective web. *Proceedings of CHI 2001,* Extended Abstracts, 165-166.

Schneider, W. & Shiffrin, R.M. (1977). Controlled and automatic human information processing: I. Detection, search, and attention. *Psychological Review,* 84, 1-66.

Schneider, W., Dumais, S.T., & Shiffrin, R.M. (1984). Automatic and control processing and attention. In *Varieties of Attention* (pp. 1-27). New York: Academic Press.

Scholtz, J. (1998). WebMetrics: A methodology for developing usable web sites. *Human Factors and Ergonomics Society Annual Meeting Proceedings,* 1612.

Schramm, W. (1973). The nature of communications between humans. In W. Schramm & D. Roberts, *The Process and Effects of Mass Communication.* Urbana: University of Illinois Press.

Schriver, K.A. (1997). Dynamics in Document Design: *Creating Text for Readers.* New York: Wiley.

Schroeder, W. (1999). *Steering users isn't easy.* Retrieved May 2003, from http://developer.netscape.com/viewsource/schroeder_ui/schroeder_ui.html.

Schwarz, E., Beldie, I.P., & Pastoor, S. (1983). A comparison of paging and scrolling for changing screen contents by inexperienced users. *Human Factors,* 24, 279-282.

Schroeder, W. (2003, April). Usability myths need reality checks. *User Interface Engineering Newsletter.* Retrieved November 2005, from http://www.uie.com/articles/usability_myths/.

Schultz, L.D. & Spyridakis, J.H. (2002). The effect of heading frequency on comprehension of online information. *Proceedings of the IEEE International Professional Communication Conference,* 513-518.

Sears, A., Jacko, J., & Borella, M. (1997). Internet delay effects: How users perceive quality, organization and ease of use information. *Proceedings of CHI'97,* 353-354.

Sefelin, R., Tscheligi, M., & Giller, V. (2003). Paper prototyping - What is it good for? A comparison of paper- and computer-based low-fidelity prototyping. *CHI 2003,* 778-779.

Selvidge, P. (2000). Before and After: How Can You Show Your New Web site is Better? *Usability News,* 2.2. Retrieved November 2005, from http://psychology.wichita.edu/surl/usabilitynews/2S/compare.htm.

Selvidge, P.R., Chaparro, B.S., & Bender, G.T. (2001). The world wide wait: Effects of delays on user performance. *International Journal of Industrial Ergonomics,* 29(1), 15-20.

Shaikh, A.D. & Chaparro, B.S. (2004). A survey of online reading habits of internet users. *Proceedings of the Human Factors and Ergonomics Society.*

Sheridan, T.B. (1997). Supervisory control. In G. Salvendy (Ed.), *Handbook of Human Factors* (2nd Edition) (pp. 1295-1327). New York: Wiley.

Shneiderman, B. (1984). Response time and display rate in human performance with computers. *Computing Surveys,* 16, 265-285.

Silvers, T.J., Voorheis, C.M., & Anders, S.H. (2004). Rapid prototyping with Microsoft PowerPoint: Page linking and animation. *Proceedings of the Human Factors and Ergonomics Society.*

Sinha, R., Hearst, M., Ivory, M., & Draisin, M. (2001). Content or graphics? An empirical analysis of criteria for award-winning Web sites. *Proceedings of the 7th Conference on Human Factors and the Web.* Retrieved November 2005, from http://www.rashmisinha.com/articles/sinha_hfw01.html.

Smith, E.E. & Goodman, L. (1984). Understanding written instructions: The role of an explanatory schema. *Cognition and Instruction,* 1, 359-396.

Smith, J.A., Bubb-Lewis, C., & Suh, Y. (2000, June). Taking order status to task: Improving usability on the ibuy Lucent Web site. *Proceedings of the 6th Conference on Human Factors and the Web.* Retrieved November 2005.

Smith, S.L. (1962). Color coding and visual search. *Journal of Experimental Psychology,* 64, 434-440.

Smith, S.L. (1963). Color coding and visual separability in information displays. *Journal of Applied Psychology,* 47, 358-364.

Smith, S.L., Farquhar, B.B., & Thomas, D.W. (1965). Color coding in formatted displays. *Journal of Applied Psychology,* 49, 393-398.

Smith, S.L. & Mosier, J.N. (1986, August). Guidelines for designing user interface software. *The MITRE Corporation Technical Report* (ESD-TR-86-278).

Snyder, H.L., Decker, J.J., Lloyd, C.J.C., & Dye, C. (1990). Effect of image polarity on VDT task performance. *Proceedings of the Human Factors Society,* 1447-1451.

Sonderegger, P., Manning, H., Souza, R.K., Goldman, H., & Dalton, J.P. (1999, December). Why most B-to-B sites fail. Forester Research.

Spain, K. (1999). What's the best way to wrap links? *Usability News,* 1.1. Retrieved November 2005, from http://psychology.wichita.edu/surl/usabilitynews/1w/Links.htm.

Spencer, H., Reynolds, L., & Coe, B. (1977a). *The effects of different kinds and intensities of background noise on the legibility of printed text and numerals.* London: Readability of Print Research Unit, Royal College of Art.

Spencer, H., Reynolds, L., & Coe, B. (1977b). *The effects of image/background contrast and polarity on the legibility of printed materials.* London: Readability of Print Research Unit, Royal College of Art.

Spencer, R. (2000). The streamlined cognitive walkthrough method, working around social constraints encountered in a software development company. *Proceedings of CHI 2000,* 353-359.

Spinillo, C.G. & Dyson, M. (2000/2001). An exploratory study of reading procedural pictorial sequences. *Information Design Journal,* 10(2), 154-168.

Spink, A., Bateman, J., & Jansen, B.J. (1999). Searching the web: A survey of Excite users. *Internet Research: Electronic Networking Applications and Policy,*

Spool, J., Schroeder, W., & Ojakaar, E. (2001, November). Users don't learn to search better. UIEtips. Retrieved November 2005, from http://www.uie.com/articles/learn_to_search/.

Spool, J.M., Klee, M., & Schroeder, W. (2000). Report 3: Designing for scent, *Designing Information-Rich Web Sites*. Bradford, MA: User Interface Engineering.

Spool, J.M., Scanlon, T., Schroeder, W., Snyder, C., & DeAngelo, T. (1997). *Web Site Usability*: A Designer's Guide. North Andover, MA: User Interface Engineering.

Spyridakis, J.H. (1989). Signaling effects: Increased content retention and new answers. *Journal of Technical Writing and Communication*, 19(4), 395-415.

Spyridakis, J.H. (2000). Guidelines for authoring comprehensible web pages and evaluating their success. *Technical Communication*, 47(3), 359-382.

Staggers, N. (1993). Impact of screen density on clinical nurses' computer task performance and subjective screen satisfaction. *International Journal of Man-Machine Studies,* 39, 775-792.

Stanton, N.A. & Stevenage, S.V. (1998). Learning to predict human error: Issues of acceptability, reliability and validity. *Ergonomics*, 41(11), 1737-1747.

Stanton, N.A., Taylor, R.G., & Tweedie, L.A. (1992). Maps as navigational aids in hypertext environments: An empirical evaluation. *Journal of Educational Multimedia and Hypermedia*, 1, 431-444.

Steinbrück, U., Schaumburg, H., Duda, S. & Krüger, T. (2002). A picture says more than a thousand words: Photographs as trust builders in e-commerce Web sites [Extended abstracts]. CHI 2002, 748-749.

Stevens, K. (1980). The effect of topic interest on the reading comprehension of higher ability students. *Journal of Educational Research*, 73, 365-368.

Stewart, T. (1980). Communicating with dialogues. *Ergonomics*, 23, 909-919.

Sticht, T. (1985). Understanding readers and their uses of texts. In T. M. Duffy & R. Waller (Eds.), *Designing Usable Texts* (pp. 315-340). Orlando, FL: Academic Press.

Sullivan, P. & Flower, L. (1986). How do users read computer manuals? Some protocol contributions to writers' knowledge. In B.T. Petersen (Ed.), *Convergences: Transactions in Reading and Writing* (pp. 163-178). Urbana, IL: National Council of Teachers of English.

Sullivan, T. & Matson, R. (2000, November). Barriers to use: Usability and content accessibility on the Web's most popular sites. *Proceedings of the Conference on Universal Usability*, 139-144. Retrieved November 2005, from http://www.pantos.org/ts/papers/BarriersToUse.pdf.

Sundar, S.S., Edgar, E., & Mayer, K. (2000, June). Multimedia effects on processing and perception of online news: A study of picture, audio and video downloads. *Proceedings of the 50th Annual Conference of the International Communication Association (ICA)*.

Tan, W-S., Dahai, L., Liu, D., Muralidhar, A., & Meyer, J. (2001). Design improvements through user testing. *Human Factors and Ergonomics Society Annual Meeting Proceedings*, 1181-1185.

Thompson, K., Rozanski, E., & Rochester, H. (2004). Here, there, anywhere: Remote usability testing that works. SIGITE'04.

Thorell, L.G. & Smith, W.J. (1990). *Using computer color effectively: An illustrated reference.* Englewood Cliffs, NJ: Prentice Hall.

Tiller, W.E. & Green, P. (1999, June). Web navigation: How to make your Web site fast and usable. *Proceedings of the 5th Conference on Human Factors and the Web.* Retrieved November 2005, from http://zing.ncsl.nist.gov/hfweb/proceedings/tiller-green/.

Tinker, M.A. (1955). Prolonged reading tasks in visual research. *Journal of Applied Psychology*, 39, 444-446.

Tinker, M.A. (1963). *Legibility of print.* Ames: Iowa State University Press.

Tinker, M.A. & Paterson, D.G. (1928). Influence of type form on speed of reading. *Journal of Applied Psychology*, 12, 359-368.

Tinker, M.A. & Paterson, D.G. (1929). Studies of typographical factors influencing speed of reading: Length of line. *Journal of Applied Psychology*, 13, 205-219.

Tinker, M.A. & Paterson, D.G. (1931). Studies of typographical factors influencing speed of reading: Variations in color of print and background. *Journal of Applied Psychology,* 15, 471-479.

Toms, E.G. (2000). Understanding and facilitating the browsing of electronic text. *International Journal of Human-Computer Studies* 52, 423-452.

Tractinsky, N. (1997, March). Aesthetics and apparent usability: Empirically assessing cultural and methodological issues. *Proceedings of CHI'97*, 115-122. Retrieved November 2005, from http://turing.acm.org/sigs/sigchi/chi97/proceedings/paper/nt.htm.

Treisman, A. (1982). Perceptual grouping and attention in visual search for features and for objects. *Journal of Experimental Psychology*, 8, 194-214.

Treisman, A. (1988). Features and objects. *Quarterly Journal of Experimental Psychology*, 40(2), 201-237.

Treisman, A. (1990). Features and objects in visual processing. In I. Rock (Ed.), *The perceptual world: Readings from Scientific American* (pp. 97-110). New York: W.H. Freeman.

Trollip, S. & Sales, G. (1986). Readability of computer-generated fill-justified text. *Human Factors*, 28, 159-164.

Tufte, E.R. (1983). *The Visual Display of Quantitative Information.* Cheshire, Connecticut: Graphics Press.

Tullis, T.S. (1981). An evaluation of alphanumeric, graphic and color information displays. *Human Factors*, 23, 541-550.

Tullis, T.S. (1983). The formatting of alphanumeric displays: A review and analysis. *Human Factors*, 25, 657-682.

Tullis, T.S. (1984). Predicting the usability of alphanumeric displays, Doctoral Dissertation, Houston, TX: Rice University.

Tullis, T.S. (1988). Screen design. In M. Helander (Ed.), *Handbook of Human-Computer Interaction* (pp. 377-411). Amsterdam, Netherlands: Elsevier Science.

Tullis, T.S. (2001). Web usability lessons learned. *Fidelity Center for Applied Technology Technical Report.* Fidelity Investments.

Tullis, T.S., Boynton, J.L., & Hersh, H. (1995). Readability of fonts in the windows environment. Proceedings of CHI'95, 127-128.

Tullis, T.S., Fleischman, S., McNulty, M., Cianchette, C., & Bergel, M. (2002). An empirical comparison of lab and remote usability testing of Web sites. *Proceedings of the Usability Professionals' Association Annual Conference, 32.*

Tullis, T.S. & Kodimer, M.L. (1992). A comparison of direct-manipulation, selection and data-entry techniques for reordering fields in a table. *Human Factors and Ergonomics Society Annual Meeting Proceedings, 298-302.*

Tullis, T.S. & Pons, A. (1997). Designating required vs. optional input fields [Extended Abstracts]. Proceedings of CHI'97, 259-260.

United States Government, Rehabilitation Act of 1973 (amended in 1998), Section 508. Retrieved November 2005, from http://www.section508.gov/.

Utting, K. & Yankelovich, N. (1989). Context and orientation hypermedia networks. ACM *Transactions on Office Information Systems*, 7, 57-84.

Van Den Haak, M.J., De Jong, M.D.T., & Schellens, P.J. (2003). Retrospective vs. concurrent think-aloud protocols: Testing the usability of an online library catalog. *Behaviour and Information Technology*, 22(5), 339-351.

Vartabedian, A.G. (1971). The effects of letter size, case and generation method on CRT display search time. *Human Factors*, 13(4), 363-368.

Vaughan, M.W. (1998). Testing the boundaries of two user-centered design principles: Metaphors and memory load. *International Journal of Human-Computer Interaction,* 10(3), 265-282.

Virzi, R.A. (1990). Streamlining the design process: Running fewer subjects. *Human Factors and Ergonomics Society Annual Meeting Proceedings*, 291-294.

Virzi, R.A. (1992). Refining the test phase of usability evaluation: How many subjects is enough? *Human Factors*, 34, 457-468.

Virzi, R.A., Sorce J.F., & Herbert, L.B. (1993). A comparison of three usability evaluation methods: Heuristic, think-aloud, and performance testing. *Proceedings of the Human Factors and Ergonomics Society 37th Annual Meeting*, 309-313.

Vischeck. Accessed November 2005, from http://www.vischeck.com/.

Vora, P. (1998). Human factors methodology for designing Web sites. In C. Forsythe, E. Grose, & J. Ratner (Eds.), *Human Factors and Web Development.* Hillsdale, NJ: Lawrence Erlbaum.

Voss, J.F., Fincher-Kiefer, R.H., Greene, T.R., & Post, T.A. (1986). Individual differences in performance: The contrastive approach to knowledge. In R.J. Sternberg (Ed.), *Advances in the Psychology of Human Intelligence* (pp. 297-2450). Hillsdale, NJ: Lawrence Erlbaum.

Walker, B.N. & Stanley, R.M. (2004). Eye movement and reaction time are both important in assessment of dialog box usability. *Proceedings of the Human Factors and Ergonomics Society Annual Meeting.*

Walker, M., Takayama, L., & Landay, J.A. (2002). High-fidelity or low-fidelity, paper or computer? Choosing attributes when testing web prototypes. *Proceedings of the Human Factors and Ergonomics Society 46th Annual Meeting, 661-665.*

Wang, E. & Caldwell, B. (2002). An empirical study of usability testing: Heuristic evaluation vs. user testing. *Proceedings of the Human Factors and Ergonomics Society 46th Annual Meeting,* 774-778.

Web Site Optimization, LLC (2003, May). May bandwidth report-US broadband penetration breaks 35%. Retrieved November 2005, from http://www.Web siteoptimization.com/bw/0305/.

Wen, C.Y. & Beaton, R.J. (1996). Subjective image quality evaluation of image compression techniques. *Human Factors and Ergonomics Society Annual Meeting Proceedings, 2,* 1188-1192.

Whissell, C. (1998). A parsimonious technique for the analysis of word-use patterns in English texts and transcripts. *Perceptual and Motor Skills, 86,* 595-613.

Williams, T.R. (1993). Text or graphic: An information processing perspective on choosing the more effective medium. *The Journal of Technical Writing and Communication,* 33-52.

Williams, T.R. (1994). Schema theory. In C.H. Sides (Ed.), *Technical Communications Frontiers: Essays in Theory* (pp. 81-102). St. Paul, MN: Association of Teachers of Technical Writing.

Williams, T.R. (2000). Guidelines for designing and evaluating the display of information on the Web. *Technical Communication, 47*(3), 383-396.

Wilson, J.R. (2000). The place and value of mental models. *Human Factors and Ergonomics Society Annual Meeting Proceedings,* 1-49-1-52.

Wixon, D. & Jones, S. (1996). Usability for fun and profit: A case study of the design of DEC Rally Version 2. In M. Rudisell, C. Lewis, P. B. Polson, & T. D. McKay (Eds.), *Human-Computer Interface Design: Success Stories, Emerging Methods, Real-World Context* (pp. 3-35). San Francisco: Morgan Kaufmann.

Wolfmaier, T.G. (1999). Designing for the color-challenged: A challenge. *Internetworking.* Retrieved November 2005, from http://www.internettg.org/ newsletter/mar99/accessibility_color_challenged.html.

Woolrych, A. & Cockton, G. (2001). Why and when five test users aren't enough. Retrieved November 2005, from http://www.cet.sunderland.ac.uk/~cs0gco/fiveusers. doc.

World Wide Web Consortium (2001). *Evaluating Web sites for accessibility.* Retrieved November 2005, from http://www.w3.org/WAI/eval/.

Wright, P. (1977). Presenting technical information: A survey of research findings. *Instructional Science, 6,* 93-134.

Wright, P. (1980). The comprehension of tabulated information: Some similarities between reading prose and reading tables. *National Society for Performance and Instruction Journal, 19*(8), 25-29.

Wright, P. (1987). Writing technical information. In E.Z. Rothkopf (Ed.), Review of Research in Education (pp. 327-385). Washington, DC: *American Educational Research Association,* 14.

Wright, R.B. & Converse, S.A. (1992). Method bias and concurrent verbal protocol in software usability testing. *Proceedings of the Human Factors Society 34th Annual Meeting,* 1285-1289.

Wu, J. & Yuan, Y. (2003) Improving searching and reading performance: the effect of highlighting and text color coding. Information and Management, 40, 617-637.

Youngman, M. & Scharff, L. (1998). Text width and margin width influences on readability of GUIs. Retrieved November 2005, from http://hubel.sfasu.edu/research/textmargin.html.

Zaphiris, P. (2000). Depth vs. breadth in the arrangement of web links. *Proceedings of the IEA 2000/HFES 2000 Congress*, 453-456.

Zellweger, P.T., Regli, S.H., Mackinlay, J.D., & Chang, B-W. (2000). The impact of fluid documents on reading and browsing: An observational study. *Proceedings of CHI 2000*, 249-256.

Zhang, B-T. & Seo, Y-W. (2001). Personalized web-document filtering using reinforcement learning. *Applied Artificial Intelligence*, 15(7), 665-685.

Ziegler, J.E., Hoppe, H.U., & Fahnrich, K.P. (1986). Learning and transfer for text and graphics editing with a direct manipulation interface: Transfer of user skill between systems. *Proceedings of CHI'86*, 72-77.

Zimmerman, D.E. & Akerelrea, C.A. (2002). A group card sorting methodology for developing an informational Web site. *Proceedings of the IEEE International Professional Communication Conference*, 437-445.

Zimmerman, D.E. & Clark, D.G. (1987). *The Random House Guide to Technical and Scientific Communication*. New York: Random House.

Zimmerman, D.E. & Prickett, T. (2000). A usability case study: Prospective students use of a university web page. *Proceedings of the 2000 Society for Technical Communication Annual Conference*.

Zimmerman, D.E., Akerelrea, C.A., Buller, D.B., Hau, B., & LeBlanc, M. (2002). Integrating usability testing into the development of a 5-a-day nutrition Web site for at-risk populations in the American Southwest. *Journal of Health Psychology*.

Zimmerman, D.E., Muraski, M., Palmquist, M., Estes, E., McClintoch, C., & Bilsing, L. (1996). Examining World Wide Web designs: Lessons from pilot studies. *Proceedings of the 2nd Conference on Human Factors and the Web*. Retrieved November 2005, from http://www.microsoft.com/usability/webconf/zimmerman.htm.

Zimmerman, D.E., Slater, M., & Kendall, P. (2001). Risk communication and a usability case study: Implications for Web site design. *Proceedings of the IEEE International Professional Communication Conference*, 445-452.

Author Index

Index

A

abbreviation, 162, 163, 203,
above the fold, 34, 41, 52, 198, 200,
to attract attention, 41,
access
  to content or information, 23, 58, 177,
  to search, 179,
accessibility, 22, 23, 26, 27, 28, 107, 195,
assistive technology and, 23, 26,
automatic evaluation tools and, 193,
  Section 508, 22, 23, 202,
accuracy
  of data entry, 120,
  of headings, 82,
  of scanning, 115,
  of selecting links, 201,
acronym, 158, 162, 164,
use of on Web sites, 162,
action
  control, 59,
  of pushbuttons, 122, 133, 202,
  of users, 39,
  possible from a homepage, 40,
activate
  radio buttons, 128,
  the default action, 133,
  the pushbutton, 202,
  using a keyboard, 26,
active portion of the screen, 62,
active voice, 167, 198, 201,
activities performed by users, 12, 203,
advertisements, 142, 147,
aid, 201,
  navigation, 24, 131,
  or usability specialists, xvi, xvii, xx, 8, 192, 193, 197,
alignment
  of page elements, 51,

alphabetical
  as an organizational method for lists, 112, 113,
alt text, 25, 27, 144,
anchor link, 61, 198, 204,
animation, 146, 153,
  as an attention-attracting feature, 100, 105,
  multimedia, 27,
  text equivalents for, 25,
annotation
  of graphics, 151,
applet, 203,
  accessibility, 22,
  Java, 198, 203,
arrows
  as clickability cues, 73, 89, 93, 199,
assistive technology, 23, 24, 26, 27, 28, 83, 198,
asterisk, 121, 124,
attention
  attracting, 41, 49, 73, 81, 89, 100, 104, 105, 109, 146, 150, 164, 198,
  user, 81, 89, 105, 141, 146, 152,
audience
  for the *Guidelines*, xv,
  multiple, 169, 177,
audio, 25, 142, 146, 201,
  accessibility issues and, 25,
auto-tab, 198,
automatic
  cursor placement, 138, 198,
  error detection, 120, 131,
  evaluation, 195,
  tabbing, 120, 141, 198,
  time-out, 14, 203,
  usability evaluation, 195,

B

Back button, 57, 59, 67,

background, 31, 53, 101, 103, 143, 173,
    and methodology for the Guidelines, xx,
    color, 53, 101, 114, 173,
    image, 143,
banner ad, 147, 198, 200,
bar
    address, 198,
    browser, 198, 201,
    navigation, 19,
    scroll, 53, 54, 72, 73, 148, 202,
    title, 78, 103, 201,
bar graph, 151, 175,
before and after, 190,
benefit
    for audiences of the *Guidelines*, xv,
    of text links, 91, 96,
bold, 53, 73, 81, 104, 105, 109, 124, 164,
bookmark, 78,
boolean, 184,
brainstorming, 7,
breadcrumbs, 19, 62, 70, 198, 201,
browser, 28, 31, 59,
    common, 30, 201, 202,
    settings, 31, 96, 107,
bullets
    clickability, 89, 93, 118, 199,
    lists, 25, 115, 118,
button
    Back, 57, 59, 67,
    radio, 23, 51, 119, 128, 129, 140, 202, 204,
bytes, 13, 142, 145,

C

"click here", 86,
capitalization, 102, 164, 203,
caption, 27, 105,
card sorting, xxi, 198,
cascading menu, 95, 199,

case
    sensitive, 123,
    upper-, 102, 123, 141, 158, 164, 179, 181,
    upper- and lower-, 102, 123, 158, 164, 179, 181,
center
    of the Web page, 44, 47, 53, 89, 93, 166, 171, 198,
characters
    limit for in text field, 127,
    per line, 56,
    spacing, 103,
    which require the use of the Shift key, 120, 141,
check box, 51, 119, 128, 134, 199,
clickability cue, 60, 61, 65, 89, 91, 93, 154, 199,
clicks
    double, 138,
    reducing user, 129, 174,
client-side, 27, 199, 203,
clutter, 45,
code
    color, 62, 108, 178,
    HTML, 6,
    user-entered, 123,
    ZIP, 131,
cognitive walkthrough, 187, 194, 195, 196,
color, 5, 24, 53, 62, 89, 110, 121, 173, 178, 199,
    accessibility issues and, 24,
    background, 53, 103, 114, 173,
    for grouping, 114, 178,
    of links, 19, 62, 89, 91, 92, 93, 199,
    to gain attention, 109,
column
    alignment, 51,
    headings, 76, 82,
    width, 56,
computer
    capabilities/strengths, 12, 125, 152,

computer, (cont.)
   error detection by, 152,
   human-computer interaction, xx,
   9,
   speed/processing time, 5, 16,
   145,
connection speed, 17, 29, 33, 142,
199,
consistency
   of alignment, 51,
   of clickability cues, 85,
   of formatting, 102,
   of important items, 44, 47, 111,
   113,
   of labels, 123,
   of link names and targets, 85, 88,
   of titles, 78,
   physical, 201,
   visual, 100, 103,
content, 1, 2, 3, 4, 5, 6, 9, 10, 26,
43, 44, 47, 54, 55, 80, 87, 90, 143,
146, 148, 150, 153, 158, 159, 160,
162, 169, 171, 177, 182, 183, 186,
192, 199,
   accessing important, 90,
   length of pages for, 54, 75,
   meta-, 6,
   organization, 169, 176, 178,
   writing Web content, 158, 163,
   166, 167, 168,
content page, 162, 171, 199,
   structuring to facilitate scanning,
   169, 171,
contents
   clickable list of page contents,
   58, 61,
   table of, 44, 68. *See also Anchor
   link and Within-page links,*
contrast
   high-contrast backgrounds, 100,
   101,
   lightness, 24,
control, *See also widgets,*
   of animation, 153,

of link wrapping, 96,
of page layout, 27,
screen-based, 120, 121,
credibility, 10,
crowding or clutter, 50,
cue
   clickability, 60, 61, 65, 85, 89,
   93, 98, 154, 199,

D

data
   comparison of, 13, 48,
   critical, highlighting of, 81,
   display of, 15, 50, 115, 124, 131,
   137,
   formatting, 15,
   re-entry of, 125,
   tables of, 82, 172,
   user-entered codes and, 123,
data entry, 121, 124, 125, 126, 132,
138,
   accuracy of, 120,
   fields, labels for, 121, 123, 124,
   126, 140,
   indicating required vs. optional
   fields, 121,
   reducing errors during, 125,
   speed of, 132, 137, 140, 141,
   user, 125, 127, 131, 132, 138,
   140,
      errors with, 125, 130, 131,
      135, 140,
      minimize, 125,
dead-end pages, 59,
default
   action, 133,
   browser, 31,
   link colors, 19, 92,
   selection, radio buttons, 128,
   value, 137,
delay
   user tolerance for, 74, 145,
density
   display, 50, 55, 199,

density, (cont.)
    page/screen, 55, 199,
design
    iterative, 1, 189,
    parallel, 1, 7,
destination page, 58, 62, 64, 88, 199,
    matching link names with, 88,
disabilities
    number of people with, 23, 28,
    See also Accessibility, Assistive technology, and Section 508,
document
    lengthy, 20, 75,
double-click, 138,
download
    convenience related to, 54,
    time for, 13, 17, 91, 143,
drop-down, 139,

E

entry field, 120, 121, 124, 126, 127, 131, 135, 138, 179, 184, 198, 199,
    labels for, 121, 123, 124, 126, 135,
    required vs. optional, 121,
errors
    automatic detection of, 120, 131,
    increasing the possibility of, 125, 140,
    reducing the number of, 64, 95, 103, 130, 131, 135, 139,
evaluation
    automatic, 195,
    heuristic, 188, 194, 195, 197, 200,
    of Web site designs, 190,
evaluator effect, 195,
evidence
    strength of, iv, xvi, xvii, xviii, xix, xx, xxi, xxii,
expert evaluation, 200. *See also heuristic evaluation,*
expert opinion, xix, xxii,

expert review, 188, 195, 197. *See also heuristic evaluation,*
eye-tracking, 47,

F

feature
    attention attracting, 100,
feedback
    providing to orient users, 58, 62, 88,
    providing while users wait, 16,
field
    data entry, indicating required, 121,
    data entry, labeling, 120, 124, 126,
    data entry, partitioning, 131,
    data entry, placing cursor in, 138,
fluid layout, 52,
fold, 200,
    above the, 41, 52, 198, 200,
    below the, 41, 54, 148, 200,
    impact on homepage design, 41,
    limit large images above, 148,
font
    attracting attention with, 105,
    emphasizing importance with, 109,
    sans serif, 106, 109,
    serif, 106,
    size and reading speed, 102, 107,
    style and reading speed, 104, 106,
form(s)
    assistive technologies and, 23,
    designing entry fields for, 63, 123, 124, 126, 131,
    displaying default values in, 137,
    making user friendly, 125, 130, 132, 138, 140, 141, 161,
    widgets and, 122, 128, 129, 133, 134, 136, 139, 140,

form(s), (cont.)
  working memory limitations and, 13,
frame(s), 200,
  accessibility issues and, 25, 28,
  appropriate use of, 67, 146,
  title, 28,
frequency, 191,

G

gloss, 200,
  assisting navigation with, 69,
graphics, decorative, 5, 105, 147, 149, 150,

H

heading, 77, 78, 79, 80, 81, 82, 83, 84, 200,
  impact on scrolling, 53, 73, 172,
  introducing lists with, 116,
  placing on the page, 60,
  providing feedback with, 53,
help, user, 92, 97, 124, 153, 171,
heuristic evaluation, 188, 194, 195, 200,
hierarchy
  information, placement of critical items in, 49,
  information, showing with site maps, 68,
  information, use of html headers and, 76, 83,
high-contrast backgrounds, reading performance and, 101,
high speed access, percent of users with, 33,
hits, 187. *See also search engine/ function,*
homepage
  announce changes to Web site on, 42,
  characteristics of, 40,
  communicating Web site purpose
    on, 38,
  conveying quality with, 37,
  enabling access to from all other pages, 35,
  length of, 41, 54,
  panels, 43,
  presenting options on, 36,
  prose text on, 39,
  horizontal scrolling, 72,
hourglass, use of to indicate waiting times, 16,
HTML order, headings and, 83,

I

IBM, 35, 41, 62,
IEEE, 86,
image, 198, 202,
  accessibility issues and, 25,
  appropriate use of, 150,
  attracting attention with, 105,
  background, 101, 143,
  conveying messages with, 149,
  decorative, 5, 93, 105, 147, 150,
  facilitating learning with, 156,
  full-size, 155,
  labeling of, 144,
  link, 91, 144, 154,
  thumbnail, 155, 203,
image map, 200,
  accessibility issues and, 25,
  clarifying clickable regions of, 98,
important items, placement of, 47, 113,
index link, 200,
information
  facilitating user performance of, 15, 126, 170, 171, 172, 173, 175, 176, 177, 178,
  hierarchy, html headings and, 83,
  quantitative, format of, 175,
  supportive, 99,
information-based Web site, xix,
instructions, writing of, 167,

italics
    attracting attention with, 105,
    emphasizing text with, 109,
iterative design process, 1, 189,

J

jargon
    avoiding the use of, 160,
    providing links to explain or
    define, 99,
Jupitermedia Corporation, 30, 32,
33, 229,

K

keyboard, entry speed and, 132,
keyword, 6, 183, 200,

L

label
    category, 77, 126,
    data entry field, 123, 124, 135,
    link, 35, 77, 86,
    list, formatting of, 114,
    tab, 64,
    widget, 122, 134, 140,
laboratory, testing in, 196,
layout
    page, horizontal scrolling and,
    72,
    page, importance to finding
    information, 49,
    page, structuring for data
    comparison, 48,
learning, using images to facilitate,
156,
left navigation, 88. *See also left
panel,*
left panel, 43, 44, 63, 67, 90, 166,
180,
letter
    case of, use in codes, 123,
    case of, use in mixed prose, 164,
    case of, use in search terms, 181,

first, capitalization of in lists, 119,
    uppercase, attracting attention
    with, 105,
Limit Homepage Length, 41,
line length, reading speed and, 56,
link
    anchor, use of on long pages, 61,
    blue, 89, 92, 93,
    clickability cues for, 93,
    embedded text, designing, 94,
    importance in site being found
    by search engines, 6,
    index, definition of, 200,
    internal vs. external, indicating,
    97,
    missing, detection by automated
    evaluation methods, 195,
    navigation, assistive technology
    skipping of, 24,
    navigation, effects of prose text
    on, 39,
    placement denoting importance,
    49,
    placement on the homepage, 36,
    40,
    repeating, 90,
    to complete printable/
    downloadable documents, 20,
    to homepage, labeling of, 35,
    to information for new users, 3,
    to related content, 87,
    to supporting information, 99,
    used, color for, 92,
    visual characteristics of, 89,
link, image
    cautions emulate on use, 91,
    importance of labels with, 144,
    real-world objects, 154,
link label
    make specific and descriptive, 77,
    text, appropriate length of, 96,
    use the user's term in, 86,
link text
    matching to destination page
    heading, 62, 88,

row
    alignment of, 51,
    headers and headings, 82, 172,

S

scanning, 202,
    accuracy, 115,
    facilitating, 169, 171,
    importance of color, 178,
    importance of headings, 79, 86,
    lists and, 113, 114, 115,
    page layout/structure and, 48,
    51, 55,
    performance, importance of
    grouping to, 173,
    prose text on the homepage and,
    39, 166,
    text link lengths and, 96,
screen, 198, 199, 200, 201, 202,
204,
    browser, 26, 28,
    density, 55,
    flicker, 28,
    locating items on, 46, 47,
    real estate, widget selection and,
    129, 136, 139,
    resolution, 33, 96, 200, 202,
screenful, 198, 202, 204,
    content page design and, 75,
    homepage length and, 41,
    large images and, 148,
    navigation page length and, 66,
screen reader, facilitating use of, 26,
27, 82, 138, 202,
script, 199, 203,
    accessibility issues and, 25, 26,
scroll bar, 54, 72, 148, 202,
scroll box, 73,
scrolling, 198, 200, 201, 202,
    data entry fields and, 127,
    facilitating, 73,
    horizontal, 72,
    impact on homepage design, 41,
    keeping functions available

during, 57,
    lists, 113, 136, 139,
    navigation pages and, 66,
    page length decisions and, 54,
    reading comprehension and, 74,
    scroll stoppers and, 53,
    searching for information and,
    75,
    versus paging, 74,
    scroll stopper, 53, 202,
search engine/function
    advanced, 184,
    best bets, 183,
    cautions when using, 182,
    functionality of, 181, 183, 184,
    185,
    page titles and, 78,
    placing on each page, 182,
    placing on homepage, 40,
    registration with, 6,
    results, making usable, 180,
    search errors, 183,
    template, design and use of, 187,
    terms used in, 181, 184,
search sequences, standardizing, 11,
secondary navigation, 63,
Section 508, 23, 25, 27, 28, 202,
sentence(s), 199, 202, 203,
    impact of on scanning, 171,
    reading comprehension and,
    165,
    use of voice in, 167,
sequential menu, 67,
server-side image map, 27, 199,
203,
severity, 191, 197,
Shift key, 120, 141,
signal, auditory, 16,
simultaneous menu, 203,
    use of frames with, 57,
    versus sequential menus, 67,
site map, 200, 203,
    link to, on homepage, 40,
    link to, placing consistently, 60,

site map, (cont.)
    use of, 60, 68,
software, 198, 201, 202,
    accessibility issues and, 26, 138,
    use of in the design process, 193,
    195,
sound, accessibility issues and, 25,
source documents, xvi,
speed
    connection, and design issues, 5,
    33,
    connection, and download times,
    17, 199,
    connection, definition of, 199,
strength of evidence, vi, xvi, xvii,
xviii, xix, xx, xxi, xxii,
style sheet, 203,
    accessibility issues and, 27,
survey
    customer, establishing user
    requirements and, 2,
    use in creating lists of user terms,
    161,

T

tab, 203,
    design and placement, 60, 65,
    labels, 64,
    ordering, 112,
table
    quantitative information and,
    175,
    row and column headings, 82,
    scrolling issues and, 172,
tag
    html heading, 83,
    pixel dimension, 145,
tagline, 38, 40, 203,
target page, 203,
    matching link names with, 88,
task(s)
    appropriate menu types for, 67,
    completion times and visual
    consistency, 103,

ordering/sequencing to maximize
user performance, 112, 159,
    sequence, standardization of, 11,
task analysis, 176, 203,
    importance in meeting user
    expectations, 3,
templates, v, 179, 187,
tertiary navigation, 63,
testing results, use of, 196,
    website, common browsers and,
    30,
    website, common screen
    resolutions and, 33,
    website, operating systems and,
    32,
test subjects, correct number of,
192,
text, 199, 202,
    alignment of, 51,
    alternatives for image maps and
    accessibility, 27,
    blocks of, 51, 53, 102,
    blue, 89, 92, 93,
    continuous, 56, 115, 199,
    formatting for emphasis, 105,
    109,
    formatting for reading
    performance, 101, 107,
    grouping with color, 173,
text box, 127, 200,
    accessibility issues and, 23,
text equivalents, accessibility issues
and, 25,
text label
    clickable images and, 144, 154,
text link
    appropriate length of, 96,
    benefits of, 91,
    embedded, 94,
    image maps and, 27,
    indicating used, 92,
    matching to destination page
    title, 62, 88,
    use of compared to image links,
    91,

text only pages, accessibility issues and, 26,
think aloud, 190,
thumbnail image, 155, 203,
time out, 14, 203,
title(s)
    abbreviating, 162,
    frame, accessibility issues and, 28,
    link, 39,
    page, 6, 78, 201,
    page, and link text consistency, 88, 201,
tool(s), xiii, 24, 193
    automatic evaluation, role in the design process, 195,
transactions, data entry, 132, 141,

U

UME, 191,
underlining
    attracting attention with, 105,
    clickability cues and, 89, 93, 109, 199,
    emphasizing importance with, 109,
    highlighting critical data and, 81,
uppercase
    attracting attention with, 105,
    use in prose text, 164,
    use with search engines, 123, 141, 181,
URL, 203,
    indicating destination of links with, 97,
    providing feedback to users with, 62,
usability, xiii, xvi, xvii, xviii, xix, xx, xxi,
    problem, 192, 194, 197, 200,
    role of 'before and after' studies in determining, 190,
    specialist, xvi, xvii, xx, 8, 192, 193, 197,

study, role in the design process, 190,
usability goal, 7,
    role in the design process, 4,
Usability Magnitude Estimation, 191. *See also UME,*
usability test(ing), xviii, xxi, 203,
    automatic evaluation and, 195,
    cognitive walkthroughs and, 196,
    determining user information needs with, 175, 176,
    expert evaluations and, 194,
    heuristic evaluations and, 194,
    performance/preference goals and, 5, 7, 192,
    role in designing headings and labels, 80, 124,
    role in the design process, 5, 71
    test subjects and, 192,
    widgets and, 129,
user(s)
    acceptance of website, text line length and, 56,
    attention, drawing with highlighting, 81,
    color deficient, designing for, 24,
    disabilities, designing for, 22, 23, 24, 25, 26, 83,
    expectations, designing to meet, 3, 191,
    experienced/frequent, designing for, 21, 141, 157,
    groups, role in establishing user requirements, 2,
    inexperienced/new, importance of clickability cues to, 93,
    inexperienced/new, paging and, 74,
    inexperienced/new, providing assistance to, 21,
    inexperienced/new, search functions and, 184,
    interface issues, 5,
    multitasking, reading performance impacts of, 19,

user(s), (cont.)
  older, importance of descriptive
  headings to, 79,
  older, scrolling behavior of, 73,
  older, widgets and, 129,
  performance, design
  considerations and, 2, 5, 7, 52,
  108, 111, 112, 120,
  requirements, 2,
  terminology, using in help
  documentation, 19,
  visual impairments, with, 25, 28,
  31,
  working memory limitations,
  designing for, 13, 57,
  workload, reducing, 12,
  younger, scrolling behavior of,
  73,

V

video
  accessibility issues and, 25,
  meaningful use of, 146,
  user control of, 153,
vision-related disabilities, 23,
visual
  consistency, importance of, 100,
  103,
  design, importance of, 2,
visual cues
  designating required data entry
  fields, 124,
  providing user feedback with, 62,
visualization techniques and
  quantitative information, 175,
visually-impaired users, 31,
vocabulary, user, designing search
terms around, 183,
voice
  active, 167, 198,
  negative, 167,
  passive, 167, 201,

W

walkthrough, cognitive, 195, 196,
199,
Web page, 55,
  attention attracting features on,
  105,
  layout, consistent alignment of
  items on, 51,
  layout, facilitating scrolling, 73,
  layout, style sheets and
  accessibility issues, 27,
  layout, white space and, 55,
  length, primary use and, 54,
  positioning important items on,
  47,
  printing options for, 20,
  titles, 78,
  visual consistency of, 103,
Web site, 26,
  accessibility issues and, 22, 23,
  24, 25, 26, 27, 28,
  attention attracting features, 105,
  designing to be found by search
  engines, 6,
  format, meeting user
  expectations for, 3,
  goal, importance in design
  process, 4,
  information, format for multiple
  audiences, 177,
  purpose, communicating, 38,
  redesign, announcing changes to
  users, 42,
  use of and help documentation,
  15,
  visual consistency across, 103,
white space
  appropriate application of, 55,
  use of in lists, 114,
widgets, 204,
  alignment of, 51,
  capitalization of labels, 119,
  check box, 199,
    appropriate use of, 134,